Swami Vivekananda: Philosophy of Man

Swami Vivekananda: Philosophy of Man

Mohit Chakrabarti

GenNext Publication

ISBN : 978-93-5128-134-4

Price : ₹ 1090

First Published, 2016

Published by

Gennext Publications
5, Ansari Road
Daryaganj, New Delhi-110002
Phones: 9811692060
E-mail: gennext@hotmail.com

Printed at: G. Print Process, Delhi.

Cataloging in Publication Data—DK

Courtesy: D.K. Agencies (P) Ltd. <docinfo@dkagencies.com>

Chakrabarti, Mohit, 1941- author.

Swami Vivekananda : philosophy of man / Mohit Chakrabarti.

pages cm

ISBN 9789380222516

1. Vivekananda, Swami, 1863-1902. 2. Philosophical anthropology. 3. Philosophy, Indic. I. Title.

BL1280.292.V58C43 2015 DDC 181.4 23

Contents

Preface

To prove the real worth of life in the world from diverse perspectives is the vision of man. To Swami Vivekananda, one of the most serene and poignant humanists the world has ever seen, it is more than that. It is to prove the real worth of life for the present in tune with the glorious past for a march ahead and beyond that. It is a never-ending process, and, as such, the true man has no holidays to while away. He must work ceaselessly to translate the divinity already in him. To manifest is to assess oneself and to assess oneself is to be on the right track of endeavour for excellence and ascent. It is a promise for man 'to strive to seek to find and not to yield' under strenuous and challenging constraints to achieve and manifest the perfection already in him. He must boldly stand up and proclaim "I am He, I am He".

The society with which man is associated is the test for his identity. It is a challenge to him to become a real partner to progress and beyond that. It is also his citadel for attuning to the pulse of the hoi polloi. It is not easy. It demands hard work and total sacrifice of personal interest. It also demands an irresistible spirit to overcome all constraints at any time without fear. The ultimate end-in-view of rebuilding the society is to put it in the proper limelight of advancement in every direction, where a man becomes men and vice versa. For this, the vision of the All Man must be a compulsory passport to realisation of man as Vivekananda time and again emphasises. Again, to be justified to all the components like education, religion, values, spirituality, aesthetics and humanism, man must march for ascent and excellence, perfection and poignance. "Conceptual Framework of Vivekananda's Philosophy of Man" encompasses all these components as characteristic pointers to Swami Vivekananda's philosophical viewpoints of man.

A good society as Vivekananda indicates must be altruistic and dynamic, living and thrilling. It necessitates disinterested service of every human being irrespective of apparent differences like caste, creed, culture etc. It also demands kindliness of the heart well balanced by sincerity and discipline, perseverance and punctuality. It is an ardent duty and responsibility of every one in the society to realise God in man living in the society and wholeheartedly work for excellence. "Man and Society: Vivekananda's Vibrant Vision" unfolds Vivekananda's philosophy of man and society from essential perspectives of fullness of man.

To be a real social being is to be truly educated, and to be truly educated is to understand and translate the fact that perfection in life and work is not an alien factor but it is already within every human being. Man must realise this and act accordingly in order to manifest it from diverse perspectives of experiences introspectively or in any way he would decide for the welfare of others. Education as Vivekananda suggests, needs a new platform of awareness that calls forth altruism. The religion of education is to cultivate and propagate with boldness: I am Knowledge, Existence and Bliss. The priorities in education from this invite the education of the soul which is the soul of education. "Man and Education: Vivekananda's Priorities" exposes some of the essential components of education hitherto and even now unduly denied more or less in the pursuit of purity and perfection of man.

Religion in the most apposite role in terms of man as Vivekananda defines and translates in unparalleled practice is "the manifestation of divinity already in man". How to manifest this inherent divinity in man? How to play the role for the practice and perfection of religion that cares for all and denies none? How to nurture religion of the right kind and also of the right mind even under challenging constraints? All these and similar other askances are illuminatingly negotiated in accordance with the serene thoughts and visions of Vivekananda in "Man and Religion: Vivekananda's Viewpoints".

"Man and Values: Vivekananda's Pointers" unfolds some of the essential values that endlessly contribute to the march of man. With rapid and alarming erosion of values now-a-days, it is high time to rethink and re-nurture the values as pointed out by Vivekananda for realisation of the real worth of man.

Spirituality stands for the essence of man for ascent and excellence. To Vivekananda, it is not a myth but a genuine reality for the identity of man who stands for the Ever Excellent. The quest for excellence begins with the spirit of undertaking an unending inner adventure to be prized with best and the beyond. "Man and

Spirituality: Vivekananda's Quest for Excellence" deals with some of the most essential inroads to inner excellence and beyond that.

"Man and Humanism: Vivekananda's Perspectives" and "Man and Aesthetics: Vivekananda's Essence of Elegance" are detailed and critical discussions on humanism and aesthetics as Vivekananda envisions and practises for ever glowing efflorescence of humanism and aesthetics in man, and might reward the revered readers with the aura of uncompromising thoughts.

"Towards the New March of Man: Vivekananda's Dynamic Vision" is an added exposition of the never-to-be-forgotten message of Vivekananda: "Whatever you think, that you will be". Let this invaluable message be the guiding spirit of the new march of man for fullness and perfection.

I convey my love and affection to Sobdo, Priyanka and Suktima, my son, daughter-in-law and grand-daughter respectively for their constant inspiration and co-operation.

If the book appeals to everyone interested in Swami Vivekananda's philosophy of man, I would ardently murmur aside: "Without / The fear of pain or search for pleasure, go / Beyond them both". (Swami Vivekananda: "Peace").

Mohit Chakrabarti
Seemantika

Seemanto Palli
Santiniketan – 731 235
West Bengal, INDIA

Dedicated to

Professor H Nandakumar Sarma
Vice Chancellor
Manipur University, Canchipur, Imphal
&
Professor E Bijoykumar Singh
Dean, School of Social Sciences
Manipur University, Canchipur, Imphal

Conceptual Framework of Vivekananda's Philosophy of Man

Man is the best creation of this universe. To Swami Vivekananda, he is more than that. He is Divine: I am He. He represents all that is best, most catholic, most glorious and most victorious. He knows no joy and sorrow, pleasure and pain, happiness and sadness because he is above all and beyond all. He is deathless because he knows how to win over death. As soon he is blessed with the spirit of winning over death, he wins over birth also because he is the Supreme Self hallowed with the essence of perfection already in him.

From the conceptual points of view, Vivekananda significantly compares man to a spring infinite and ever flowing with its own inherent spirit:

> *Man is like an infinite spring, coiled up in a small box, and that spring is trying to unfold itself; and all the social phenomena that we see the result of this trying to unfold. All the competitions and struggles and evils that we see around us are neither the causes of these unfoldments, nor the effects. As one of our great philosophers says— in the case of the irrigation of a field, the tank is somewhere upon a higher level, and the water is trying to rush into the field, and is barred by a gate. But as soon as the gate is opened, the water rushes in by its own nature; and if there is dust and dirt in the way, the water rolls over them. But dust and dirt are neither the result nor the cause of this unfolding of the divine nature of man. They are co-existent circumstances, and, therefore, can be remedied.*[1]

That man is the highest and best creation of all is undeniable. He is the 'greatest being', greater even than the gods or the angels. As Vivekananda strongly observes:

> *Man is higher than all animals, than all angels; none is greater than man. Even the Devas (gods) will have to come down again and attain to salvation through a human body. Man alone attains to perfection, not even the Devas. According to the Jews and Mohammedans, God created man after creating the angels*

and everything else, and after creating man He asked the angels to come and salute him, and all did so except Iblis; so God cursed him and he became Satan. Behind this allegory is the great truth that this human birth is the greatest birth we can have. The lower creation, the animal, is dull, and manufactured mostly out of Tamas. Animals cannot have any high thoughts; nor can the angels, or the Devas, attain to direct freedom without human birth. In human body, in the same way, too much wealth or too much poverty is a great impediment to the higher development of the soul. It is from the middle classes that the great ones of the world come. Here the forces are very equally adjusted and balanced.[2]

Admittedly, man stands out as the 'most representative being in this universe'. From the Sankhya philosophy, it is obvious that man is the concept of Mahat— universal consciousness— well embodied in the spirit of greatness. Analysing man in terms of the 'body', Vivekananda exposes the real identity of man, the most celebrated 'thinking being' and the universe the 'Om':

It naturally follows that if the universe is built upon the same plan as the body, the universe also must have the same divisions of form, name, and thought. The "thought" is the finest part of the universe, the real motive power. The thought behind our body is called soul, and the thought behind the universe is called God. Then after that is the name, and last of all is the form which we see and feel. For instance, you are a particular person, a little universe in this universe, and behind that is the name, what is called the "Word" in all religions, and behind that is God. The universal thought is Mahat, as the Sankhyas call it, universal consciousness. What is that name? There must be some name. The world is homogeneous, and modern science shows beyond doubt that each atom is composed of the same material as the whole universe. If you know one lump of clay you know the whole universe. Man is the most representative being in the universe, the microcosm, a small universe in himself. So in man we find there is the form, behind that the name, and behind that the thought, the thinking being. So this universe must be on exactly the same plan. The question is: What is that name? According to the Hindus, that word is Om. The old Egyptians also believed that. The Katha Upanishad says, "That, seeking

> *which a man practises Brahmacharya, I will tell you in short what that is, that is Om.*[3]

The new concept of man as God—*Narayana*— as Vivekananda emphasises is the highest form of reverence with which man is identified. This not only ensures the true identity of man but also glorifies him as the living God. From a report published in *The Tribune*, it is explicit that Vivekananda characteristically interprets this role of man towards man in terms of worship:

> *The highest form of worship that had been laid down by the Bhakta was the worship of man. Really, if there were to be any sort of worship, he would suggest getting a poor man, or six, or twelve, as their circumstances would permit, every day to their homes, and serving them, thinking that they were Narayanas. He had seen charity in many countries and the reason it did not succeed was that it was not done with a good spirit. "Here, take this, and go away"— that was not charity, but the expression of the pride of the heart, to gain the applause of the world, that the world might know they were becoming charitable. Hindus must know that, according to the Smritis, the giver was lower than the receiver, for the receiver was for the time being God Himself. Therefore he would suggest such a form of worship as getting some of these poor Narayanas into every house every day, and giving them the worship they would give to an image, feeding them and clothing them, and the next day doing the same to others. He did not condemn any form of worship, but he went to say was that the highest form and the most necessary at present in India was this form of Narayana worship.*[4]

That a man should possess and maintain his own identity by crystallising himself through erudition and perseverance is the genesis of man as the symbol of excellence and ascent. It is his earnest endeavour to continually upgrade himself in terms of truth. He should never surrender himself to anything that serves as a constraint to his right thinking. Vivekananda explains this point in a very radical way in terms of man and religion:

> *The peculiar tendencies with which a person is born must remain with him. This is the chief reason why the world cannot be of one religion— and God forbid that there should be one religion only—for the world would then be a chaos and not a cosmos. A*

> *man must follow the tendencies peculiar to himself; and if he gets a teacher to help him to advance along his own lines, he will progress. We should let a person go the way he intends to go, but if we try to force him into another path, he will lose what he has already attained and will become worthless. As the face of one person does not resemble that of another, so the nature of one differs from that of another, and why should he not be allowed to act accordingly? A river flows in a certain direction; and if you direct the course into a regular channel, the current becomes rapid and the force is increased, but try to divert it from its proper course, and you will see the result; the volume as well as the force will be lessened. This life is very important, and it, therefore, ought to be guided in the way one's tendency prompts him.*[5]

An ardent believer in the sternness of man, Vivekananda prioritises man's sanity as one of the most significant components of personality. His vision of man is deeply influenced by Buddha's philosophy of man. As he frankly submits:

> *He [Buddha] died at a ripe old age. All his life he was a most stern man: he never yielded to weakness. I do not believe many of his doctrines; of course, I do not. I believe that the Vedantism of the old Hindus is much more thoughtful, is a grander philosophy of life. I like his method of work, but what I like [most] in that man is that, among all the prophets of mankind, here was a man who never had any cobwebs in his brain, and [who was] sane and strong. When kingdoms were at his feet, he was still the same man, maintaining "I am the man amongst men."*[6]

What, then, is man? Man, as Vivekananda identifies in terms of the Advaita philosophy, is Brahman:

> *According to the Advaita philosophy, there is only one thing real in the universe, which it calls Brahman; everything else is unreal, manifested, and manufactured out of Brahman by the power of Maya. To reach back to that Brahman is our goal. We are, each one of us, that Brahman, that Reality, plus this Maya. If we can get rid of this Maya or ignorance, then we become what we really are. According to this philosophy, each man consists of three parts— the body, the internal organ or the mind, and*

behind that, what is called the Atman, the Self. The body is the external coating and the mind is the internal coating of the Atman who is the real perceiver, the real enjoyer, the being in the body who is working the body by means of the internal organ or the mind.[7]

Tracing the whole history of man, Vivekananda unfolds the concept of man in terms of the cosmos and the Self. He also associates the whole history of man with the whole history of nature and the whole history of life:

> *Everything in nature rises from some fine seed-forms, becomes grosser and grosser, exists for a certain time, and again goes back to the original fine form. Our earth, for instance, has come out of a nebulous form which, becoming colder and colder, turned into this crystallised planet upon which we live, and in the future it will again go to pieces and return to its rudimentary nebulous form. This is happening in the universe, and has been through time immemorial. This is the whole history of man, the whole history of nature, the whole history of life.*[8]

The concept of man endearing and glorifying the vision of ascent and excellence through the progress of the soul is a new philosophy of man. While explaining the circular movement of the soul in human body, Vivekananda points out:

> *Every soul moves in a circle, as it were, and will have to complete it; and no soul can go so low but that there will come a time when it will have to go upwards. It may start straight down, but it has to take the upward curve to complete the circuit. We are all projected from a common centre, which is God, and will come back after completing the circuit to the centre from which we started.*
>
> *Each soul is a circle. The centre is where the body is, and the activity is manifested there. You are omnipresent, though you have the consciousness of being concentrated in only one point. That point has taken up particles of matter and formed them into a machine to express itself. That through which it expresses itself is called the body. You are everywhere. When one body or machine fails you, the centre moves on and takes up other particles of matter, finer or grosser, and works through them. Here is man.*[9]

Again, the concept of man from the standpoint of perfection is endless but interesting, tireless and challenging. The science of the study of the human mind is always in quest of the real end where the higher mind of man gets its signal and input of perfection.

Vivekananda emphasises on the utility of the science of the mind because it never allows us to remain under the dominance of nature but to conquer nature and march ahead beyond life. This is the true identity of man:

> *Now, can we not hasten the growth of individuals? We can. Can we limit to the hastening? We cannot say how much a man can grow in one life. You have no reason to say that this much a man can do and no more. Circumstances can hasten him wonderfully. Can there be any limit then, till you come to perfection? So, what comes of it? – That a perfect man, that is to say, the type that is to come of this race, perhaps millions of years hence, that man can come today. And this is what the Yogis say, that all great incarnations and prophets are such men; that they reached perfection in this one life. We have such men at all periods of the world's history and at all times. Quite recently, there was such a man who lived the life of the whole human race and reached the end— even in this life. Even this hastening of the growth must be under laws. Suppose we can investigate these laws and understand their secrets and apply them to our own needs; it follows that we grow. We hasten our growth, we hasten our development, and we become perfect, even in this life. This is the higher part of our life, and the science of the study of mind and its powers has this perfection as its real end. Helping others with money and other material things and teaching them how to go on smoothly in their daily life are mere details.*
>
> *The utility of this science is to bring out the perfect man, and not let him wait and wait for ages, just a plaything in the hands of the physical world, like a log of drift-wood carried from wave to wave and tossing about in the ocean. This science wants you to be strong, to take the work in your own hand, instead of leaving it in the hands of nature, and get beyond this little life.*[10]

The destiny of man lies in his own hands. It is man who shapes his destiny in accordance with his devotion to duties and responsibilities. None else can be made responsible for framing and re-framing his present, past and future. In explaining the role of man in relation to his duties and responsibilities in life, Vivekananda elegantly observes:

> *We see in this life that we can shape and form our future; every one of us, every day, is trying to shape the morrow. Today we fix the fate of the morrow; tomorrow we shall fix the fate of the day after, and so on. It is quire logical that this reasoning can be pushed backward too. If by our own deeds we shape our destiny in the future, why not apply the same rule to the past? If, in an infinite chain, a certain number of links are alternately repeated, then, if one of these groups of links be explained, we can explain the whole chain. So, in this infinite length of time, if we can cut off one portion and explain that portion and understand it, then, if it be true that nature is uniform, the same explanation must apply to the whole chain of time. If it be true that we are working out our own destiny here within this short space of time, if it be true that everything must have a cause as we see it now, it must also be true that that which we are now is the effect of the whole of our past; therefore, no other person is necessary to shape the destiny of mankind but man himself.*[11]

The Real Man is Universal. He is the Universal Being. Man is never bound by any limited vision. He enjoys the broad and boundless spectrum of reality. From the spiritual points of view, man is present everywhere in every thought and action, word and motion. Vivekananda's spiritual and mystic vision of the Real Man is clear and explicit:

> *The body is not the Real Man, neither is the mind, for the mind waxes and wanes. It is the Spirit beyond, which alone can live for ever. The body and mind are continually changing, and are, in fact, only names of series of changeful phenomena, like rivers whose waters are in a constant state of flux, yet presenting the appearance of unbroken streams. Every particle in this body is continually changing; no one has the same body for many minutes together, and yet we think of it as the same body. So with the mind; one moment it is happy, another moment unhappy; one moment strong, another weak; an ever-changing whirlpool. That cannot be the Spirit which is infinite. Change can only be in the limited. To say that the infinite changes in*

any way is absurd; it cannot be. You can move and I can move, as limited bodies; every particle in this universe is in a constant state of flux, but taking the universe as a unit, as one whole, it cannot move, it cannot change. Motion is always a relative thing. I move in relation to something else. Any particle in this universe can change in relation to any other particle; but take the whole universe as one, and in relation to what can it move? There is nothing besides it. So this infinite Unit is unchangeable, immovable, absolute, and this is the Real Man. Our reality, therefore, consists in the Universal and not in the limited. These are old delusions, however comfortable they are, to think that we are limited beings, constantly changing. People are frightened when they are told that they are Universal Being, everywhere present. Through everything you work, through every foot you move, through every lip you talk, through every heart you feel.[12]

The conceptual vision of man the infinite is always looked upon as one of the most significant components of the celebration of man. That man is always in quest of infinite desire and its endless fulfilment is a characteristic vision of the ascent of man. In one of the lectures delivered in New York at the Vedanta Society in June 1900, Vivekananda strongly upholds:

We seek neither misery nor happiness, but freedom. This one aim is the secret of the insatiable thirst of man. Man's thirst, says the Hindu, man's thirst, says the Buddhist, is a burning, unquenchable thirst for more and more. You Americans are always looking for more pleasure, more enjoyment. You cannot be satisfied, true; but at bottom what you seek is freedom.

This vastness of his desire is really the sign of man's own infinitude. It is because he is infinite, that he can only be satisfied when his desire is infinite and its fulfilment infinite.

What then can satisfy man? Not gold. Not enjoyment. Not beauty. One Infinite alone can satisfy him, and that Infinite is Himself. When he realises this then alone comes freedom.

"This flute, with the sense-organs as its keyholes,

With all its sensations, perceptions, and song.

Is singing only one thing. It longs to go back to the wood whence it was cut!"

"Deliver thou thyself by thyself!
Ah, do not let thyself sink!
For thou art thyself thy greatest friend,
And thou thyself thy greatest enemy."[13]

With freedom as the ultimate reality of man the Infinite, Vivekananda, draws our attention to the cultivation of love, sympathy and infinite patience for the welfare of others. And to cultivate all these invaluable components we must be free with free will. Only freedom, genuine and serene, marks the victory of man the Infinite. Let us pronounce with promise of perfection the soul-stirring and poignant words of Vivekananda:

> *Give up the notion that man is a responsible being, only the perfect man is a responsible being, only the perfect man is responsible. The ignorant have drunk deep of the cup of delusion and are not sane. You, who* know, *must have infinite passion with these. Have nothing but love for them and find out the disease that has made them see the world in a wrong light, then help them to cure it and see a right. Remember always that only the free have free will; all the rest are in bondage and are not responsible for what they do. Will as will is bound. The water when melting on the top of the Himalayas is free, but becoming the river, it is bound by the banks; yet the original impetus carries it to the sea, and it regains its freedom. The first is the "fall of man", the second is the "resurrection". Not one atom can rest until it finds freedom.*[14]

What, then, should be the role of man in terms of freedom and love? How should these be really meaningful for manifestation of fullness and perfection? How should we be really justified to the real being within every one of us? Vivekananda's viewpoints clarify all these queries:

> *Freedom and highest love must go together, then neither can become a bondage. We can give nothing to God; he gives all to us. He is the Guru of Gurus. Then we find that He is the "Soul of our souls", our very Self. No wonder we love Him, He is the Soul of our souls; whom or what else can we love? We want to be the "steady flame, burning without heat and without smoke". To whom can you do good, when you see only God? You cannot*

do good to God! All doubt goes, all is, "sameness". If you do good at all, you do it to yourself; feel that the receiver is the higher one. You serve the other because you are lower than he, not because he is low and you are high. Give as the rose gives perfume, because it is its own nature, utterly unconscious of giving.[15]

The concept of man varied but distinct as Vivekananda unfolds in diverse and different dimensions by encapsulating education, society, religion, spirituality and aesthetics has no parallel in the history of interpreting the philosophy of man. Man, the ever glorious one, knows how to overcome all constraints, however difficult these might be. He also knows how to challenge alone without being assisted by anyone at any time anywhere. He is ever optimistic, ever patient, ever loving, ever good and and ever sacrificing. His only duty and responsibility is to spread the aroma of excellence and perfection like a violet. In the vibrant and stimulating words of Vivekananda:

What though thy bed be frozen earth,
Thy cloak the chilling blast;
What though no mate to cheer thy path,
Thy sky with gloom o'ercast;
What though if love itself doth fail,
Thy fragrance strewed in vain;
What though if bad o'er good prevail,
And vice o'er virtue reign:
Change not thy nature, gentle bloom,
Thou violet, sweet and pure,
But ever pour thy sweet perfume
Unasked, unstinted, sure![16]

When would everyone rise up to translate the meaning of man in the light of the above?

1. Swami Vivekananda: *The Complete Works of Swami Vivekananda*, Advaita Ashrama, Kolkata, Mayavati Memorial Edition, 1989, Vol. I, p. 389.
2. *Ibid.*, p. 142.
3. *Ibid.*, Vol. IV, pp. 49-50.
4. *Ibid.*, Vol. III, p. 391.
5. *Ibid.*, pp. 358-359.
6. *Ibid.*, p. 527.
7. *Ibid.*, Vol. II, p. 254.
8. *Ibid.*, Vol. V, p. 255.
9. *Ibid.*, p. 271.
10. *Ibid.*, Vol. II, pp. 18-19.
11. *Ibid.*, p. 242.
12. *Ibid.*, pp. 79-80.
13. *Ibid.*, Vol. VIII, pp. 250-251.
14. *Ibid.*, Vol. VII, p.99.
15. *Ibid.*, p. 86.
16. *Ibid.*, Vol. VIII, pp. 169-170.

MAN AND SOCIETY: VIVEKANANDA'S VIBRANT VISION

Man is an essential part of the society. He is also inseparable from the society in which he lives as well as from all other societies in the whole world. In fact, a man to be men and *vice versa* must explore a universal identity of man and society. An ever radical thinker and iconoclast, Swami Vivekananda has pointed out time and again the real relationship between man and society. If man stands apart from society, man turns out to be absolutely useless as being gifted with rationality and humane sensibilities. Again, if society is dissociated from human habitation and is solely at the mercy of other living creatures and nature, it loses the fullness and cadence of living.

Man is not only the living spirit of society but also an incomparable force to promote and illumine the latter in terms of religion, aesthetics, morality, spirituality and mystic grandeur. Indeed, when we say that a man is social, it not only indicates that he is a part and parcel of the society but also points out and highlights the fact that he is dedicated to the spirit of altruism. As such, a truly social man never cares for his own health, happiness and prosperity but sacrifices everything for the welfare of everyone of the society to which he belongs and finds out the true meaning of man and society in the harmony of humane and catholic relationship.

To educate and raise the masses to be conscious of themselves is the key to making a harmonious relationship between man and society. Vivekananda draws our attention to the importance of mass education for the real awakening of fullness of man already in him in terms of individuality. As he emphasises on his own mission of mass education:

> *Everyone must work out his own salvation. Our duty is to put the chemicals together, the crystallisation will come through God's laws. Let us put ideas into their heads, and they will do the rest. Now this means educating the masses. Here are these difficulties. A pauper government cannot, will not do anything; so no help from that quarter.*

Even supposing we are in a position to open schools in each village free, still the poor boys would rather go to the plough to earn their living than come to your school. Neither have we the money, nor can we make them come to education. The problem seems hopeless. I have found a way out. It is this. If the mountain does not come to Mohammed, Mohammed must go to the mountain. If the poor cannot come to education, education must reach them at the plough, in the factory, everywhere. How? You have seen my brethren. Now I can get hundreds of such, all over India, unselfish, good, and educated. Let these men go from village to village bringing not only religion to the door of everyone but also education.[1]

A healthy and ideal relationship between man and society is the cultivation of intelligence and culture by one and all. Intelligence is never a monopoly of a few sections of people of the society where the spirit of intelligence is dwarfed. At the same time, true culture should never be the monopoly of a few people in the society. This will lead to anarchy in the society. Vivekananda inspires on the importance of advancement of intelligence and culture amongst everyone in the society because that alone highlights the true spirit of democracy, which has served as a pathfinder of India's march for crowning glory in the all-round welfare of man and society everywhere:

Intelligence must not remain the monopoly of the cultured few; it will be disseminated from higher to lower classes. Education is coming and compulsory education will follow. The immense power of our people for work must be utilised. India's potentialities are great and will be called forth.[2]

To eliminate the distinction between the high and the low, the advantaged and the disadvantaged, the haves and the have-nots in the society, Vivekananda has emphasised on the spirit of sympathy to be cultivated in all sections of the society irrespective of caste or creed, colour or culture, this will create a healthy and living social atmosphere bereft of which human progress is impossible. In response to a point made by one of his disciples on the constraints in making a harmonious bond of relationship between the higher and the lower classes in the society, he strongly observes:

But without that there is no well-being for your upper classes. You will be destroyed by internecine quarrels and fights— which you have been having so long. When the masses will wake up, they will come to understand your oppression of them, and by a puff of their mouth you will be entirely blown away! It is they who have introduced civilisation amongst you; and it is they who will then pull it down. Think how at the hands of the Gauls the mighty ancient Roman civilisation crumbled into dust! Therefore I say, try to rouse these lower classes from slumber by imparting learning and culture to them. When they will awaken— and awaken one day they must— they also will not forget your good services to them and will remain grateful to you.[3]

For a new birth of the society in honouring everyone to have a free access to the study and practice of religious scriptures, Vivekananda is always radical and iconoclastic. He has protested against the autocratic power of the Brahmins in religious ceremonies and in reply to a query made by one of his disciples on the dominance of the Brahmins everywhere, he categorically observes:

I don't find it. Where do the tenfold Samskaras or purifying ceremonies enjoined by the Shastras obtain still? Well, I have travelled the whole of India, and everywhere I have found society to be guided by local usages which are condemned by the Shrutis and Smritis. Popular customs, local usages, and observances prevalent among women only— have not these taken the place of the Smritis everywhere? Who obeys, and whom? If you can but spend enough money, the priest-class is ready to write out whatever sanctions or prohibitions you want! How many of them read the Vedic Kalpa (Ritual), Grihya and Shrauta Sutras? Then, look, here in Bengal the code of Raghunandana is obeyed: a little farther on you will find the code of Mitakshara in vogue; while in another part the code of Manu holds sway! You seem to think that the same laws hold good everywhere! What I want therefore is to introduce the study of the Vedas by stimulating a greater regard for them in the minds of the people, and to pass everywhere the injunctions of the Vedas.[4]

A new society always means a dedicated group of parsons or a community always ready for service to others. This broadens the vision of man the ever altruistic and benevolent, self-sacrificing and transparent. Vivekananda upholds the vision of man and *vice versa* in terms of a society that promises man the ever victorious against all odds and constraints symbolising challenges in different and diverse dimensions. As a practical visionary of man, society and the world at large, he significantly points out

> *Our duty to others means helping others; doing good to the world. Why should we do good to the world? Apparently to help the world, but really to help ourselves. We should always try to help the world, that should be the highest motive in us; but if we consider well, we find that the world does not require our help at all. This world was not made that you or I should come and help it. I once read a sermon in which it was said, "All this beautiful world is very good, because it gives us time and opportunity to help others." Apparently, this is a very beautiful sentiment, but is it not a blasphemy to say that the world needs our help? We cannot deny that there is much misery in it; to go out and help others is, therefore, the best thing we can do, although in the long run, we shall find that helping others is only helping ourselves. As a boy I had some white mice. They were kept in a little box in which there were little wheels, and when the mice tried to cross the wheels, the wheels turned and turned, and the mice never got anywhere. So, it is with the world and our helping it. The only help is that we get moral exercise. This world is neither good nor evil; each man manufactures a world for himself. If a blind man begins to think of the world, it is either as soft or hard, or as cold or hot. We are a mass of happiness or misery; we have seen that hundreds of times in our lives. As a rule, the young are optimistic and the old pessimistic. The young have life before them; the old complain their day is gone; hundreds of desires, which they cannot fulfil struggle in their hearts. Both are foolish nevertheless. Life is good or evil according to the state of mind in which we look at it, it is neither by itself. Fire, by itself, is neither good nor evil. When it keeps us warm we say, "How beautiful is fire!" When it burns our fingers, we blame it. Still, in itself it is neither good nor bad. According as we use it, it produces in us the feeling of good or bad; so also is this world. It is perfect. By perfection is meant that it is perfectly fitted to meet its ends. We may all be perfectly sure that it will go on beautifully well without us, and we need not bother our heads wishing to help it.*[5]

The 'salvation of humanity' as the basic principle of man in every society is the true identity of man. For this, everyone must be buoyant with the spirit of patriotism. It is a great burden for every individual to seriously think and awaken within everyone the inherent divinity for the welfare of the world society. In his address delivered at Kumbakonam on the mission of the Vedanta, Vivekananda's clarion call for 'the salvation of humanity' is a definite pointer to paving the path for this end-in-view:

> *Great has been our nation's work in the past; and if we cannot do greater things in the future, let us have this consolation that we can sink and die together in peace. Be patriots, love the race which has done such great things for us in the past. Ay, the more I compare notes, the more I love you, my fellow-countrymen; you are good and pure and gentle. You have been always tyrannised over, and such is the irony of this material world of Maya. Never mind that; the Spirit will triumph in the long run. In the meanwhile let us work and let us not abuse our country, let us not curse and abuse the weather-beaten and work-worn institutions of our thrice-holy motherland. Have no word of condemnation even for the most superstitious and the most irrational of its institutions, for they also must have served some good in the past. Remember always that there is not in the world any other country whose institutions are really better in their aims and objects than the institutions of this land. I have seen castes in almost every country in the world, but nowhere is their plan and purpose so glorious as here. If caste is thus unavoidable, I would rather have a caste of purity and culture and self-sacrifice, than a caste of dollars. Therefore utter no words of condemnation. Close your lips and let your hearts open. Work out the salvation of this land and of the whole world, each of you thinking that the entire burden is on your shoulders. Carry the light and the life of the Vedanta to every door, and rouse up the divinity that is hidden within every soul. Then, whatever may be the measure of your success, you will have this satisfaction that you have lived, worked, and died for a great cause. In the success of this cause, howsoever brought out, is centred the salvation of humanity here and hereafter.*[6]

In our ideal of working for the good of the society, we must be free from all attachments, all personal pleasure and pain, all sorrow and happiness. This will enable us to learn the secret of how to work best for the society. This is really challenging for every one of us wishing to be truly social and altruistic, controlled and calm. If any one of us succeeds, he truly becomes an ideal worker of man and society.

In Karma-Yoga, Vivekananda spells out the secret of how to work for the society in all excellence and perfection:

> *Intense activity is necessary; we must always work. We cannot live a minute without work. What then becomes of rest? Here is one side of the life-struggle— work, in which we are whirled rapidly round. And here is the other— that of calm, retiring renunciation: everything is peaceful around, there is very little of noise and show, only nature with her animals and flowers and mountains. Neither of them is a perfect picture. A man used to solitude, if brought in contact with the surging whirlpool of the world, will be crushed by it; just as the fish that lives in the deep sea water, as soon as it is brought to the surface, breaks into pieces, deprived of the weight of water on it that had kept it together. Can a man who has been used to the turmoil and the rush of life live at ease if he comes to a quiet place? He suffers and perchance may lose his mind. The ideal man is he who, in the midst of the greatest silence and solitude, finds the intensest activity, and in the midst of the intensest activity finds the silence and solitude of the desert. He has learnt the secret of restraint, he has controlled himself. He goes through the streets of a big city with all its traffic, and his mind is as calm as if he were in a cave, where not a sound could reach him; and he is intensely working all the time. That is the ideal of Karma-Yoga, and if you have attained to that you have really learnt the secret of work.*
>
> *But we have to begin from the beginning, to take up the works as they come to us and slowly make ourselves more unselfish every day. We must do the work and find out the motive power that prompts us; and, almost without exception, in the first years, we shall find that our motives are always selfish; but gradually this selfishness will melt by persistence, till at last will come the time when we shall be able to do really unselfish work. We may all hope that some day or other, as we struggle through the*

paths of life, there will come a time when we shall become perfectly unselfish; and the moment we attain to that, all our powers will be concentrated, and the knowledge which is ours will be manifest.[7]

The socio-spiritual vision of man as Vivekananda highlights in the spirit of Vedantism necessitates a look afresh in the context of the relation between man and society at present. To love every human being as one's very own is the hallmark of socio-spiritual advancement. The vision of the Impersonal God becomes more transparent and accessible in fusion with the living society. Every human being becomes aware of the well-being of the society even at the cost of self-denial and self-sacrifice so that a man becomes men in the society and *vice versa*.

The altruistic socio-spiritual advancement of man in the marvellous manifestation of Bhakti or renunciation of the highest order in the midst of multi-dimensional constraints is really vibrant and pulsating. Unless there is a call from within for the all-round welfare of man and society, the vision of altruism becomes a myth. It is time to address the fusion and solidarity of all life so that man and society are in cohesion with each other anywhere.

Vivekananda characteristically unfolds the vision of the socio-spiritual man in terms of the Impersonal God:

It is only through the idea of the Impersonal God that you can have any system of ethics. In every nation the truth has been preached from the most ancient times— love your fellow-beings as yourselves— I mean, love human beings as yourselves. In India it has been preached, "Love all beings as yourselves"; we make no distinction between men and animals. But no reason was forthcoming, no one knew why it would be good to love other beings as ourselves. And the reason, why, is there in the idea of the Impersonal God; you understand it when you learn that the whole world is one— the oneness of the universe— the solidarity of all life— that in hurting any one I am hurting myself, in loving any one I am loving myself. Hence we understand why it is that we ought not to hurt others. The reason for ethics, therefore, can only be had from this ideal of the Impersonal God. Then there is the question of the position of the Personal God in it. I understand the wonderful flow of love that comes from the idea of a Personal God, I thoroughly appreciate the power and potency of Bhakti on men to suit the needs of different times. What we now want in our country, however, is not so much of weeping, but a little strength. What a mine of strength is in this Impersonal God, when all have been thrown overboard, and man stands on his feet with the knowledge— I am the Impersonal Being of the world! What can make me afraid? I care not for nature's laws. Death is a joke to me.[8]

Activity—Rajas—is the prime need for man for social advancement. Unless there is an inner urge in every one for sincere involvements in diverse social activities, there is no hope for regeneration of man and society. Activity is life, inactivity is death. When a person is sincere in discharging his duties and responsibilities as a social being, he enters the world of service as the blessings of the All Serene. Then the society to which he belongs no longer remains as a mere society but an embodiment of the living God. He adores and worships every human being as the representative of the All Serene.

In explaining the role of work in our life and society to one of his disciples, Vivekananda strongly asserts:

In this human life, one cannot help doing some kind of work always. When man has perforce to do some work, Karma-Yoga enjoins on him to do it in such a way as as will bring freedom through the realisation of the Atman. As to your objection that none will be induced to work— the answer is, that whatever work you do has some motive behind it; but when by the long performance of work, one notices that one work merely leads to another, through a round of births and rebirths, then the awakened discrimination of man naturally begins to question itself, "Where is the end to this interminable chain of work?" It is then that he appreciates the full import of the words of the Lord in the Gita: "Inscrutable is the course of work." Therefore when the aspirant finds that work with motive brings no happiness, then he renounces action. But man is so constituted that to him the performance of work is a necessity, so what work should he take up? He takes up some unselfish work, but gives up all desire for its fruits.[9]

Man must dedicate himself to the well-being of the society. This is an arduous task. But this is really very challenging. Despite many constraints we have no alternative but to accept and negotiate that inevitable challenge. Addressing one of his disciples on how to bring about harmony among people of different sections in the society, Vivekananda observes:

> *If you think any work difficult, then do not come here. Through the grace of God all paths become easy. Your work is to serve the poor and miserable, without distinction of caste or colour, and you have no need to think about the results. Your duty is to go on working, and then everything will follow of itself. My method of work is to construct and not to pull down. Read the history of the world, and you will find that a great soul stood as the central figure in a certain period of a country. Animated by his ideas, hundreds of people did good to the world. You are all intelligent boys, and have been coming here for a long time. Say, what have you done? Couldn't you give one life for the service of others? In the next life you may read Vedanta and other philosophies. Give this life for the service of others, then I shall know that your coming here has not been in vain.*[10]

For the dawn of a new and living socio-spiritual consciousness, man must untiringly strive for endless service for all-round well-being of humankind. The dream that evokes a vibrant vision of man and society is yet to be dreamt. It is the dream that shines in the success of an enlightened and glorious society where every one is unique with the vision of fullness in self-sacrifice and self-excellence.

In realising the dream as above, Vivekananda places this promise of poignancy before us to boldly assert:

> *If things go ill or well—*
>
> *If joy rebounding spreads the face,*
>
> *Or sea of sorrow swells—*
>
> *A play— we each have part,*
>
> *Each one to weep or laugh as may;*
>
> *Each one his dress to don—*
>
> *Its scenes, alternative shine and rain.*
>
> *Thou dream, O blessed dream!*
>
> *Spread far and near thy veil of haze,*

Tone down the lines so sharp,
Make smooth what roughness seems.
No magic but in thee!
Thy touch makes desert bloom to life.
Harsh thunder, sweetest song,
Fell death, the sweet release.[11]

Love for the society to which one belongs leads to love for the country. One must wake up for the well-being of the society. It is a call from within and does not wait for any instruction from outside. This is a force that fully assures elimination of 'hypocrites and brutes' who are always engaged in bringing down the progress and excellence of any society.

In a letter to Shrimati Sarala Ghosal, editor, the *Bharati,* written on 6th April, 1897, Vivekananda significantly states:

> *There are many things to be done, but means are wanting in this country. We have brains, but no hands. We have the doctrine of Vedanta, but we have not the power to reduce to practice. In our books there is the doctrine of universal equality, but in work we make great distinctions. It was in India that unselfish and disinterested work of the most exalted type was preached; but in practice* we *are awfully cruel, awfully heartless— unable to think besides our own mass-of-flesh bodies.*
>
> *Yet it is only through the present state of things that it is possible to proceed to work. There is no other way. Every one has the power to judge of good and evil, but he is the hero who undaunted by the waves of Samsara— which is full of errors, delusions, and miseries— with one hand wipes the tears, and with the other, unshaken, shows the path of deliverance. On the other hand, there is the conservative society, like a mass of inert matter; on the other, the restless, impatient, fire-darting reformer; the way to good lies between the two. I heard in Japan that it was the belief of the girls of that country that their dolls would be animated if they were loved with all their heart. The Japanese girl never breaks her doll. O you of great fortune! I too believe that India will awake again if anyone could love with all his heart the people of the country— bereft of the grace of affluence, of blasted fortune, their discretion totally lost, downtrodden,*

ever-starved, quarrelsome, and envious. Then only India will awake, when hundreds of large-hearted men and women, giving up all desires of enjoying the luxuries of life, will long and exert themselves to their utmost for the well-being of the millions of their countrymen who are gradually sinking lower and lower in the vortex of destitution and ignorance. I have experienced even in my insignificant life that good motives, sincerity, and infinite love can conquer the world. One single soul possessed of these virtues can destroy the dark designs of millions of hypocrites and brutes.[12]

A rebirth of man and society always depends on alertness, sincerity, devotion and dedication. It is never a miracle but action—positive, pure, purposeful and pointed. It must be a matter of selfless service that never cares for name and fame, power and position, vanity and appreciation. What it always cares and strives for is all-round altruism and advancement.

In a letter written on 28th May, 1894 from Chicago, Vivekananda advises Alisinga:

Act on the educated young men, bring them together, and organise them. Great things can be done by great sacrifices only. No selfishness, no name, no fame, yours or mine, nor my Master's even! Work, work the idea, the plan, my boys, my brave, noble, good souls— to the wheel, to the wheel put your shoulders! Stop not to look back for name , or fame, or any such nonsense. Throw self overboard and work. Remember, "The grass when made into a rope by being joined together can even chain a mad elephant." The Lord's blessings on you all! His power be in you all— as I believe it is already. *"Wake up, stop not until the goal is reached", say the Vedas. Up, up, the long night is passing, the day is approaching, the wave has risen, nothing will be able to resist its tidal fury. The spirit, my boys, the spirit; the love, my children, the love; the faith, the belief; and fear not! The greatest sin is fear.*

My blessings on all. Tell all the noble souls in Madras who have helped our cause that I send them my eternal love and gratitude, but I beg of them not to slacken. Throw the idea broadcast. Do not be proud; do not insist upon anything dogmatic; do not go against anything— ours is to put chemicals together, the Lord

> *knows how and when the crystal will form. Above all, be not inflated with my success or yours. Great works are to be done; what is this small success in comparison with what is to come? Believe, believe, the decree has gone forth, the fiat of the Lord has gone forth— India must rise, the masses and the poor are to be made happy. Rejoice that you are the chosen instruments in His hands. The flood of spirituality has risen. I see it is rolling over the land resistless, boundless, all-absorbing. Every man to the fore, every good will be added to its forces, every hand will smooth its way, and glory be unto the Lord!*[13]

While cultivation of sympathy is the watchword of man and society, it is obligatory to ignore personal sorrow or happiness at the time of devotion to work for the cause of anyone or anything in the society. The world is a great school for learning man and society. Here the struggle for the lowly and the lost, the poor and the ignorant demands tireless and unyielding self-determination, self-dependence and self-advancement by totally ignoring personal calamity that might befall at any time under any circumstances. The great sacrifice thus undertaken will definitely usher forth a new dawn of awakening of man and society.

In another letter written earlier to Alasinga on 20th August, 1893, Vivekananda ventilates the vision of man and society in the light of the above:

> *I have been dragged through a whole life full of crosses and tortures, I have seen the the nearest and dearest die, almost of starvation; I have been ridiculed, distrusted, and have suffered for my sympathy for the very men who scoff and scorn. Well, my boy, this is the school of misery, which is also the school of great souls and prophets for the cultivation of sympathy, of patience, and, above all, of an indomitable iron will which quakes not even if the universe be pulverised at our feet. I pity them. It is not their fault. They are children, yea, veritable children, though they be great and high in society. Their eyes see nothing beyond their little horizon of a few yards— the routine-work, eating, drinking, earning, and begetting, following each other in mathematical precision. They know nothing beyond— happy little souls! Their sleep is never disturbed, their nice little brown studies of lives never rudely shocked by the wail of woe, of*

misery, of degradation, and poverty, that has filled the Indian atmosphere— the result of centuries of oppression. They little dream of the ages of tyranny, mental, moral, and physical, that has reduced the image of God to a mere beast of burden; the emblem of the Divine Mother, to a slave to bear children; and life itself, a curse. But there are others who see, feel, and shed tears of blood in their hearts, who think that there is a remedy for it, and who are ready to apply this remedy at any cost, even to the giving up of life. And "of such is the kingdom of Heaven". Is it not then natural, my friends, that they have no time to look down from their heights to the vagaries of these contemptible little insects, ready every moment to spit their little venoms?

Trust not to the so-called rich, they are more dead than alive. The hope lies in you— in the meek, the lowly, but the faithful. Have faith in the Lord; no policy, it is nothing. Feel for the miserable and look up for help— it shall come..[14]

A new vision of man in the true spirit of social equality as Vivekananda suggests is a religion of religions yet to be adored and practised with earnestness from everyone everywhere. It is a social religion that pays more attention to the dignity of man. It is also a social religion that re-frames social power and justice in terms of protest against religion that overrides the sovereignty of a society. As Vivekananda emphasises:

We believe that it is the duty of every soul *to treat, think of, and behave to other* souls *as such, i.e., as* Gods, *and not hate or despise, or vilify, or try to injure them by any manner or means. This is the duty not only of the Sannyasin, but of all men and women.*

** ** **

Social laws were created by economic conditions under the sanction of religion. The terrible mistake of religion was to interfere in social matters but how hypocritically it says and thereby contradicts itself, "Social reform is not the business of religion"! True, what we want is that religion should not be a social reformer, but we insist at the same time that society has no right to become a religious law-giver. Hands off! Keep yourself to your own bounds and everything would come right.[15]

Man, as Vivekananda strongly asserts, must be the true emblem of the society. It is the duty of every human being to guarantee every society freedom from the tyranny of the minority. How to bring about a change so desired? Vivekananda draws our attention towards an enlightened and spirited society through education. It is the only viable way out. Otherwise, social reforms will ever remain a myth.

Referring to the importance of education for advancement of man and social change, Vivekananda categorically remarks:

> *We do stand in need of social reform. At times great men would evolve new ideas of progress, and kings would give them the sanction of law. Thus social improvements had been in the past made in India, and in modern times to effect such progressive reforms, we will have first to build up such an authoritative power. Kings having gone, the power is the people's. We have, therefore, to wait till the people are educated, till they understand their needs and are ready and able to solve their problems. The tyranny of the minority is the worst tyranny in the world. Therefore, instead of frittering away our energies on ideal reforms, which will never become practical, we had better go to the root of the evil and make a legislative body, that is to say, educate our people, so that they may be able to solve their own problems. Until that is done all these ideal reforms will remain ideals only. The new order of things is the salvation of the people by the people, and it takes time to make it workable especially in India..*[16]

What type of men do we require for such an enlightened society as above? Are we really in a position to say that our education is directed towards fulfilment of the minimum ends-in-view of education that guarantees a vibrant and progressive society? Are we assured of the fact that energy and will-force, diligence and dedication are natural and spontaneous in man and society? How to become a real Yogi to serve the purpose of real manhood and a genuine urge for an altruistic society? Here are Vivekananda's classic and incomparable words of advice:

> *First hear, then understand, and then, leaving all distractions, shut your minds to outside influences, and devote yourselves to developing the truth within you. There is the danger of frittering away your energies by taking up an idea only for its novelty,*

and then giving it up for another that is newer. Take one thing up and do it, and see the end of it, and before you have seen the end, do not give it up. He who can become mad with an idea, he alone sees light. Those that only take a nibble here and a nibble there will never attain anything. They may titillate their nerves for a moment, but there it will end. They will be slaves in the hands of nature, and will never get beyond the senses.

Those who really want to be Yogis must give up, once for all, this nibbling at things. Take up one idea. Make that one idea your life— think of it, dream of it, live on that idea. Let the brain, muscles, nerves, every part of your body, be full of that idea, and just leave every other idea alone. This is the way to success, and this is the way great spiritual giants are produced. Others are mere talking machines. If we really want to be blessed, we must go deeper. The first step is not to disturb the mind, not to associate with persons whose ideas are disturbing. All of you know that certain persons, certain places, certain foods, repel you. Avoid them; and those who want to go to the highest, must avoid all company, good or bad. Practise hard; whether you live or die does not matter. You have to plunge in and work, without thinking of the result. If you are brave enough, in six months you will be a perfect Yogi. But those who take up just a bit of it and a little of everything else make no progress. It is of no use simply to take a course of lessons. To those who are full of Tamas, ignorant and dull— those whose minds never get fixed on any idea, who only crave for something to amuse them— religion and philosophy are simply objects of entertainment. These are the unpersevering. They hear a talk, think it very nice, and then go home and forget all about it. To succeed, you must have tremendous perseverance, tremendous will. "I will drink the ocean," says the persevering soul, "at my will mountains will crumble up." Have that sort of energy, that sort of will, work hard, and you will reach the goal.[17]

Admittedly, the role of the individual in the society determines the quality of man and society. No individual survives in a society where he remains isolated from others and thinks and acts for personal interest alone. He must become a part and parcel of the society at least to which he belongs. It is a crime to deceive the society which has given refuge to his very becoming and being.

A new society with new individuals nurturing love and compassion, service and dedication ennobles both man and society. Unless there is self-motivation and self-involvement on the part of every one in the society, the quality of social enrichment becomes impossible. Vivekananda reminds us of the desirable role of the individual in the society very clearly and explicitly:

> *To move slowly towards the infinite whole, bearing a constant feeling of intense sympathy and sameness with it, being happy with its happiness and being distressed with its affliction, is the individual's sole duty. Not only is it his duty, but in its transgression is his death, while compliance with this great truth leads to life immortal. This is the law of nature, and who can throw dust into her ever-watchful eyes? None can hoodwink society and deceive it for any length of time. However much there may have accumulated heaps of refuse and mud on the surface of society— still, at the bottom of those heaps the life-breath of society is ever to be found pulsating with the vibrations of universal love and self-denying compassion for all. Society is like the earth that patiently bears incessant molestation; but she wakes up one day, however long that may be in coming, and the force of the shaking tremors of that awakening hurls off to a distance the accumulated dirt of self-seeking meanness piled up during millions of patient and silent years!*[18]

An unparalleled visionary of man and society in terms of religion of the right kind that finds its true meaning in the poor and the destitute, the illiterate and the ignorant, Vivekananda encourages service to man and society as service to God. His socio-humanistic religion is the religion of service for the welfare of the have-nots and the down-trodden. In a letter written to Swami Akhandananda, the nephew of Shri Ramakrishna, he instructs:

> *Go from door to door amongst the poor and lower classes of the town of Khetri and teach them religion. Also, let them have oral lessons on geography and such other subjects. No good will come of sitting idle and having princely dishes, and saying "Ramakrishna, O Lord!"— unless you can do some good to the poor. Go to other villages from time to time, and teach the people the arts of life as well as religion. Work, worship, and Jnana (knowledge)— first work, and your mind will be purified;*

> *otherwise everything will be fruitless like pouring oblations on a pile of ashes instead of in the sacred fire. When Gunanidhi comes, move from door to door of the poor and the destitute in every village of Rajputana . If people object to the kind of food you take, give it up immediately. It is preferable to live on grass for the sake of doing good to others. The Gerua robe is not for enjoyment. It is the banner of heroic work. You must give your body, mind, and speech to "the welfare of the world" .you have read—* "Matridevo bhava, pitridevo bhava—*Look upon your mother as God, look upon your father as God"— but I say* "Daridradevo bhava, murkhadevo bhava— *the poor, the illiterate, the ignorant, the afflicted— let these be your God." Know that service to these alone is the highest religion.*[19]

Vivekananda's vision of man and society as above finds its exemplary reality when he himself after serving the Santals, the *Narayanas*, God manifest has addressed the Sannyasins of the Math:

> *See, how simple they are. Can you mitigate their misery a little? Otherwise, of what good is the wearing of the Gerua robe? Sacrifice of everything for the good of others is real Sannyasa. They have never enjoyed any good thing in life. Sometimes I feel a desire to sell the Math and everything, and distribute the money to the poor and destitute. We have made the tree our shelter, alas! The people of the country cannot get anything to eat, and how can we have the heart to raise food to our mouths? When I was in the Western countries, I prayed to the Divine Mother, "People here are sleeping on a bed of flowers, they eat all kinds of delicacies, and what do they not enjoy, while people in our country are dying of starvation. Mother, will there be no way for them! One of the objects of my going to the West to preach religion was to see if I could find any means for feeding the people of this country.*
>
> *"Seeing the poor people of our country starving for food, a desire comes to me to overthrow all ceremonial worship and learning, and go round from village to village collecting money from the rich by convincing them through force of character and Sadhana, and to spread the whole life serving the poor."*[20]

The new image of man in society must usher forth a new hope of emancipation and fulfilment, quest for excellence and perfection.

What, then, should be the end-in-view of man in terms of society? Here is an incomparable and essential suggestion which highlights Vivekananda's own profound vision of man and society and which ought to inspire the young generation from time to time:

> *There are two sorts of persons in the world. The one— strong-nerved, quiet, yielding to nature, not given to much imagination, yet good, kind, sweet, etc. For such is the world; they alone are born to be happy. There are others again with high-strung nerves, tremendously imaginative, with intense feeling, always going high one moment and coming down the next. For them there is no happiness. The first class will have almost an even terror of happiness; the last will have to run between ecstasy and misery. But of these alone what we call geniuses are made. There is some truth in the recent theory that "genius is a sort madness".*
>
> *Now, persons of this class if they want to be great, they must fight to finish— clear out the deck for battle. No encumbrance— no marriage, no children, no undue attachment to anything except the one* idea, *and live and die for that. I am a person of this sort. I have taken up the idea of "Vedanta" and I have "cleared the deck for action".*[21]

Restraint in consonance with will-force and sacrifice is the key to the progress of man and society as we need for quality and advancement. Unless man is efficient in controlling the self, he will be overpowered by passivity and inaction. He will also be a victim to obsession and indecision which terribly affect the society in which he lives. Vivekananda warns man against all these forms of ills writ large in the society and strongly upholds:

> *In our system it is accepted that a man cannot have all he desires. Life is subjected to many restraints. This is ugly, yet it brings out points of light and strength. Our liberals see only the ugliness and try to throw it off. But they substitute quite as bad; and the new custom takes as long as the old for us to work to its centres of strength.*
>
> *Will is not strengthened by change. It is weakened and enslaved by it. But we must be always absorbing. Will goes stronger by absorption. And consciously, or unconsciously, will is the one thing in the world that we admire. ..*

It is selfishness that we must seek to eliminate. I find that whenever I have made a mistake in my life, it has always been because self *entered into the calculation. Where self has not been involved, my judgement has gone straight to the mark.*[22]

The new vision of man must be service to everyone in the society irrespective of caste, creed, religion etc. His God is man, the Living God, and none else. He must not be a worshipper of silliness in the name of worship. As a transparent and practical worshipper, he must be dynamic and realistic in envisioning and realising the real God, the Living God—Man-God— in and around him.

In a letter written to his brother-disciples, Vivekananda explicitly states:

If you want any good to come, just throw your ceremonials overboard and worship the Living God, the Man-God— every being that wears a human form— God in His universal as well as individual aspect. The universal aspect of God means this world, and worshipping it means serving it—this indeed is work, not indulging in ceremonials. Neither is it work to cogitate as to whether the rice-plate should be placed in front of the God for ten minutes or for half an hour—that is called lunacy. Millions of rupees have been spent only that the temple-doors of Varanasi or Vrindaban may play at opening and shutting all day long! Now the Lord is having His toilet, now He is taking His meals, now He is busy on something else we know not what. ... And all this, while the Living God is dying for want of food, for want of education! The banias of Bombay are erecting hospitals for bugs— while they would do nothing for men even if they die! You have not the brain to understand this simple thing— that is a plague in our country, and lunatic asylums are rife all over. ... Let some of you spread like fire, and preach this worship of the universal aspect of the Godhead— a thing that was never undertaken before in our country. No quarrelling with people, we must be friends with all. ...

Spread ideas— go from village to village , from door to door— then only there will be real work. Otherwise, lying complacently on the bed and ringing the bell now and then is a sort of disease, pure and simple.[23]

The well-being of man and society can never be made through denunciation of evils but by doing good by devotion to sincerity and respect to everybody. As a promoter of development and enrichment of man and society, a positive approach to dynamism is the primary need. Not narrowness but expansion of vision man and society is the touchstone of social reformation. While explaining the mission of the Vedanta for the welfare of the society, Vivekananda observes:

> *That there are evils in our society even a child can see; and in what society are there no evils? And let me take this opportunity, my countrymen, of telling you that in comparing the different races and nations of the world I have been among, I have come to the conclusion that our people are on the whole the most moral and the most godly, and our institutions are, in their plan and purpose, best suited to make mankind happy. I do not, therefore, want any reformation. My ideal is growth, expansion, development on national lines. As I look back upon the history of my country, I do not find in the whole world another country which has done quite so much for the improvement of the human mind. Therefore I have no words of condemnation for my nation. I tell them, "You have done well; only try to do better." Great things have been done in the past in this land, and there is both time and room for greater things to be done yet. I am sure you know that we cannot stand still. If we stand still, we die. We have either to go forward or to go backward. We have either to progress or degenerate. Our ancestors did great things in the past, but we have to grow into a fuller life and march beyond even their great achievements. How can we now go back and degenerate ourselves? That cannot be; that must not be; going back will lead to national decay and death. Therefore let us go forward and do yet greater things.*[24]

To have faith in man is to have faith in society. A good society always demands cultivation of faith and elimination of desolation and disappointment, darkness and denunciation. This brings about a sea change in man and society. Man no longer remains isolated from the society to which he belongs. He becomes eager to be really and essentially justified to the latter.

Vivekananda clarifies the importance of having faith in man and society to uphold truth under any circumstances whatsoever and howsoever:

Let us preach where we all agree and leave the differences to remedy themselves. As I have said to the Indian people again and again, if there is the darkness of centuries in a room and we go into the room and begin to cry, "Oh, it is dark, it is dark!", will darkness go? Bring in the light and the darkness will vanish at once. This is the secret of reforming men. Suggest to them higher things; believe in man first. Why start with the belief that man is degraded and degenerated? I have never failed in my faith in man in any case, even taking him at his worst. Wherever I had faith in man, thought at first the prospect was not always bright, yet it triumphed in the long run. Have faith in man whether he appears to you to be a very learned one or a most ignorant one. Have faith in man, whether he appears to be an angel or the very devil himself. Have faith in man first, and then having faith in him, believe that if there are defects in him, if he makes mistakes, if he embraces the crudest and the vilest doctrines, believe that it is not from his real nature that they come, but from the want of higher ideals. If a man goes towards what is false, it is because he cannot get what is true. Therefore, the only method of correcting what is false is by supplying him with what is true. Do this, and let him compare. You give him the truth, and there your work is done. Let him compare it in his own mind with what he has already with him; and, mark my words, if you have really given him the truth, the false must vanish, light must dispel darkness, and truth will bring the good out. This is the way if you want to reform the country spiritually; this is the way, and not fighting , not even telling people that what they are doing is bad. Put the good before them, see how eagerly they take it, see how the divine that never dies, that is always living in the human, comes up awakened and stretches out its hand for all that is good, and all that is glorious.[25]

Indeed, for advancement of man and society, there is no alternative to goodness and glory derived from cultivation of faith and truth.

From a higher level of appreciating the role of man in society and *vice versa*, what is very significant is to delve deep into the heart of their mutual relationship. All differences are apparent and in reality there is unity inherent and assured in everything. This spirit of unity or oneness brings forth the true image of man and society.

Vivekananda adroitly spells out this unity or oneness from the standpoint of the theme of the Vedanta:

> *When all life and the whole universe are seen in this Atman, then alone man has attained the secret. There is no more delusion for him. Where is any more misery for him who sees this Oneness in the universe?*
>
> *This is another great theme of the Vedanta, this Oneness of life, this Oneness of everything. We shall see how it demonstrates that all our misery comes through ignorance, and this ignorance is the idea of manifoldness, this separation between man and man, between nation and nation, between earth and moon, between moon and sun. out of this idea of separation between atom and atom comes all misery. But the Vedanta says this separation does not exist, it is not real. It is merely apparent, on the surface. In the heart of things there is Unity still. If you go below the surface, you find that Unity between man and man, between races and races, high and low, rich and poor, gods and men, and men and animals. If you go deep enough, all will be seen as variations of the One, and he who has attained to this variation of Oneness has no more delusion. What can delude him? He knows the reality of everything, the secret of everything. Where is there any more misery for him? What does he desire? He has traced the reality of everything to the Lord, the Centre, the Unity of everything, and that is Eternal Existence, Eternal Knowledge, Eternal Bliss.*[26]

The quest for inwardness amidst man and society is long overdue. This is not because there is no urge for man and, for that end-in-view, social ascent and excellence. Nor is it true that man suffers from indolence in thought and action. What really prompts man and society is to heavily bank upon the grossness of what Vivekananda characteristically identifies as "outward presentation". In one of his famous poems he ventilates this truth:

> *Lo! The sun, the moon,*
>
> *The moving planets and the shining stars,*
>
> *Spheres of abode by myriads in the skies,*

The comet swift, the glimmering lightning-flash,
The firmament, expanded, infinite—
These all, observant watchful eyes behold.
Anger, desire, greed, Moha, and the rest,
Whence issues forth the waving of the play
Of this existence; the home wherein dwells
Knowledge, and non-knowledge— whose centre is
The feeling of small self, the "Aham!" " Aham!"
Full of the dual sense of pleasure and pain,
Teeming with birth and life, decay and death,
Whose arms are "The External" and "The Internal",
All things that are, down to the ocean's depths,
Up to sun, moon, and stars in spanless space—
The Mind, the Buddhi, Chitta, Ahamkar,
The Deva, Yaksha, man and demon, all,
The quadruped, the bird, the worm, all insect life,
The atom and its compound, all that is,
Animate and inanimate, all, all—
The Internal and the External— dwell
In that one common plane of existence!
This outward presentation is of order gross,
As hair on human brow, Ay! Very gross.[27]

The inherent philosophy of man and society should be like a spectrum consisting of all hues, all opinions, all forms, all ideas and all visions. It must welcome all thoughts, all sentiments, all viewpoints and all criticisms where freedom and individuality always enjoy a fair play of transparency and transcendence.

In explaining the highest ideal of the Vedanta philosophy, Vivekananda refers to the fact as above, and points out the role of every one in terms of all in the society:

The highest ideal of the Vedanta is very difficult to understand, and people are always quarrelling about it, and the greatest difficulty is that when they get hold of certain ideas, they deny and fight other ideas. Take up what suits you, and let others take up what they need. If you are desirous of clinging to this little individuality, to this limited manhood, remain in it, have all these desires, and be content and pleased with them. If your experience of manhood has been very good and nice, retain it as long as you like; and you can do so, for you are the makers of your own fortunes; none can compel you to give up your manhood. You will be men as long as you like; none can prevent you. If you want to be angels, you will be angels, that is the law. But there may be others who do not want to be angels even. What right have you to think that theirs is a horrible notion? You may be frightened to lose a hundred pounds, but there may be others who would not even wink if they lost all the money they had in the world. There have been such men and still there are. Why do you dare to judge them according to your standard? You cling on to your limitations, and these little worldly ideas may be your highest ideal. You are welcome to them. It will be to you as you wish. But there are others who have seen the truth and cannot rest in these limitations, who have done with these things and want to get beyond. The world with all its enjoyments is a mere mud-puddle for them. Why do you want to bind them down to your ideas? You must get rid of this tendency once for all. Accord a place to everyone.[28]

The devotion to service to man and society as Vivekananda emphasises is the essence of spirituality. It is that devotion which teaches us how to learn the lesson of self-denial and self-sacrifice as significant components of socio-spiritual advancement.

It is interesting to note in this connection how Vivekananda in his lecture delivered at the Triplicane Literary Society has inspired to work for the welfare of others by sacrificing self-interest for emancipation of man and society:

There have been great conquering races in the world. We also have been great conquerors. The story of our conquest has been described by that noble Emperor of India, Asoka, as the conquest of religion and of spirituality. Once more the world must be conquered by India. This is the dream of my life, and I wish that each one of you who hear me today will have the same dream in your minds, and stop not till you have realised the dream. They will tell you every day that we will better look to our own homes first and then go to work outside. But I will tell you in plain

> *language that you work best when you work for others. The best work that you ever did for yourselves was when you worked for others, trying to disseminate your ideas in foreign languages beyond the seas, and this very meeting is proof how the attempt to enlighten other countries with your thoughts is helping your own country. One-fourth of the effect that has been produced in this country by going to England and America would not have been brought about, had I confined my ideas only to India. This is the great ideal before us, and every one must be ready for it— the conquest of the whole world by India— nothing less than that, and we must get ready for it, strain every nerve for it. Let foreigners come and flood the land with their armies, never mind. Up, India, and conquer the world with your spirituality! Ay, as has been declared in this soil first, love must conquer hatred, hatred cannot conquer itself. Materialism and all its miseries can never be conquered by materialism. Armies when they attempt to conquer armies only multiply and make brutes of humanity. Spirituality must conquer the West. Slowly they are finding out that what they want is spirituality to preserve them as nations. They are waiting for it, they are eager for it. Where is the supply to come from? Where are the men ready to go out to every country in the world with the messages of the great sages of India? Where are the men who are ready to sacrifice everything, so that this message shall reach every corner of the world? Such heroic souls are wanted to help the spread of truth. Such heroic workers are wanted to go abroad and help to disseminate the great truths of the Vedanta . The world wants it; without it the world will be destroyed.*[29]

In our service to man and society what is of absolute importance is to sincerely consider every work as worship. There should be neither any room for self-interest nor should there be any exercise of passion and partiality. In the event of service to man and society, there are numerous constraints and hardships which are nothing but challenges to success through display of dispassionate temperament. The goal we should seek in performing any work is to rise above all narrowness and strive as best as possible for a higher plane of existence by means of denying desires for personal interest. The real identity of man indicates this truth of broadening our vision and crystallising our finer sensibilities by considering and realising service to man and society as service through love and sympathy, reverence and modesty. As an incomparable connoisseur of ascent of man and society, Vivekananda elegantly elucidates:

> *We shall find that the philosophy of duty, whether it be in the form of ethics or of love, is the same as in every other Yoga— the object being the attenuating of the lower self, so that the real higher Self may shine forth— the lessening of the frittering away of energies on the lower plane of existence, so that the soul may manifest itself on the higher ones. This is accomplished by the continual denial of low desires, which duty rigorously requires. The whole organisation of society has thus been developed, consciously or unconsciously, in the realms of action and experience, where, by limiting selfishness, we open the way to an unlimited expansion of the real nature of man.*
>
> *Duty is seldom sweet. It is only when love greases its wheels that it runs smoothly; it is a continuous friction otherwise. How else could parents do their duties to their children, husbands to their wives, and* vice versa? *Do we not meet with cases of friction every day in our lives? Duty is sweet only through love, and love shines in freedom alone. Yet is it freedom to be a slave to the senses, to anger, to jealousies and a hundred other petty things that must occur every day in human life? In all these little roughnesses that we meet with in life, the highest expression of freedom is to forbear.*[30]

For an ideal of man and society buoyant with the spirit of freedom and duty for the welfare as desired, the spirit of religion must be directed towards this end-in-view. There is neither any room for ignorance nor should superstitions be allowed to have the upper hand. Love, selflessness and burning character manifested in bold deeds and straightforwardness in vision and action should always be the essential guidelines for advancement of man and society.

In a letter to Miss Noble on 7th June 1896 what Vivekananda has written demands re-thinking:

> *My ideal indeed can be put into a few words and that is: to preach unto mankind their divinity, and how to make it manifest in every moment of life.*

This world is in chain of superstition. I pity the oppressed, whether man or woman, and I pity more the oppressors.

One idea that I see clear as daylight is that misery is caused by ignorance and nothing else. Who will give the world light? Sacrifice in the past has been the Law, it will be, alas, for ages to come. The earth's bravest and best will have to sacrifice themselves for the good of many, for the welfare of all. Buddhas by the hundred are necessary with eternal love and pity.

Religions of the world have become lifeless mockeries. What the world wants is character. The world is in need of those whose life is one burning love, selfless. That love will make every word tell like thunderbolt.[31]

The dream of man and society as Vivekananda significantly highlights should act as an indomitable force in us to undergo a radical change. It should always be crystallised by new ideals and involvements of man and society that care for victory and fulfilment, freedom and ascent.

Are we ready for a new journey of man with a radiant and altruistic society?

1. Swami Vivekananda: *The Complete Works of Swami Vivekananda*, Advaita Ashrama, Kolkata, Mayavati Memorial Edition, 1989, Vol. VIII, pp. 307-308.
2. *Ibid.*, Vol. III, p. 199.
3. *Ibid.*, Vol. VII, p. 150.
4. *Ibid.*, pp. 173-174.
5. *Ibid.*, Vol. I, pp. 75-76.
6. *Ibid.*, Vol. III, p. 199.
7. *Ibid.*, Vol. I, pp. 34-35.
8. *Ibid.*, Vol. III, pp. 129-130.
9. *Ibid.*, Vol. VII, pp. 179-180.
10. *Ibid.*, pp. 246-247
11. *Ibid.*,Vol. VIII, p. 168.
12. *Ibid.*,Vol. VI, pp. 126-127.
13. *Ibid.*, Vol. V, pp. 34-35.
14. *Ibid.*, pp.15-16.
15. *Ibid.*, Vol. IV, pp. 357-358.
16. *Ibid.*, Vol. V, pp. 215-216.
17. *Ibid.*, Vol. I, pp. 177-178.
18. *Ibid.*, Vol. IV, pp. 463-464.
19. *Ibid.*, Vol. VI, p. 288.
20. *Ibid.*, Vol. VII, pp. 245-246
21. *Ibid.*, Vol. VIII, pp. 390-391.
22. *Ibid.*, p. 265.
23. *Ibid.*, Vol. VI, pp. 264-265.
24. *Ibid.*, Vol. III, pp. 195-196.
25. *Ibid.*, pp. 383-384.
26. *Ibid.*, Vol. II, pp. 153-154.
27. *Ibid.*, "A Song I Sing to Thee", Vol. IV, pp. 512-513.
28. *Ibid.*, Vol. II, pp. 350-351.
29. *Ibid.*, Vol. III, pp. 276-277.
30. *Ibid.*, Vol. I, pp. 66-67.
31 *Ibid.*, Vol. VII, p. 501.

Man and Education: Vivekananda's Priorities

The true identity of man is education. It is best reflected in manifestation. What manifestation is referred to, and why? Where is that reflection which naturally takes place? For answers to these questions and the like, Swami Vivekananda's oft-quoted saying is the best answer that glorifies man:

Education is the manifestation of the perfection already in man.[1]

Man perfect and serene is free from any delusion. He is blessed with the realisation of the Self. He is the perfect Being reflected in all splendour everywhere. Education is the means of visualising the reflection of that perfection already in man. That the perfect man through knowledge is free from all delusions and reflects the Being is the true meaning of man. Vivekananda characteristically elucidates:

> *The Self, the Knower, the Lord of all the Real Being, is the cause of all the vision that is in the universe, but it is impossible for Him to see Himself, excepting through reflection. You cannot see your own face except in a mirror, and so the Self cannot see Its own nature until It is reflected, and this whole universe therefore is the Self trying to realise Itself. This reflection is thrown back first from the protoplasm, then from plants and animals, and so on and on from better and better reflectors, until the best reflector, the perfect man, is reached— just as a man who, wanting to see his face, looks first in a little pool of muddy water, and sees just an outline; then he comes to clear water, and sees a better image; then to a piece of shining metal, and sees a still better image; and at last to a looking-glass, and sees himself reflected as he is. Therefore the perfect man is the highest reflection of that Being who is both subject and object. You now find why man instinctively worships everything, and how perfect men are instinctively worshipped as God in every country.*

** ** ** **

A perfect man is much higher than such conceptions. In him the circle becomes complete; the subject and the object become one. In him all delusions go away and in their place comes the realisation that he has always been that perfect Being. How came this bondage then? How was it possible for this perfect Being to degenerate into the imperfect? How was it possible that the free became bound? The Advaitist says, he was never bound, but was always free. Various clouds of various colours come before the sky. They remain there a minute and then pass away. It is the same eternal blue sky stretching there for ever. The sky never changes: it is the cloud that is changing. So you are always perfect, eternally perfect. Nothing ever changes your nature, or ever will. All these ideas that I am imperfect, I am a man, or a woman, or a sinner, or I am the mind, I have thought, I will think—all are hallucinations; you never think, you never had a body; you never were imperfect. You are the blessed Lord of this universe, the one Almighty ruler of everything that is and ever will be, the one mighty ruler of these suns and stars and moons and earths and planets and all the little bits of our universe. It is through you that the sun shines and the stars shed their lustre, and the earth becomes beautiful. It is through your blessedness that they all love and are attracted to each other. You are in all and you are all. Whom to avoid and whom to take? You are the all in all. When this knowledge comes, delusion immediately vanishes.[2]

To be a perfect man is to prove oneself as a mirror to eliminate all delusions and hallucinations through devotion to knowledge perfect and serene. The purpose of education is to eliminate all littleness and adorn vastness in oneself to enlighten vastness spontaneously among every one as one's own Self. That we are always learning is the essence of eduction and at the same time the permanent end-in-view of man. As knowledge is man's inherent entity, it is his ardent duty to explore knowledge unendingly from different perspectives. Vivekananda distinctly asserts:

What we say a man "knows", should, in strict psychological language, be what he "discovers" or "unveils"; what a man "learns" is really what he "discovers", by taking the cover off his own soul, which is a mine of infinite knowledge.

* * * * * * * *

All knowledge that the world has ever received comes from the mind; the infinite library of the universe is in your own mind. The external world is simply the suggestion, the occasion, which sets you to study your own mind, but the object of your study is always your own mind.

****

All knowledge, therefore, secular or spiritual, is in the human mind. In many cases it is not discovered, but remains covered, and when the covering has been slowly taken off, we say, "We are learning", and the advance of knowledge is made by the advance of this process of uncovering. The man from whom this veil is being lifted is the more knowing man, the man upon whom it lies thick is ignorant, and the man from whom it has entirely gone is all-knowing, omniscient. There have been omniscient men, and, I believe, there will be yet; and there will be myriads of them in the cycles to come. Like fire in a piece of flint, knowledge exists in the mind; suggestion is the friction which brings it out. So with all our feelings and action— our tears and our smiles, our joys and our griefs, our weeping and our laughter, our curses and our blessings, our praises and our blames— every one of these we may find, if we calmly study our own selves, to have been brought out from within ourselves by so many blows.[3]

The role of education in relation to man and vice versa has very often been confused. The importance of the consolidation of our thoughts and actions by exercising concentration of our mind cannot at all be ignored. Education is neither meant for accumulation of facts by reading books nor is it a mere attachment to certain things. It becomes meaningful and worthwhile in leading us to have a perfect control over our mind. As Vivekananda straightforwardly observes on education for the purpose of manhood:

Education is not filling the mind with a lot of facts. Perfecting the instrument and getting complete mastery of my own mind [is the ideal of education]. If I want to concentrate my mind upon a point, it goes there, and the moment I call, it is free again.

****

That is the great difficulty. By great struggle we get a certain power of concentration, the power of attachment of the mind to certain things. But then there is not the power of detachment. I would give half my life to take my mind off that object! I cannot. It is the power of concentration and attachment as well as the power of detachment [that we must develop].[If] the man [is]equally powerful in both— that man has attained manhood. You cannot make him miserable even if the whole universe tumbles about his ears. What books can teach you that?[4]

With detachment as one of the invaluable components of education to be, the cultivation of education of strength is also very important. An assured change in the body from weakness to strength brings forth faith which is the key to success in man. Vivekananda strongly urges on the strength of the body to increase the strength of the mind, the strength of faith in oneself:

You must change your body. Physical weakness is the cause and nothing else. You have talked of reforms, of ideals, and all these things for the past hundred years; but when it comes to practice, you are not to be found anywhere— till you have disgusted the whole world, and the very name of reform is a thing of ridicule! And what is the cause? Do you not know? You know too well. The only cause is that you are weak, weak, weak; your body is weak, your mind is weak, you have no faith in yourselves! Centuries and centuries, a thousand years of crushing tyranny of castes and kings and foreigners and your own people have taken out all your strength, my brethren. Your backbone is broken, you are like downtrodden worms. Who will give you strength? Let me tell you, strength, strength is what we want. And the first step in getting strength is to uphold the Upanishads, and believe— "I am the Soul", "Me the sword cannot cut; nor weapons pierce; me the fire cannot burn; me the air cannot dry; I am the Omnipotent, I am the Omniscient." so repeat these blessed, saving words. Do not say we are weak; we can do anything and everything. What can we not do? Everything can be done by us; we all have the same glorious soul, let us believe in it. Have faith, as Nachiketa. At the time of his father's sacrifice, faith came unto Nachiketa; ay, I wish that faith would come to each of you; and every one of you would stand up a giant, a world-mover with a gigantic intellect—an infinite God in every respect. This is what I want you to become. This is the strength that you get from the Upanishads, this is the faith that you get from there.[5]

The education of the mind must be the true education and identity of man. It is the passport to control and advancement, creative impulse and efflorescence. It indicates how education should become living and meaningful. It also indicates awakening of "the inner teacher" and "an opening of the book of the heart" to respond to the inner voice represented by man's will. As Vivekananda poignantly advises:

Control the mind, cut off the senses, then you are a Yogi; after that, all the rest will come. Refuse to hear, to see, to smell, to taste; take way the mental power from the external organs. You continually do it unconsciously as when your mind is absorbed; so you can learn to do it consciously. The mind can put the senses where it pleases. Get rid of the fundamental superstition that we are obliged to act through the body. We are not. Go into your own room and get the Upanishads out of your own Self. You are the greatest book that ever was or ever will be, the infinite depository of all that is. Until the inner teacher opens, all outside teaching is in vain. It must lead to the opening of the book of the heart to have any value.

The will is the "still small voice", the real Ruler who says "do" and "do not". It has done all that binds us. The ignorant will leads to bondage, the knowing will can free us. The will can be made strong in thousands of ways; every way is a kind of Yoga, but the systematised Yoga accomplishes the work more quickly. Bhakti, Karma, Raja, and Jnana-Yoga get over the ground more effectively. Put on all powers, philosophy, work, prayer, meditation— crowd all sail, put on all head of steam— and reach the goal. The sooner, the better.[6]

The new thoughts and visions of man will show the new ways of challenging all odds and constraints of life and make life glorious through self-help and self-sacrifice like a true hero. The only way to success is to be free from all bondage and fear. Man to be really justified as man must under any circumstances be brave and fearless. This is one of the most practical and effective education of man. In the vibrant words of Vivekananda:

If there is no strength in body and mind, the Atman cannot be realised. First you have to build the body by good nutritious food— then only will the mind be strong. The mind is but the subtle part of the body. You must retain great strength in your mind and words. "I am low, I am low"— repeating these ideas in the mind, man belittles and degrades himself.

* * * * * * * *

He alone who is always awake to the idea of freedom, becomes free. He who thinks he is bound, endures life after life in the state of bondage. It is a fact. This truth holds good both in spiritual and temporal matters. Those who are always down-hearted and dispirited in this life can do no work; from life to life they come and go wailing and moaning. "The earth is enjoyed by heroes"— this is the unfailing truth. Be a hero. Always say, "I have no fear." Tell this to everybody— "Have no fear." Fear is death, fear is sin, fear is hell, fear is unrighteousness, fear is wrong life. All the negative thoughts and ideas that are in this world have proceeded from this evil spirit of fear.[7]

What type of man would we endear as one who has the true education of freedom? Here is Vivekananda's splendid response:

He is free, he is great, who turns his back upon the world, who has renounced everything, who has controlled his passion, and who thirsts for peace. One may gain political and social independence, but if one is a slave to his passions and desires, one cannot feel the pure joy of real freedom.[8]

To eliminate all selfishness and work for the good of all is the prized outcome of education. Such education strengthens us to exercise freedom in a communicated and conjoint manner of human welfare. Vivekananda welcomes the endeavour to inspire the young to march ahead in the education for all without fear:

Act on the educated young men, bring them together, and organise them. Great things can be done by great sacrifices only. No selfishness, no name, no fame, yours or mine, nor my Master's even! Work, work for the idea, the plan, my boys, my brave, noble, good souls— to the wheel, to the wheel put your shoulders! Stop not to look back for name, or fame, or any such nonsense. Throw self overboard and work. Remember, "The grass when made into a rope by being joined together can even chain a mad elephant." The Lord's blessings on you all— as I believe it is already. *"Wake up, stop not until the goal is reached", say the*

Vedas. Up, up, the long night is passing, the day is approaching, the wave has risen, nothing will be able to resist its tidal fury. The spirit, my boys, the spirit; the love, my children, the love; the faith, the belief; and fear not! The greatest sin is fear.[9]

As the greatest being of this universe, man is gifted with the rarest of rare qualities. He is the knower and and known, worshipper and worshipped at the same time. He is the emblem of divinity. At the same time, he is the teacher and taught. He is purified because he is always in the process of self-purification without being deluded by honour, pride, strength, fame, vanity and selfishness. As Vivekananda inspires us:

To identify the sun with the spots on the object-glass is the fundamental error. Know the sun, the "I", to be ever unaffected by anything, and devote yourself to cleansing the spots. Man is the greatest being that ever can be. The highest worship there is, is to worship man as Krishna, Buddha, Christ. What you want, you create. Get rid of desire.

* * * * * * * *

The angels and the departed are all here, seeing this world as heaven. The same "x" is seen by all according to their mental attitude. The best vision to be had of the "x" is here on this earth. Never want to go to heaven, that is the worst delusion. Even here, too much wealth and grinding poverty are both bondages and hold us back from religion. Three great gifts we have: first, a human body. (The human mind is the nearest reflection of God, we are "His own image".) Second, the desire to be free. Third, the help of a noble soul, who has crossed the ocean of delusion, as a teacher. When you have these three, bless the Lord; you are sure to be free.[10]

In the true spirit of education, Vivekananda explains the role of freedom in terms of work and worship. This has enriched the vision of freedom as education of the whole man, the man as a human being and the one with spiritual excellence. Referring to Shankara's philosophy of the Advaita-Vedanta as the "crowning glory of the Vedas", Vivekananda observes:

No law can make you free, you are free. Nothing can give you freedom, if you have it not already. The Atman is self-illumined. Cause and effect do not reach there, and this disembodiedness is freedom. Beyond what was, or is, or is to be, is Brahman. As an effect, freedom would have no value; it would be a compound, and as such would contain the seeds of bondage. It is the one real factor, not to be attained, but the real nature of the soul.

Work and worship, however, are necessary to take away the veil, to lift off the bondage and illusion. They do not give us freedom; but all the same, without effort on our own part we do not open our eyes and see what we are. Shankara says further that Advaita-Vedanta is the crowning glory of the Vedas; but the lower Vedas are also necessary, because they teach work and worship, and through these many come to the Lord. Others may come without any help but Advaita. Work and worship lead to the same result as Advaita.[11]

The Darwinian theory of struggle for existence is never a match for man and education. It goes against the very nature of man whose primary duty is to educate himself how to manifest rationality. He alone knows that the education that prepares him to sacrifice is his true identity. It is sacrifice that indicates man's spirit of rationality and complete control over his mind. Vivekananda's elucidation on this point is clear and explicit:

In the animal kingdom we really see such laws as struggle for existence , survival of the fittest, etc., evidently at work. Therefore, Darwin's theory seems true to a certain extent. But in the human kingdom, where there is the manifestation of rationality, we find just the reverse of those laws. For instance, in those whom we consider really great men or ideal characters, we scarcely observe any external struggle. In the animal kingdom instinct prevails; but the more a man advances, the more he manifests rationality. For this reason progress in the rational human kingdom cannot be achieved, like that in the animal kingdom, by the destruction of others! The highest evolution of man is effected through sacrifice alone. A man is great among his fellows in proportion as he can sacrifice for the sake of others, while in the lower strata of the animal kingdom, that animal is the strongest which can kill the greatest number of animals. Hence the struggle theory is not equally applicable to both kingdoms. Man's struggle is in the mental sphere. A man is greater in proportion as he can control his mind. When the mind's activities are perfectly at rest, the Atman manifests Itself. The struggle which we observe in the animal kingdom for the preservation of the gross body obtains in the human plane of existence for gaining mastery over the mind or for attaining the state of balance. Like a living tree and its reflection in the water of a tank, we find opposite kinds of struggle in the animal and human kingdoms.[12]

The education of man in terms of freedom necessitates an outlook always crystallised anew and afresh , where man must prove his depth of vision under the bondage of human life. As human life seeks fullness of education in the efflorescence of the soul pure, indivisible and unalloyed by any force internal or external, the education of man that enables him to eliminate all constraints of exercising freedom of the soul is the only passport to prove our divine right inherent in every one of us. Vivekananda clarifies the concept of man's education in the light of freedom of the soul very significantly:

You may find many fools in this country at the present time, saying, "I am not bound; I am God Himself; let me do anything I like." This is not right, although it is true that the soul is beyond all laws, physical, mental, or moral. Within law is bondage; beyond law is freedom. It is also true that freedom is of the nature of the soul, it is its birthright: that real freedom of the soul shines through veils of matter in the form of the apparent freedom of man. Every moment of your life you feel that you are free. We cannot live, talk, or breathe for a moment without feeling that we are free; but, at the same time, a little thought shows us that we are like machines and not free. What is true then? Is this idea of freedom a delusion? One party holds that the idea of freedom is a delusion; another says that the idea of bondage is a delusion. How does this happen? Man is really free, the real man cannot but be free. It is when he comes into the world of Maya, into name and form, that he becomes bound. Free will is a misnomer. Will can never be free. How can it be? It is only when the real man has become bound that his will comes into existence, and not before. The will of man is bound, but that which is the foundation of that will is eternally free. So, even in the state of bondage which we call human life or god-life, on earth or in heaven, there yet remains to us that recollection of the freedom which is ours by divine right. And consciously or unconsciously we are all struggling towards it. When a man attained his own freedom, how can he be bound by any law? No law in this universe can bind him, for this universe itself is his.[13]

The real education of man starts with the exercise of mental activity. If he remains passive and purposeless, drab and dull, disinterested and devoid of sincere self-involvement, education becomes meaningless. Man must prove his novelty and marked points of departure in the exercise of mental activity by means of education of love and inwardness that goes beyond mere rules and regulations to be strictly followed by any means. Vivekananda adroitly explains this fact:

If living by rule ensures excellence, if it be virtue to follow strictly the rules and customs handed down through generations, say then, who is more virtuous than a tree, who is a greater devotee, a holier saint, than a railway train? Who has ever seen a piece of stone transgress a natural law? Who has ever known cattle to commit sin?

The huge steamer, the mighty railway engine— they are non-intelligent; they move, turn, and run, but they are without intelligence. And yonder tiny worm which moved away from the railway line to save its life, why is it intelligent? There is no manifestation of will in the machine, the machine never wishes to transgress law; the worm wants to oppose law— rises against law whether it succeeds or not; therefore it is intelligent. Greater is the happiness, higher is the Jiva, in proportion as this will is more successfully manifest.[14]

The new vision of man in terms of education must be steadfastness to truth and logical analysis. There are only two main dangers for man— the one from frauds and the other from fools. How to be free from these two dangers? Vivekananda's advice to think before we act upon anything is invaluable:

Sometimes I find persons perfectly wanting in logical analysis of anything. A man comes and says, "I have a message from such and such a god", and asks, "Can you deny it? Is it not possible that there will be such and such a god, and that he will give such a message?" And 90 per cent of fools will swallow it.

They think that that is reason enough. But one thing you ought to know, that it is possible for anything to happen— quite possible that the earth may come into contact with the Dog star in the next year and go to pieces. But if I advance this proposition, you have the right to stand up and ask me to prove it to you. What the lawyers call the onus probandi *is on the man who made the proposition. It is not your duty to prove that I got my inspiration from a certain god, but mine, because I produced the proposition to you. If I cannot prove it, I should better hold my tongue. Avoid both these dangers, and you can get anywhere you please. Many of us get many messages in our lives, or think we get them, and as long as the message is regarding our own selves, go on doing what you please; but when it is in regard to our contact with and behaviour to others, think a hundred times before you act upon it; and then you will be safe.*[15]

Learning to think as one of the most essential components of education also calls forth learning to feel. The education of sympathy is the real indicator of the education of the heart. It denotes man in quest of excellence. Unless there is a total overhauling of education that cares for the advancement of man in search of fullness and perfection, it is meaningless. Vivekananda poignantly reminds us:

If you wish to be a true reformer, three things are necessary. The first is to feel. Do you really feel for your brothers? Do you really feel that there is so much misery in the world, so much ignorance and superstition? Do you really feel that men are your brothers? Does this idea come into your whole being? Does it run with your blood? Does it tingle in your veins? Does it course through every nerve and filament of your body? Are you full of that idea of sympathy? If you are, that is only the first step. You must think next if you have found any remedy. The old ideas may be all superstition, but in and round these masses of superstition are nuggets of gold and truth. Have you discovered means by which to keep that gold alone, without any of the dross? If you have done that, that is only the second step; one more thing is necessary. What is your motive? Are you really sure that you can stand to your ideals and work on, even if the hole world wants to crush you down? Are you sure you know what you want and will perform your duty, and that alone, even if your life is at stake? Are you sure that you will persevere so long as life endures, so long as there is one pulsation left in the heart? Then you are a real reformer, you are a teacher, a Master, a blessing to mankind. But man is so impatient, so short-sighted! He has not the patience to wait, he has not the power to see. He wants to rule, he wants results immediately. Why? He wants to reap the fruits himself, and does not really care for others. Duty for duty's sake is not what he wants.[16]

The education of doing one's duty even under dire constraints is the true ideal of man. He must not nurse contempt towards anybody, and instead, must act upon the truth that all is One. This will widen the real identity of man and the broadened canvas would make every action and experience crystallised in the spirit of altruism and equality of man. As Vivekananda points out:

We must not look down with contempt on others. All of us are going towards the same goal. The difference between weakness and strength is one of degree; the difference between virtue and vice is one of degree; the difference between heaven and hell is one of degree; the difference between life and death is one of degree; all differences in this world are of degree, and not of kind, because oneness is the secret of everything. All is One, which manifests Itself, either as thought, or life, or soul, or body, and the difference is only of degree. As such, we have no right to look down with contempt upon those who are not developed exactly in the same degree as we are. Condemn none; if you can stretch out a helping hand, do so. If you cannot, fold your hands, bless your brothers, and let them go their own way. Dragging down and condemning is not the way to work. Never is work accomplished in that way. We spend our energies in condemning others. Criticism and condemnation is a vain way of spending our energies , for in the long run we come to learn that all are seeing the same thing, are more or less approaching the same ideal, and that most of our differences are merely differences of expression.[17]

The vision of man in the light of true education undergoes a series of steps till it is complete in true perception. Ordinarily, there is a half-hearted attempt on the part of every human being to jump into conclusion in this regard but a little endeavour to delve deep into the matter of perception unfolds the disciplined and error-free process of perception. Vivekananda spells out this point very clearly:

> *I am looking at you. How many things are necessary for this vision? First, the eyes. For if I am perfect in every other way, and yet have no eyes, I shall not be able to see you. Secondly, the real organ of vision. For the eyes are not the organs. They are but the instruments of vision, and behind them is the real organ, the nerve centre in the brain. If that centre be injured, a man may have the clearest pair of eyes, yet he will not be able to see anything. So, it is necessary that this centre, or the real organ, be there. Thus, with all our senses. The external ear is but the instrument for carrying the vibration of sound inward to the centre. Yet, that is not sufficient. Suppose in your library you are intently reading a book, and the clock strikes, yet you do not hear it. The sound is there, the pulsations in the air are there, the ear and the centre are also there, and these vibrations are carried through the ear to the centre, and yet you do not hear it. What is wanting? The mind is not there. Thus we see that the third thing necessary is, that the mind must be there. First the external instruments, then the organ to which this external instrument will carry the sensation, and lastly the organ itself must be joined to the mind. When the mind is not joined to the organ, the organ and the ear may take the impression, and yet we shall not be conscious of it. The mind, too, is only the carrier; it has to carry the sensation still forward, and present it to the intellect. The intellect is the determining faculty and decides upon what is brought to it. Still this is not sufficient. The intellect must carry it forward and present the whole thing before the ruler in the body, the human soul, the king on the throne. Before him this is presented, and then from him comes the order, what is to do or what not to do; and the order goes down in the same sequence to the intellect, to the mind, to the organs, and the organs convey it to the instruments, and the perception is complete.*[18]

The importance of rising above our sense-perception is the right approach to education. Unless we are in a position to win over our senses, we will remain slaves to ourselves and will fail to do justice to the infinite possibilities of efflorescence of man in diverse and thrilling directions. From the psychological points of view between man and education, Vivekananda observes:

> *We are constantly doing things against the better side of our nature, and afterwards we upbraid ourselves for so doing and wonder what we could have been thinking of, how we could do such a thing! Yet again and again we do it, and again and again we suffer for it and upbraid ourselves, at the time, perhaps, we think we desire to do it, but we only desire it because we are forced to desire it. We are forced onward, we are helpless! We are all slaves to our own and to everybody else's mind; whether we are good or bad, that makes no difference. We are led here and there because we cannot help ourselves. We say we think, we do, etc. It is not so. We think because we have to think. We act because we have to. We are slaves to ourselves and to others. Deep down in our subconscious mind are stored up all the thoughts and acts of the past, not only of this life, but of all other lives we have lived. This great boundless ocean of subjective mind is full of all the thoughts and actions of the past. Each one of these is striving to be recognised, pushing outward for expression, surging, wave after wave, out upon the objective mind, the conscious mind. These thoughts, the stored-up energy, we take for natural desires, talents, etc. It is because we do not realise their true origin. We obey them blindly, unquestioningly; and slavery, the most helpless kind of slavery, is the result; and we call ourselves free. Free! We who cannot for a moment govern our own minds, nay, cannot hold our minds on a subject, focus it on a point to the exclusion of everything else for a moment! Yet we call ourselves free. Think of it! We cannot do as we know we ought to do even for a very short space of time. Some sense-desire will crop up, and immediately we obey it. Our conscience smites us for such weakness, but again and again we do it, we are always doing it. We cannot live up to a high standard of life, try as we will. The ghosts of past thoughts, past lives hold us down. All the misery of the world is caused by this slavery to the senses. Our inability to rise above the sense-life – the striving for physical pleasures, is the cause of all the horrors and miseries of the world.*[19]

To uphold individuality through exercise of one's own personality is the true education for which one should always strive.

Not aping others but proving one's inwardness is the greatest spirit of education which calls forth one's lifelong and genuine realisation. Citing his own experience and learning from Shri Ramakrishna, an incomparable and unparalleled teacher par excellence, Vivekananda writes:

> *The man at whose feet I sat all my life— and it is only a few ideas of his that try to teach— could [hardly] write his name at all. All my life I have not seen another man like that, and I have travelled all over the world. When I think of that man, I feel like a fool, because I want to read books and he never did. He never wanted to lick the plates after other people had eaten. That is why he was his own book. All my life I am repeating what Jack said and John said, and never say anything myself. What glory is it that you know what John said twenty-five years ago and what Jack said five years ago? Tell me what* you *have to say.*[20]

The education of man has its identity in fullness as an Infinite Being. The spirit of monism is enriched with this vision of man in terms of education for manifestation of perfection. When we speak about the evolution of man as an Infinite Being, the education that we have out of our own encapsulates the fact that we possess infinite power, existence and blessedness within ourselves and not from any external source. Vivekananda's explanation on this point clarifies the relationship between man and education as an intensive, introspective and inward revelation of the Infinite Being— man:

> *The finite, manifested man forgets his source and thinks himself to be entirely separate. We, as personalised, differentiated beings, forget our reality, and the teaching of monism is not that we shall give up these differentiations, but we must learn to understand what they are. We are in reality that Infinite Being, and our personalities represent so many channels through which this Infinite Reality is manifesting Itself; and the whole mass of changes which we call evolution is brought about by the soul trying to manifest more and more of its infinite energy. We cannot stop anywhere on this side of the Infinite; our power, and blessedness, and wisdom, cannot but grow into the Infinite. Infinite power and existence and blessedness are ours, and we have not to acquire them; they are our own, and we have only to manifest them.*[21]

The new world of human knowledge and existence welcomes education of the origin of man in terms of evolution and involution. This is a very interesting chapter of man and civilisation which is very often misunderstood. Vivekananda clarifies this as follows:

> *Out of what has this universe been produced then? From a preceding fine universe. Out of what has man been produced? The preceding fine form. Out of what has the tree been produced? Out of the seed; the whole of the tree was in the seed. It comes out and becomes manifest. So, the whole of this universe has been created out of this very universe existing in a minute form. It has been made manifest now. It will go back to that minute form, and again will be made manifest. Now we find that the fine forms slowly come out and become grosser and grosser until they reach their limit, and when they reach their limit they go back further and further, becoming finer and finer again. This coming out of the fine and becoming gross, simply changing the arrangements of its parts, as it were, is what in modern times called evolution. This is very true, perfectly true; we see it in our lives. No rational man can possibly quarrel with these evolutionists. But we have to learn one thing more. We have to go one step further, and what is that? That every evolution is preceded by an involution. The seed is the father of the tree, but another tree was itself the father of the seed. The seed is the fine form out of which the big tree comes, and another big tree was the form which is involved in that seed. The whole of this universe was present in the cosmic fine universe. The little cell, which becomes afterwards the man, was simply the involved man and becomes evolved as a man. If this is clear, we have no quarrel with the evolutionists, for we see that if they admit this step, instead of their destroying religion, they will be the greatest supporters of it.*[22]

Man christened in the true spirit of education as Vivekananda strongly asserts, must be active, knowing and loving. The combination of head, heart and hand is the hallmark of man. What type of man do we want? Here is Vivekananda's distinct answer:

> *What we want is to see the man who is harmoniously developed ...great in heart, great in mind, [great in deed] ...We want the man whose heart feels intensely the miseries and sorrows of the*

> *world. . . .And [we want] the man who not only can feel but can find the meaning of things, who delves deeply into the heart of nature and understanding. [We want] the man who will not even stop there, [but] who wants to work out [the feeling and meaning by actual deeds]. Such a combination of head, heart, and hand is what we want. There are many teachers in this world, but you will find [that most of them] are one-sided. [One] sees the glorious midday sun of intellect [and] sees nothing else. Another hears the beautiful music of love and can hear nothing else. Another is [immersed] in activity, and has neither time to feel nor time to think. Why not [have] the giant who is equally active, equally knowing, and equally loving? Is it impossible? Certainly not. This is the man of the future, of whom there are [only a] few at present. [The number of such will increase] until the whole world is humanised.*[23]

The education that man should always seek and adore, nurse and disseminate is the education of self-reliance and self-strength. That he is the mightiest of all should always be rooted to his own identity as a man. Vivekananda unfolds this optimistic vision of man firmly:

> *You are lions, you are souls, pure, infinite, and perfect. The might of the universe is within you. "Why weepest thou, my friend? There is neither birth nor death for thee. Why weepest thou? There is no disease nor misery for thee, but thou art like the infinite sky; clouds of various colours come over it, play for a moment, then vanish. But the sky is ever the same eternal blue." Why do we see wickedness? There was a stump of a tree, and in the dark, a thief came that way and said, "That is a policeman." A young man waiting for his beloved saw it and thought that it was his sweetheart. A child who had been told ghost stories took it for a ghost and began to shriek. But all the time it was the stamp of a tree. We see the world as we are.*[24]

To assert and manifest the inherent nature is the true education of man. It is also the highest education that honours and upholds man as the best creation of all. When a man seeks a perfect ideal he must remember that it is inherent in his own self and nowhere else. Vivekananda puts this essence of man and education very characteristically:

No perfection is going to be attained. You are already free and perfect. What are these ideas of religion and God and searching for the hereafter? Why does man look for a God? Why does man, in every nation, in every state of society, want a perfect ideal somewhere, either in man, or God, or elsewhere? Because that idea is within you. It was your own heart beating and you did not know; you were mistaking it for something external. It is the God within your own self that is propelling you to seek for Him, to realise Him. After long searches here and there, in temples and in churches, in earths and in heavens, at last you come back, completing the circle from where you started, to your own soul and find that He for whom you have been seeking all over the world, from whom you have been weeping and praying in churches and temples, on whom you were looking as the mystery of all mysteries shrouded in the clouds, is nearest of the near, is your own Self, the reality of your life, body, and soul. That is your own nature. Assert it, manifest it. Not to become pure, you are pure already. Nature is like that screen which is hiding the reality beyond. Every good thought that you think or act upon is simply tearing the veil, as it were; and the purity, the Infinity, the God behind manifests Itself more and more.[25]

The real nature of man is that he is free; he is the true embodiment of freedom. The study of books most often forces us to be baptised in knowledge not of our own and not even cared by us. We take it for granted that whatever is written there is to be accepted as our own and whatever we think and act is to be rejected as abstractions. This makes us passive and irresponsible to our own freedom in education. Vivekananda significantly elucidates this point in education by means of "book-worship" that appallingly affects freedom:

To worship is inherent in every man's nature; only the highest philosophy can rise to pure abstraction. So man will ever personify his God in order to worship. This is very good, as long as the symbol, be it what it may, is worshipped as a symbol of the Divinity and not in and for itself. Above all, we need to free ourselves from the superstition of believing because "it is in the books". To try to make everything— science, philosophy, and all— conform to what any book says, is a most horrible tyranny. Book-worship is the worst form of idolatry. There was once a stag, proud and free, and he talked in a lordly fashion to his child, "Look at me, see my powerful horns! With one thrust I can kill a man; it is a fine thing to be a stag!" Just then the sound of the huntsman's bugle was heard in the distance, and the stag precipitately fled, followed by his wondering child. When they had reached a place of safety, he inquired, "Why do you fly before man, O my father, when you are so strong and brave?" The stag answered, "My child, I know I am strong and powerful, but when I hear that sound, something seizes me and makes me fly whether I will or no." So with us. We hear the "bugle sound" of the laws laid down in the books, habits and old superstitions lay hold of us; and before we know it, we are fast bound and forget our real nature which is freedom.[26]

Education is a matter of esteem, adoration and respect which brings forth man in his true perspective. What we mean *Shraddha* in *Sanskrit* signifies that connotation by which man reveals his true identity. It is only alternative to regain our loss of faith in ourselves. Unless self-respect is revived, man loses his rationality in honouring the Atman which is incomparable and unparalleled.

Vivekananda rightly points out that our education has lost its inherent strength of self-respect for self-identity and fullness of man:

We want Shraddha, we want faith in our own selves. Strength is life, weakness is death. 'We are the Atman, deathless and free; pure, pure by nature. Can we ever commit any sin? Impossible!' – such a faith is needed. Such a faith makes men of us, makes gods of us. It is by losing this idea of Shraddha that the country has gone to ruin.[27]

Vivekananda further clarifies:

We have had a negative education all along from our boyhood. We have only learnt that we are nobodies. Seldom are we given to understand that great men were ever born in our country. Nothing positive has been taught to us. We do not even know how to use our hands and feet! We master all the facts and figures concerning the ancestors of the English, but we are sadly unmindful about our own. We have learnt only weakness. Being a conquered race, we have brought ourselves to believe that we are weak and we have no independence in anything. So, how can it be but that the Shraddha is lost? The idea of true Shraddha must be brought back once more to us, the faith in our own selves must be reawakened, and, then only, all the problems which face our country will gradually be solved by ourselves.[28]

The march of man in terms of education should be a continual striving from instinct to reason and from reason to transcendence towards super-consciousness. There must be a regularity and discipline in this striving where the basis should always be ensured by every approach and every strategy undertaken in the most scientific and unbiased manner. Only then education is directed towards the meaning of man. As Vivekananda poignantly observes:

To get any reason out of the mass of incongruity we call human life, we have to transcend our reason, but we must do it scientifically, slowly, by regular practice, and we must cast off all superstition. We must take up the study of the super-conscious state just as any other science. On reason we must have to lay our foundation, we must follow reason as far as it leads, and when reason fails, reason itself will show us the way to the highest plane. When you hear a man say, "I am inspired", and then talk irrationally, reject it. Why? Because these three states – instinct, reason, and super-consciousness, or the unconscious, conscious, and super-conscious states— belong to one and the same mind. There are not three minds in one man, but one state of it develops into the others. Instinct develops into reason, and reason into the transcendental consciousness; therefore, not one of the states contradicts the others. Real inspiration never contradicts reason, but fulfils it. Just as find great prophets saying, "I come not to destroy but to fulfil," so inspiration always comes to fulfil reason, and is in harmony with it.[29]

The essence of education is derived from experience. It is what every human being necessitates to be justified to education that is far above book-learning. Books are not the minds but man possesses the infinite power to regenerate and revitalise himself for all-round efflorescence by dint of his experience. When would education come out of the book of the mind of man? When would man be free from the constraints of belief that stifles the mind through nursing book-knowledge? Vivekananda draws our attention to this fact by elucidating the importance of experience in education of the right type that allows education of man with the right mind:

Experience is the only teacher we have. We may talk and reason all our lives, but we shall not understand a word of truth, until we experience it ourselves. You cannot hope to make a man a surgeon by simply giving him a few books. You cannot satisfy my curiosity to see a country by showing me a map; I must have actual experience. Maps can only create curiosity in us to get more perfect knowledge. Beyond that, they have no value whatever. Clinging to books only degenerates the human mind. Was there ever a more horrible blasphemy than the statement that all the knowledge of God is confined to this or that book? How dare men call God infinite, and yet try to compress Him within the covers of a little book! Millions of people have been killed because they did not believe what the books said, because they would not see all the knowledge of God within the covers of a book. Of course this killing and murdering has gone by, but the world is still tremendously bound up in a belief in books.[30]

The education of man is the education of the sense-organs. How to control the sense-organs is a very important activity. This activity requires perseverance and sincerity of purpose. It also requires diligence and right exercise of the mind. The internal and external senses can very well be exercised by two very important components in education – discipline and self-control.

As an educational thinker par excellence, Vivekananda inspires us to stick to truth under any circumstances. This enables us to be duly alert in responding to and enriching our senses by exercising good thoughts, good principles, good operations and good involvements in dissemination. As truth always remains above narrowness in exercising senses, the education of man becomes self-controlled and self-disciplined. That there is a great link between truth and self-control is very well elucidated by Vivekananda as follows:

The external senses are the visible organs situated in different parts of the body; the internal senses are intangible. We have the external eyes, ears, nose, and so on; and we have the corresponding internal senses. We are continually at the beck and call of both these groups of senses. Corresponding to the senses are sense-objects. If any sense-objects are nearby, the senses compel us to perceive them; we have no choice or independence. There is the big nose. A little fragrance is there; I have to smell it. If there were a bad odour, I would say to myself, "Do not smell it"; but nature says "Smell", and I smell it. Just think what we have become! We have bound ourselves.

****

All these senses, external and internal, must be under the disciple's control. By hard practice he has to arrive at the stage where he can assert his mind against the senses, against the commands of nature. He should be able to say to his mind, "You are mine; I order you, do not see or hear anything", and the mind will not see or hear anything— no form or sound will react on the mind. In that state the mind has become free of the domination of the senses, has become separated from them. No longer is it attached to the senses and the body. The external things cannot order the mind now; the mind refuses to attach itself to them. Beautiful fragrance is there. The disciple says to the mind, "Do not smell", and the mind does not perceive the fragrance. When you have arrived at that point, you are just beginning to be a disciple. That is why when everybody says, "I know the truth", I say, "If you know the truth, you must have self-control; and if you have control of yourself, show it by controlling these organs."[31]

The education that man receives out of knowledge should be in terms of truth. If truth is absent, knowledge becomes meaningless. The teaching of the Vedanta as Vivekananda reminds us is to make a quest for truth in one's own self, because it lies within and inherent in every one under any circumstances. So, it is futile to have knowledge about truth by eliminating individuality. At the same time, knowing the past and the future is entirely dependent on knowing the present well, because time past and time future are best known through time present:

What does Vedanta teach us? In the first place, it teaches that you need not even go out of yourself to know the truth. All the past and all the future are here in the present. No man ever saw the past. Did any one of you see the past? When you think you are knowing the past, you only imagine the past in the present moment. To see the future, you would have to bring it down to the present, which is the only reality— the rest is imagination.

This present is all that is. There is only the One. All is here right now. One moment in infinite time is quite as complete and all-inclusive as every other moment. All that is and was and will be is here in the present. Let anybody try to imagine anything outside of it— he will not succeed.[32]

In exercising knowledge in terms of truth in education, man must be faithful to his work. Truth is a matter of self-realisation in terms of utilisation of sense-organs and a thorough verification of ideas and experiences received or likely to be received in course of time and a favourable time for introspection. Vivekananda characteristically explains the role of man in quest of truth in terms of the science of Raja-Yoga:

The science of Raja-Yoga proposes to put before humanity a practical and scientifically worked-out method of reaching the truth. In the first place, every science must have its own method of investigation. If you want to become an astronomer and sit down and cry "Astronomy! Astronomy!" it will never come to you. The same with chemistry. A certain method must be followed. You must go to a laboratory, take different substances, mix them up, compound them, experiment with them, and out of them will come a knowledge of chemistry. If you want to be an astronomer, you must go to an observatory, take a telescope, study the stars and planets, and then you will become an astronomer. Each science must have its own methods. I could preach you thousands of sermons, but they would not make you religious, until you practised the method. These are the truths of the sages of all countries, of all ages, of men pure and unselfish, who had no motive but to do good to the world. They all declare that they have found some truth higher than what the senses can bring to us, and they invite verification. They ask us to take up the method and practise honestly, and then, if we do not find this higher truth, we will have the right to say there is no truth in the claim, but before we have done that, we are not rational in denying the truth of their assertions. So we must work faithfully, using the prescribed methods, and light will come.

In acquiring knowledge we make use of generalisations, and generalisation is based upon observation. We first observe facts, then generalise, and then draw conclusions or principles. The knowledge of the mind, of the internal nature of man, of thought, can never be had until we have first the power of observing the facts that are going on within. It is comparatively easy to observe facts in the external world, for many instruments have been invented for the purpose, but in the internal world we have no instrument to help us. Yet we know we must observe in order to have a real science. Without a proper analysis, any science will be hopeless— mere theorising. And that is why all the psychologists have been quarrelling among themselves since the beginning of time, except those few who found out the means of observation.[33]

Vivekananda prioritises the importance of good teachers in imparting education that ensures man par excellence. He, therefore, advises us to have teachers who are selfless workers without any motive or greed for wealth and fame, money and name. As he categorically states:

The teacher must not teach with any ulterior selfish motive— for money, name, or fame; his work must be simply out of love, out of pure love for mankind at large. The only medium through which spiritual force can be transmitted is love. Any selfish motive, such as the desire for gain or for name, will ultimately destroy this conveying medium. God is love, and only he who has known God as love can be a teacher of godliness and God to man.[34]

Education enables man to build a strong foundation of knowledge by means of a harmonious blending of theory and practice in teaching-learning. It may sometime appear difficult to introduce psychical subjects through demonstration because we are, at the very outset, confused with the meaning of demonstration. Viewing the manifestation of perfection man already possesses, Vivekananda extends the spirit of demonstration in appreciating psychic things in a wider horizon of perfection in the human society:

About the psychical things that have been the subject of discussion, I have very little to say here, for in the first place, the question is whether psychical subjects are capable of scientific demonstration. What do you mean by this demonstration? First of all, there will be the subjective and the objective side necessary. Taking chemistry and physics, with which we are so familiar, and of which we have read so much, is it true that everyone in this world is able to understand the demonstration even of the commonest subjects? Take any boor and show him one of your experiments. What will he understand of it? Nothing. It requires a good deal of previous training to be brought up to the point of understanding an experiment. Before that he cannot understand it at all. That is a great difficulty in the way. If scientific demonstration means bringing down certain facts to a plane which is universal for all human beings, where all beings can understand it, I deny that there can be any such scientific demonstration for any subject in the world. If it were so, all our universities and education would be in vain. Why are we educated if by birth we can understand everything scientific? Why so much study? It is of no use whatsoever. So, on the face of it, it is absurd if this be the meaning of scientific demonstration, the bringing down of intricate facts to the plane on which we are now. The next meaning should be the correct one, perhaps, that certain facts should be adduced as proving certain more intricate facts. There are certain more complicated, intricate phenomena, which we explain by less intricate ones, and thus get, perhaps, nearer to them; in this way they are gradually brought down to the plane of our present ordinary consciousness. But even this is very complicated and very difficult, and means a training also, a tremendous amount of education. So all I have to say is that in order to have scientific explanation of psychical phenomena, we require not only perfect evidence on the side of the phenomena themselves, but a good deal of training on the part of those who want to see. All this being granted, we shall be in a position to say yea or nay, about the proof or disproof of any phenomena which are presented before us. But, before that, the most remarkable phenomena or the most oft-recorded phenomena that have happened in human society, in my opinion, would be very hard indeed to prove even in an offhand manner.[35]

The essence of man and education is inspiration. More often than not, we fail to understand what true inspiration means. It is loosely interpreted by many people many a time. It is also not known to many people that it is the highest form of knowledge which is superior to instinct and reason. Vivekananda significantly spells out:

There is such a thing as instinct in us, which we have in common with the animals, a reflex mechanical movement of the body. There is again a higher form of guidance, which we call reason, when the intellect obtains facts and then generalises them. There is still a higher form of knowledge which we call inspiration, which does not reason, but knows things by flashes. That is the highest form of knowledge. But how shall we know it from instinct? That is the great difficulty. Everyone comes to you, nowadays, and says he is inspired, and puts forth superhuman claims. How are we to distinguish between inspiration and deception? In the first place, inspiration must not contradict reason. The old man does not contradict the child, he is the development of the child. What we call inspiration is the development of reason. The way to intuition is through reason. Instinctive movements of your body do not oppose reason. As you cross a street, how instinctively you move your body to save yourself from the cars. Does your mind tell you it was foolish to save your body that way? It does not. Similarly, no genuine inspiration ever contradicts reason. Where it does it is no inspiration. Similarly, inspiration must be for the good of one and all, and not for name or fame, or personal gain. It should always be for the good of the world, and perfectly unselfish. when these rests are fulfilled, you are quite safe to take it as inspiration.[36]

Prioritising education in the making of man is a very challenging task. The teacher alone can take this challenge as the living and genuine quest for education. His sole aim is to properly and intelligently ignite the learners to be on the right track of education. To identify such a teacher, to recognise him from the fundamental objectives and principles of teaching learning of the right kind and for the right mind is really very difficult. Let us pay attention to Vivekananda's invaluable words:

How are we to know a teacher, then? The sun requires no torch to make him visible, we need not light a candle in order to see him. When the sun rises, we instinctively become aware of the fact, and when a teacher of men comes to help us, the soul will instinctively know that truth has already begun to shine upon it. Truth stands on its own evidence, it does not require any other testimony to prove it true, it is self-effulgent. It penetrates into the innermost corners of our nature, and in its presence the whole universe stands up and says, "This is truth." The teachers whose wisdom and truth shine like the light of the sun are the very greatest the world has known, and they are worshipped as God by the major portion of mankind. But we may get help from comparatively lesser ones also; only we ourselves do not possess intuition enough to judge properly of the man from whom we receive teaching and guidance; so there ought to be certain tests, certain conditions, for the teacher to satisfy, as there are also for the taught.[37]

Education is man. To study man is to educate oneself. Man, as Vivekananda appreciates, is "a living poem". Books are dead objects. That we are living books and our words are simply conveyed by them are most often forgotten. Vivekananda directs our attention towards this fact:

Books are useless to us until our own book opens; then all other books are good so far as they confirm our book. It is the strong that understand strength, it is the elephant that understands the lion, not the rat. How can we understand Jesus until we are his equals? It is all in the dream to feed five thousand with two loaves, or to feed two with five loaves; neither is real and neither affects the other. Only grandeur appreciates grandeur, only God realises God. The dream is only the dreamer, it has no other basis. It is not one thing and the dreamer another. The keynote running through the music is— "I am He, I am He", all other notes are but variations and do not affect the real theme. We are the living books and books are but the words we have spoken. Everything is the living God, the living Christ; see it as such. Read man, he is the living poem. We are the light that illumines all the Bibles and Christs and Buddhas that ever were. Without that, these would be dead to us, not living.[38]

When would we be really radical in our vision of man and education in the light of the above?

1. Swami Vivekananda: *The Complete Works of Swami Vivekananda,* Advaita Ashrama, Kolkata, Mayavati Memorial Edition, 1989, Vol. IV, p. 358.
2. *Ibid.*, Vol. III, pp. 8-9.
3. *Ibid.*, Vol. I, pp. 28-29.
4. *Ibid.*, p. 510.
5. *Ibid.*, Vol. III, pp. 243-244.
6. *Ibid.*, Vol. VII, p. 71.
7. *Ibid.*, Vol. I, p. 78.
8. *Ibid.*, Vol. V, p. 419.
9. *Ibid.*, pp. 34-35.
10. *Ibid.*, Vol. VII, pp. 76-77.
11. *Ibid.*, pp. 52-53.
12. *Ibid.* pp. 154-155.
13. *Ibid.*, Vol. II, pp. 282-283.
14. *Ibid.*, Vol. IV, pp. 489-490,
15. *Ibid.*, pp. 214-215.
16. *Ibid.*, pp. 158-159.
17. *Ibid.*, Vol. II, p. 299.
18. *Ibid.*, pp. 213-214.
19. *Ibid.*, Vol. VI, pp. 29- 30.
20. *Ibid.*, p. 64.
21. *Ibid.*, Vol. II, p. 339.
22. *Ibid.*, pp. 207-208.
23. *Ibid.*, Vol. VI, pp. 49-50.
24. *Ibid.*, Vol. II, pp. 86-87.
25. *Ibid.*, pp. 81-82.
26. *Ibid.*, Vol. VIII, pp. 33-34.
27. *Ibid.*, Vol. V, p. 332.
28. *Ibid.* p. 332.
29. *Ibid.*, Vol. I. pp. 184-185.
30. *Ibid.*, pp. 185-186.
31. *Ibid.*, Vol. VIII, pp. 108-109.
32. *Ibid.*, p. 128.
33. *Ibid.*, Vol. I, pp. 128-129.
34. *Ibid.*, Vol. III, p. 51.
35. *Ibid.*, Vol. IV, pp. 192-193.
36. *Ibid.*, pp. 58-59.
37. *Ibid.*, Vol. III, pp. 47-48.
38. *Ibid.*, Vol. VII, p. 89.

Man and Religion: Vivekananda's Viewpoints

Religion is, somehow or other, the identity of man. To anyone who cares to be religious in the true sense of the term ought to unfold the inherent vision of man. What is that vision? What is actually signified with that vision? How to be justified with it, and why? All these queries and other allied ones contribute to the essence and significance of man in terms of religion and vice versa.

As an ever abiding and earnest backdrop to the above and to be very distinct and transparent, Swami Vivekananda describes religion as "the manifestation of the Divinity already in man."[1] All religions of the world convey this invaluable message of the glory of man. This broad vision of man as an exponent of religion finds its finest expression as follows:

> *Religion is not the outcome of the weakness of human nature; religion is not here because we fear a tyrant; religion is love, unfolding, expanding, growing. Take the watch— within the little case is machinery and a spring. The spring, when wound up, tries to regain its natural state. You are like the spring in the watch, and it is not necessary that all watches have the same kind of a spring, and it is not necessary that we all have the same religion. And why should we quarrel? If we all had the same ideas the world would be dead. External motion we call action; internal motion is human thought. The stone falls to the earth. You say it is caused by the law of gravitation. The horse draws the cart and God draws the horse. This is the law of motion. Whirlpools show the strength of the current; stop the current and stagnation ensues. Motion is life. We must have unity and variety. The rose would smell sweet by any other name, and it does not matter what your religion is called.*[2]

The true religion of man is to realise 'the trinity of existence' which means nature, man and God in unison to be visualised by every one of us. The idea of religion thus in symphony of man and nature makes man more in relation to the living existence of God as he visualises in him. This clarifies religion in relation to man from three points of view: first, the concept of God becomes a matter of individual realisation; second, religion becomes natural and liberal without being a constraint to man; third, the excellence of relation between man and religion becomes living and spontaneous.

Vivekananda clarifies the above in elucidating the role of man in terms of the spirit of religion of love:

> *Man does not manufacture God out of his own brain; but he can only see God in the light of his own capacity, and he attributes to Him the best of all he knows. Each attribute is the whole of God, and this signifying the whole by one quality is the metaphysical explanation of the personal God. Ishvara is without form yet has all forms, is without qualities yet has all qualities. As human beings, we have to see the trinity of existence— God, man, nature; and we cannot do otherwise.*
>
> *But to the Bhakta all these philosophical distinctions are mere idle talk. He cares nothing for argument, he does not reason, he "senses", he perceives. He wants to lose himself in pure love of God, and there have been Bhaktas who maintain that this is more to be desired than liberation, who say, "I do not want to be sugar. I want to taste sugar; I want to love and enjoy the Beloved."*[3]

Religion in relation to man and vice versa cannot but remain as a vision, a perception introspective endless always in the process of crystallisation with best thoughts and emotions, consciousness and devotion. It never cares for constraints because all forms of constraints are symbols to success in realisation.

The claims of religion in terms of the above becomes more explicit from Vivekananda's viewpoints:

> *This universe of ours, the universe of the senses, the rational, the intellectual, is bounded on both side by the illimitable, the unknowable, the ever unknown. Herein is the search, herein are the inquiries, here are the facts; from this comes the light which is known to the world as religion. Essentially, however, religion belongs to the supersensuous and not to the sense plane. It is beyond all reasoning, and not on the plane of intellect. It is a*

vision, an inspiration, a plunge into the unknown and unknowable, making the unknowable more than known, for it can never be "known". This search has been in the human mind, as I believe, from the very beginning of humanity. There cannot have been human reasoning and intellect in any period of the world's history without this struggle, this search beyond. In our little universe, this human mind, we see a thought arise. Whence it rises we do not know, and when it disappears, where it goes we do not know either. The macrocosm and the microcosm are, as it were, in the same groove, passing through the same stages, vibrating in the same key. ...

It is my belief that religious thought is in man's very constitution, so much so that it is impossible for him to give up religion until he can give up his mind and body, until he can stop thought and life. As long as a man thinks, this struggle must go on, and so long man must have some form of religion. Thus we see various forms of religion in the world. It is a bewildering study; but it is not, as many of us think, a vain speculation. Amidst this chaos there is harmony, throughout these discordant sounds there is a note of concord; and he who is prepared to listen to it, will catch the tone.[4]

Religion should always be a stepping stone of human progress and civilisation. It should be the mouthpiece of man in thought and action, behaviour and manifestation. It should highlight the spirit of man. Its motto in terms of man should be: "Be and make". As Vivekananda proclaims:

Be not deluded by your religion teaching original sin, for the same religion teaches original purity. When Adam fell, he fell from purity, purity is our real nature, and to regain that is the object of all religion. All men are pure; all men are good. Some objections can be raised to them , and you ask why some men are brutes? That man you call a brute is like the diamond in the dirt and dust— brush the dust off and it is a diamond, just as pure as if the dust had never been on it, and we must admit that every soul is a big diamond.

Nothing is baser than calling our brother a sinner. A lioness once fell upon a flock of sheep and killed a lamb. A sheep found a very young lion, and it followed her, and he gave it suck, and it grew up with the sheep and learned to eat grass like a sheep. One day an old lion saw the sheep lion and tried to get it away from the sheep, but it ran away as he approached. The big lion waited till he caught the sheep lion alone, and he seized it and carried it to a clear pool of water and said, 'You are not a sheep, but a lion; look at your picture in the water.' The sheep lion seeing its picture reflected from the water, said, 'I am a lion and not a sheep.' Let us not think we are sheep, but be lions, and don't bleat and eat grass like a sheep.[5]

The goal of man in terms of religion is very often misunderstood. Religion is never an end but a means to an end in the quest for the truth it eternally denotes. The point of appreciating religion for the good of man varies from man to man but the ultimate end-in-view of religion is what man ought to be from what stands now as best to man. Therefore, religion entertains new ideas, new concepts, new policies and new principles of the welfare of mankind. If that fails, it is due to paucity of vision and transparency in application.

The progress of man in relation to religion depends on approaches to perfection. Do we believe in the science of religion? When would we be able to appreciate religion in terms of perfect unity as an ever dynamic and continuous progress to further progress. But prior to that, are we sure about the importance of the new discovery of truth that religion fosters? Here are Vivekananda's viewpoints:

Nowadays it is asserted that man is progressing infinitely, forward and forward, and there is no goal of perfection to attain to. Ever approaching, never attaining, whatever that may mean, and however wonderful it may be, it is absurd on the face of it. Is there any motion in a straight line? A straight line infinitely projected becomes a circle, it returns back to the starting point. You must end where you begin; and as you began in God, you must go back to God. What remains? Detail work. Through eternity you have to do the detail work.

Yet another question: Are we to discover new truths of religion as we go on? Yea and nay. In the first place, we cannot know anything more of religion; it has been all known. In all the religions of the world you will find it claimed that there is a unity within us. Being one with the Divinity, there cannot be any further progress in that sense. Knowledge means finding this unity in variety. I see you as men and women, and this is variety. It becomes scientific knowledge when I group you together and call you human beings. Take the science of chemistry, for instance. Chemists are seeking to resolve all known substances into their original elements, and if possible, to find the one element from which all these are derived. The time has come when they will find the one element. That is the source of all other elements. Reaching that, they can go no further; the science of chemistry will have become perfect. So it is with the science of religion. If we can discover this perfect unity, then there cannot be any further progress.[6]

A radical thinker par excellence in religion, Vivekananda has never allowed any authoritarianism and blind faith. He strongly asserts on logical and scientific concept of religion. He has categorically stated that religion is never a matter of 'believing' but always a quest for 'being and becoming'. In this connection, one might recall his forceful and vibrant words well substantiated by the Buddha's invaluable words on religion:

Believe what? To believe blindly is to degenerate the human soul. Be an atheist if you want, but do not believe in anything unquestioningly. Why degrade the soul to the level of animals? You not only hurt yourselves thereby, but you injure society, and make danger for those that come after you. Stand up and reason out, having no blind faith. Religion is a question of being and becoming, not of believing. This is religion, and when you have attained to that, you have religion. Before that you are no better than the animals. "Do not believe in what you have heard," says the great Buddha, "do not believe in doctrines because they have been handed down to you through generations; do not believe in anything because it is followed blindly by many; do not believe because some old sage makes a statement; do not believe in truths to which you have become attached by habit; do not believe merely on the authority of your teachers and elders. Have deliberation and analyse, and when the result agrees with reason and conduces to the good of one and all, accept it and live up to it."[7]

To understand and appreciate religion as the true identity of man is an infinite challenge. That religion is strength can only be understood in terms of freedom. Freedom is the only passport to religion par excellence. It is freedom from worldly happenings like life and death and exploring the Atman, the true nature. It is freedom that allows us to be on the right track to understand the Divine Self within every one of us. In the words of Vivekananda, it is 'the one and only God'.

What, then, should be the role of man in quest of freedom as the exponent of religion? Let us ponder over the answer we receive from Vivekananda's viewpoints:

> *What we want is freedom, not life, nor pleasure, nor good. Creation is infinite, without beginning and without end— the ever-moving ripple in an infinite lake. There are yet unreached depths and others where the equilibrium has been regained; but the ripple is always progressing, the struggle to regain the balance is eternal. Life and death are only different names for the same fact, the two sides of the one coin. Both are Maya, the inexplicable state of striving at one time to live, and a moment later to die. Beyond this is the true nature, the Atman. While we recognise a God, it is really only the Self which we have separated ourselves from and worship as outside of us; but it is our true Self all the time— the one and only God.*
>
> *To regain the balance we must counteract Tamas by Rajas; then conquer Rajas by Sattva, the calm, beautiful state that will grow and grow until all else is gone. Give up bondage; become a son, be free, and then you can "see the Father", as did Jesus. Infinite strength is religion and God. Avoid weakness and slavery. You are only a soul,* if *you are free; there is immortality for you,* if *you are free; there is God,* if *He is free. ...*
>
> *The world for me, not I for the world. Good and evil are our slaves, not we theirs. It is the nature of the brute to remain where he is (not to progress); it is the nature of man to seek good and avoid evil; it is the nature of God to seek neither, but just to be eternally blissful. Let us be God! Make the heart like an ocean, go beyond all the trifles of the world, be mad with joy even at evil; see the world as a picture and then enjoy its beauty, knowing that nothing affects you. Children finding glass beads in a mud*

puddle, that is the good of the world. Look at it with calm complacency; see good and evil as the same— both are merely "God's play"; enjoy all.[8]

The new vision of man in terms of religion and vice versa finds its truest foundation on Truth. "That God is in us and we are in God" as Vivekananda clearly asserts, is the sum and substance of all religions. If we fail to believe in this truth and do not uphold religion from this point of view, religion loses its true identity of man and turns into dogmatism, sectarianism, parochialism, and a mere process of nurturing ritualism. In this connection, Vivekananda's transparent viewpoints may be recalled:

We believe in one God, the Father of us all, who is omnipresent and omnipotent, and who guides and preserves His children with infinite love. We believe in a Personal God as the Christians do, but we go further: we believe that we are He! That His personality is manifested in us, that God is in us, and that we are in God. We believe there is a germ of truth in all religions, and the Hindu bows down to them all; for in this world, truth is to be found not in subtraction but in addition. We would offer God a bouquet of the most beautiful flowers of all the diverse faiths. We must love God for love's sake, not for the hope of reward. We must do our duty for duty's sake, not for the hope of reward. We must worship the beautiful for beauty's sake, not for the hope of reward. Thus in the purity of our heart shall we see God. Sacrifices, genuflexions, mumblings, and mutterings are not religion. They are only good if they stimulate us to the brave performance of beautiful and heroic deeds and lift our thoughts to the apprehension of the divine perfection.

What good is it, if we acknowledge in our prayers that God is the Father of us all, and in our daily lives do not treat every man as our brother? Books are only made so that they may point the way to a higher life; but no good results unless the path is trodden with unflinching steps![9]

The concept of man in relation to God as true religion indicates is oneness. This not only ennobles man but also enriches religion. Man becomes an inseparable part of religion. He strives more and more for a higher and higher vision of religion by dint of introspection and accomplishment. As Vivekananda poignantly states:

> *Man is the highest being that exists, and this is the greatest world. We can have no conception of God higher than man, so our God is man, and man is God. When we rise and go beyond and find something higher, we have to jump out of the mind, out of body and the imagination and leave this world; when we rise to be the Absolute, we are no longer in this world. Man is the apex of the only world we can ever know. All we know of animals is only by analogy, we judge them by what we do and feel ourselves.*
>
> ********
>
> *Those who have attained sameness are said to be living in God. All hatred is killing the "Self by the self", therefore love is the law of life. To rise to this is to be perfect; but the more perfect we are, less work (so-called) can we do. The Sattvika see and know that all is mere child's play and do not trouble themselves about anything.*
>
> *It is easy to strike a blow, but tremendously hard to stay the hand, stand still, and say, "In Thee, O Lord, I take refuge", and then wait for Him to act.*[10]

The true spirit of religion in the light of the above further encompasses the greatness of man. Each individual is unique in his concept of religion as the means of realisation of God. Each has the unique role to foster individuality in the exercise of religion he considers his very own. He must prove his sincerity of purpose in highlighting and enriching his own religion that enriches the spirit of altruism. Therefore, a variety of religions will provide man with multidimensional opportunities for exercising the best avenues of efflorescence of individuality.

Vivekananda significantly elucidates the point as above with an emphasis on the role of different religions for man to consolidate and strengthen his own religion:

> *The human mind is not homogeneous like the external world. According to the different nature, there must be different methods. As some special sense predominates in a person— one person will see most, another will hear most— so there is a*

predominant mental sense; and through this gate must each reach his own mind. Yet through all minds runs a unity, and there is a science which may be applied to all. This science of religion is based on the analysis of the human soul. It has no creed.

No one form of religion will do for all. Each is a pearl on a string. We must be particular above all else to find individuality in each. No man is born to any religion; he has a religion in his own soul. Any system which seeks to destroy individuality is in the long run disastrous. Each life has a current running through it, and this current will eventually take it to God. The end and aim of all religions is to realise God. The greatest of all training is to worship God alone. If each man chose his own ideal and stuck to it, all religious controversy would vanish.[11]

The diversity of religions as man adores and ennobles places both man and religion on a sound platform of excellence and ascent. Man finds religion as "the soul of humanity". It also proves the fact that we express religions in different ways but, essentially, all religions are one and the same for the advancement of man. As Vivekananda appropriately observes:

Religion is fundamental in the very soul of humanity; and as all life is the evolution of that which is within, it, of necessity, expresses itself through various peoples and nations.

The language of the soul is one, the languages of nations are many; their customs and methods of life are widely different. Religion is of the soul and finds expression through various nations, languages, and customs. Hence, it follows that the difference between the religions of the world is one of expression and not of substance; and their points of similarity and unity are of the soul, are intrinsic, as the language of the soul is one, in whatever peoples and under whatever circumstances it manifests itself. The same sweet harmony is vibrant there also, as it is on many and diverse instruments.[12]

Religion is intense realisation. It is the realisation through which man feels, talks, and sees God. To the Western people, it might appear absurd; but to the people of the East, it is as normal, natural and desirable as religion is never apart from man. At the same time, religion is never an abstraction but a reality— a living, thriving, spontaneous and thrilling realisation of man, the Divine Being.

Referring to the exercise of religion by Shri Ramakrishna, his Master, Vivekananda narrates:

> *There have been various poets in Bengal whose songs have passed down to the people; they are sung in the streets of Calcutta and in every village. Most of these are religious songs, and their one central idea, which is perhaps peculiar to the religions of India, is the idea of realisation. There is not a book in India on religion which does not breathe this idea. Man must realise God, feel God, see God, talk to God. That is religion. The Indian atmosphere is full of stories of saintly persons having visions of God. Such doctrines form the basis of their religion; and all these ancient books and scriptures are the writings of persons who came in direct contact with spiritual facts. These books were not written for the intellect, nor can any reasoning understand them, because they were written by men who saw the things of which they wrote, and they can be understood only by men who have raised themselves to the same height. They say there is such a thing as realisation even in this life, and it is open to everyone, and religion begins with the opening of this faculty, if I may call it so. This is the central idea of all religions, and this is why we may find one man with the most finished oratorical powers, or the most convincing logic, preaching the highest doctrines and yet unable to get people to listen to him, while we may find another, a poor man, who scarcely can speak the language of his own motherland, yet half the nation worships him in his own lifetime as God. When in India the idea somehow or other gets abroad that a man has raised himself to that state of realisation, that religion is no more a matter of conjecture to him, that he is no more groping in the dark in such momentous questions as religion, the immortality of the soul, and God, and people come from all quarters to see him and gradually they begin to worship him.*[13]

Faith in man and religion for cultivation of intense insight, not fanaticism, knowledge for sincerity and devotion and not exercise of drab intellectualism, and love sans display of sentimentalism— all these must be synchronised for exercise of religion par excellence.

Any effective endeavour in the practice of religion should be supported by an impartial approach well backed by the exercise of a generous vision of human character.

In a letter written to "Kidi" on March 3, 1894, Vivekananda distinctly spells out:

> *I agree with you so far that faith is a wonderful insight and that it alone can save; but there is the danger in it of breeding fanaticism and barring further progress.*
>
> *Jnana is all right; but there is the danger of its becoming dry intellectualism. Love is great and noble; but it may die away in meaningless sentimentalism.*
>
> *A harmony of all these is the thing required. Ramakrishna was such a harmony. Such beings are few and far between; but keeping him and his teachings as the ideal, we can move on. And if amongst us, each one may not individually attain to that perfection, still we may get it collectively by counteracting, equipoising, adjusting, and fulfilling one another. This would be* harmony *by a number of persons and a decided advance on all other forms and creeds.*
>
> *For a religion to be effective, enthusiasm is necessary. At the same time we must try to avoid the danger of multiplying creeds. We avoid that by being a non-sectarian sect, having all the advantages of a sect and the broadness of a universal religion.*
>
> *God, though everywhere, can be known to us in and through human character. No character was ever so perfect as Ramakrishna's, and that should be the centre round which we ought to rally, at the same time allowing everybody to regard him in his own light, either as God, saviour, teacher, model, or great man, just as he pleases. We preach neither social equality nor inequality, but that every being has the same rights, and insist upon freedom of thought and action in every way.*
>
> *We reject none, neither theist, nor pantheist, monist, polytheist, agnostic, nor atheist; the only condition of being a disciple is modelling a character at once the broadest and the most intense. Nor do we insist upon particular codes of morality as to conduct, or character, or eating and drinking, except so far as it injures others.*[14]

A generous approach to man and religion not only paves path to understanding and appreciating the importance of both the concepts but also allows greater and more intensive culture of progress and ascent, purity and excellence. To man, religion is never equivalent to a few creeds, dogmas, principles etc. It is a human essence— "a constitution of the human mind"— which varies from person to person, from community to community, and from country to country. A study of different religions enables any one to be empowered with transparency and catholicity of vision. Vivekananda himself has admitted that in his own boyhood life he has for a particular period of time suffered from scepticism but a study of different religions has widened the vision of looking at and honouring all religions as the stepping stones of excellence and ascent of man. In his invaluable words:

> *Under the tremendous sledge-hammer blows of scientific research, old superstitions were crumbling away like masses of porcelain. Those to whom religion meant only a bundle of creeds and meaningless ceremonials were in despair; they were at their wits' end. Everything was slipping between their fingers. For a time it seemed inevitable that the surging tide of agnosticism and materialism would sweep all before it. There were those who did not dare utter what they thought. Many thought the case hopeless and the cause of religion lost once and for ever. But the tide has turned and to the rescue has come— what? The study of comparative religions. By the study of different religions we find that in essence they are one. When I was a boy, this scepticism reached me, and it seemed for a time as if I must give up all hope of religion. But fortunately for me I studied the Christian religion, the Mohammedan, the Buddhistic, and others, and what was my surprise to find that the same foundation principles taught by my religion were also taught by all religions. It appealed to me this way. What is the truth? I asked. Is this world true? Yes. Why? Because I see it. Are the beautiful sounds we just heard (the vocal and instrumental music) true? Yes. Because we heard them. We know that a man has body, eyes, and ears, and he has a spiritual nature which we cannot see. And with his spiritual faculties he can study the different religions and find that whether a religion is taught in the forests and*

jungles of India or in a Christian land, in essentials all religions are one. This only shows us that religion is a constitutional necessity of the human mind. The proof of one religion depends on the proof of all the rest. For instance, if I have six fingers, and no one else has, you may well say that is abnormal. The same reasoning may be applied to the argument that only one religion is true and all others false. One religion only, like one set of six fingers in the world, would be unnatural. We see, therefore, that if one religion is true, all other must be true. There are differences in non-essentials, but in essentials they are all one. If my five fingers are true, they prove that your five fingers are true too. Wherever man is, he must develop a belief, he must develop his religious nature.[15]

The quest for real religion indicates the fact that it is one. This is the real bond between man and religion. To move away from it is to dissociate man from the real perception of the oneness of religion. Therefore, there is no antagonism between man and man, religion and religion, and man and religion.

From the point of view of the Atman as an exponent of personality in relation to the freedom of man, Vivekananda adroitly elucidates the real nature of religion:

We must get beyond all differentiation and reach eternal "sameness" or homogeneity or Brahman. The Atman is the unity of all personalities and is unchangeable, the "one without a second". It is not life, but it is coined into life. It is beyond life and death and good and bad. It is the Absolute Unity. Dare to seek Truth even through hell. Freedom can never be true of name and form, of the related. No form can say, "I am free as a form." Not until all idea of form is lost, does freedom come. If our freedom hurts others, we are not free there. We must not hurt others. While real perception is only one, relative perceptions must be many. The fountain of all knowledge is every one of us— in the ant as in the highest angel. Real religion is one; all quarrel is with the forms, the symbols, the "illustrations". The millennium exists only for those who find it. The truth is, we have lost ourselves and think the world to be lost. "Fool! Hearest not thou? In thine own heart, day and night, is singing that Eternal Music— Sachchidananda, Soham, Soham, (Existence, Knowledge, and Bliss, I am He, I am He)!"

To try to think without a phantasm is to try to make the impossible possible. Each thought has two parts—the thinking and the word, and we must have both. Neither idealists nor materialists are able to explain the world; to do that, we must take both idea and expression. All knowledge is of the reflected as we can only see our own faces reflected in a mirror. So no one can know his Self or Brahman; but each is that Self and must see it reflected in order to make it an object of knowledge.[16]

The real identity of man in terms of religion is that religion is not apart from man. It is not an abstraction but a living reality. When a man does not differentiate himself from religion and makes no difference between man and everything in and around, he is blessed with encountering the Living God which is the highest manifestation of religion. As Vivekananda characteristically describes in his poem "The Living God":

He who is at once the high and low,
The sinner and the saint,
Both God and worm,
Him worship—visible, knowable, real, omnipresent,
Break all other idols!
In whom is neither past life
Nor future birth nor death,
In whom we always have been
And always shall be one,
Him worship. Break all other idols!
Ye fools! Who neglect the living God,
And His infinite reflections with which the world is full.
While ye run after imaginary shadows,
That lead alone in fights and quarrels,
Him worship, the only visible!
Break all other idols![17]

Admittedly, Vivekananda emphasises on the fact that religion is inherent in man. It cannot be had by any external objects or individuals like books or teachers because the knowledge necessary for learning religion is within every human being, and that inherent knowledge is to be exercised with all sincerity and devotion. That is religion sans bondage sans artificiality. It is direct and spontaneous, living and inspiring to encounter the All Free by exercising freedom and love supreme.

In explaining the true concept of man in relation to religion for which there is no room for absence of exercise of his own powers of freedom and love, Vivekananda strongly stresses on the existence of religion in man alone, and advises for extinction of personality and self-interest for the well-being of others without banking upon books any more than mere suggestions and a method to exercise 'the inner light':

> *Books suggest the inner light and the method of bringing that out, but we can only understand them when we have earned the knowledge ourselves. When the inner light has flashed for you, let the books go, and look only within. You have in you all and a thousand times more than is in all the books. Never lose faith in yourself, you can do anything in this universe. Never weaken, all power is yours.*
>
> *If religion and life depend upon books or upon the existence of any prophet whatsoever, then perish all religion and books! Religion is in us. No books or teachers can do more than help us to find it, and even without them we can get all truth within. You have gratitude for books and teachers without bondage to them; and worship your Guru as God, but do not obey him blindly; love him all you will, but think for yourself. No blind belief can save you, work out your own salvation. Have only one idea of God— that He is an eternal help.*
>
> *Freedom and highest love must go together, then neither can become a bondage. We can give nothing to God; He gives all to us. He is the Guru of Gurus. Then we find that He is the "Soul of our souls", our very Self. No wonder we love Him, He is the Soul of our souls; whom or what else can we love? We want to be the "steady flame, burning without heat and without smoke". To whom can you do good, when you see only God? You cannot do good to God! All doubt goes, all is, "sameness". If you do good at all, you do it to yourself; feel that the receiver is the higher one. You serve the other because you are lower than he, not because he is low and you are high. Give as the rose gives perfume, because it is its own nature, utterly unconscious of giving.*[18]

The concept of Brahman as Vivekananda elucidates in the light of the Vedanta eliminates the difference between man and man along with that in other aspects and things like angels, animals, plants or stones as the so-called difference is in degree only. What is more important is manifestation. The better the manifestation, the greater is the efflorescence of the Brahman within.

Indeed, the religion of the Vedanta with its most scientific vision and practice comes closest to its relation to man irrespective of so-called individual differences in efflorescence. As Vivekananda makes an in-depth observation:

> *The Self is the essence of this universe, the essence of all souls; He is the essence of your own life, nay, "Thou art That". You are one with this universe. He who says he is different from others, even by a hair's breadth, immediately becomes miserable. Happiness belongs to him who knows this oneness, who knows he is one with this universe.*
>
> *Thus we see that the religion of the Vedanta can satisfy the demands of the scientific world, by referring it to the highest generalisation and to the law of evolution. That the explanation of a thing comes from within itself is still more completely satisfied by Vedanta. The Brahman, the God of the Vedanta, has nothing outside of Himself; nothing at all. All this indeed is He: He is the universe: He is the universe Himself. "Thou art the man, Thou art the woman, Thou art the young man walking in the pride of youth, Thou art the old man tottering in his step". He is here. Him we see and feel: in Him we live, and move, and have our being. You have that conception in the New Testament. It is that idea, God immanent in the universe, the very essence, the heart, the soul of things. He manifests Himself, as it were, in this universe. You and I are little bits, little points, little channels, like expressions, all living inside of that infinite ocean of Existence, Knowledge, and Bliss. The difference between man, between angels and man, between man and animals, between animals and plants, between plants and stones is not in kind, because everyone from the highest angel to the lowest particle and matter is but an expression of that one infinite ocean, and the difference is only in degree. I am a low manifestation, you may be a higher, but in both the materials are the same. You and*

I are both outlets of the same channel, and that is God; as such, your nature is God, and so is mine. You are of the nature of God by your birthright; so am I. You may be an angel of purity, and I may be the blackest of demons. Nevertheless, by birthright is that infinite ocean of Existence, Knowledge, and Bliss. So is yours. You have manifested yourself more today. Wait; I will manifest myself more yet, for I have it all within me.[19]

Religion is realisation of man in and through contact of the senses. The search for the means of what religion truly stands for is to be made with a conscious mind. This will gradually inspire man to be on the right track of sensing the super-conscious mind.

In most cases, man loses the sense of scientific thinking as the basis of finding out the genesis of religion. As a result, what is apparent and superficial vainly adorns religion. It is the outcome of unscientific and split thinking that leads to ambiguities and misconception of religion.

The best way to know the basis of religion is to follow the footprints of great teachers of religion and thoroughly understand the avenues of realisation of religion. Everyone's religion is precious and everyone should strive for realising it from diverse perspectives. As Vivekananda clearly observes:

Religion is based upon sense contact, upon seeing, the only basis of knowledge. What comes in contact with the super-conscious mind is fact. Aptas are those who have "sensed" religion. The proof is that if you follow their method, you too will see. Each science requires its own particular method and instruments. An astronomer cannot show you the rings of Saturn by the aid of all the pots and pans in the kitchen. He needs a telescope. So, to see the great facts of religion, the methods of those who have already seen must be followed. The greater the science the more varied the means of studying it. Before we came into the world, God provided the means to get out; so all we have to do is to find the means. But do not fight over methods. Look only for realisation and choose the best method you can find to suit you.[20]

Man learns the true concept of religion by means of realisation of the true concept of nature. Nature eludes us in our day-to-day life. We fail to realise that the spirit within every one of us never dies. That realisation is possible through renunciation and meditation which are the essence of religion. Man fails to accept the truth that it is futile to run after wealth and pleasure, happiness and worldly attractions which are very transitory and bound to be perishable. He also fails to accept the fact that everything in this world changes but true religion is eternal, unchangeable, imperishable, unfathomable, unending and everlasting.

In analysing the role of Nature vis-a-vis religion and man, Vivekananda unfolds the importance of concentration and meditation as the most potent factor of understanding human power:

> *Nature grinds all of us. Keep count of the ounce of pleasure you get. In the long run, nature did her work through you, and when you die your body will make other plants grow. Yet we think all the time that we are getting pleasure ourselves. Thus the wheel goes round.*
>
> *Therefore to realise the spirit as spirit is practical religion. Everything else is good so far as it leads to this one grand idea. That [realisation] is to be attained by renunciation, by meditation— renunciation of all the senses, cutting the knots, the chains that bind us down to matter. "I do not want to get material life, do not want the sense-life, but something higher." that is renunciation. Then, by the power of meditation, undo the mischief that has been done.*
>
> ********
>
> *What is meditation? Meditation is the power which enables us to resist all this. Nature may call us, "Look, there is a beautiful thing!" I do not look. Now she says, "There is a beautiful smell; smell it!" I say to my nose, "Do not smell it", and the nose doesn't. "Eyes, do not see!" Nature does such an awful thing— kills one of my children, and says, "Now, rascal, sit down and weep! Go to the depths!" I say, "I don't have to." I jump up. I must be free. Try it sometimes.... [In meditation], for a moment, you can change this nature. Now, if you had that power in yourself, would not that be heaven, freedom? That is the power of meditation.*[21]

That each man is potentially divine is the essence of man and religion. What is of utmost importance for man is to properly manifest this divinity. There are endless ways to manifest but each way should be entirely free from rituals, dogmas, rigidities, ambiguities, rites, superstitions and absurdities. The role of man in practising religion, therefore, signifies the fact that there must be purity, sincerity, work, worship, and dedication in the pursuit of religion. Only then there would be an ideal relation between man and religion.

Vivekananda consolidates his viewpoints on the above by taking recourse to Yoga philosophy as follows:

> *According to Yoga philosophy, it is through ignorance that the soul has been joined with nature. The aim is to get rid of nature's control over us. That is the goal of all religions. Each soul is potentially divine. The goal is to manifest this Divinity within, by controlling nature, external and internal. Do this either by work, or worship, or psychic control, or philosophy— by one or more or all of these— and be free. This is the whole of religion. Doctrines, or dogmas, or rituals, or books, or temples, or forms, are but secondary details. The Yogi tries to reach this goal through psychic control. Until we can free ourselves from nature, we are slaves; as she dictates so we must go. The Yogi claims that he who controls mind controls matter also. The internal nature is much higher than the external and much more difficult to grapple with, much more difficult to control. Therefore he who has conquered the internal nature controls the whole universe; it becomes his servant. Raja-Yoga propounds the methods of gaining this control. Forces higher than we know in physical nature will have to be subdued. This body is just the external crust of the mind. They are not two different things; they are just the oyster and its shell. They are but two aspects of one thing; the internal substance of the oyster takes up matter from outside, and manufactures the shell. In the same way the internal fine forces which are called mind take up gross matter from outside, and from that manufacture this external shell, the body. If, then, we have control of the internal, it is very easy to have control of the external. Then again, these forces are not different. It is not that some forces are physical, and some mental; the physical forces are but the gross manifestations of the fine forces, just as the physical world is but the gross manifestation of the fine world.*[22]

A broader and finer vision of man in terms of religion and vice versa is yet to be envisioned and translated into reality. We are yet to be explicit in the goal of mankind. As we are always in the quest for religion for the sake of religion which is never in fusion with, and the true identity of, man, we fall back upon vagueness, absurdities and meaninglessness whereby neither man nor religion becomes our very own, very familiar, very much endearing and enlivening.

In expounding the goal of man and that of religion, and the relation between religion and man, Vivekananda characteristically observes:

> *What right have you to say, "Here is my standard, and the whole universe must be governed by my standard?" What right have you to say that every truth shall be judged by this standard of yours— the standard that preaches mere bread, and money, and clothes as God?*
>
> *Religion does not live in bread, does not dwell in a house. Again and again you hear this objection advanced: "What good can religion do? Can it take away the poverty of the poor and give them more clothes?" Supposing it cannot, would that prove the untruth of religion? Suppose a baby stands up among you, when you are trying to demonstrate an astronomical theory, and says, "Does it bring gingerbread?" "No, it does not," you answer. "Then," says the baby, "it is useless." Babies judge the whole universe from their own standpoint, that of producing gingerbread, and so do the babies of the world.*
>
> **********
>
> *We must not judge of higher things from the low standpoint of ours. Everything must be judged by its own standard, and the infinite must be judged by the standard of infinity. Religion permeates the whole of man's life, not only the present, but the past, present, and future. It is therefore the eternal relation between the eternal Soul, and the eternal God.*[23]

Religion is never a mere theory. It is realisation from all true perspectives of goodness, nobility and welfare of man. The great teachers of religion nurture and culture intense faith, deep love, absolute purity, self-abnegation and self-identity. They are truest man-Gods. In the soul-stirring words of Vivekananda:

> *These great Teachers are the living Gods on this earth. Whom else should we worship? I try to get an idea of God in my mind,*

and I find what a false little thing I conceive: it would be a sin to worship that God. I open my eyes and look at the actual life of these great ones of the earth. They are higher than any conception of God that I could ever form. For, what a conception of mercy could a man like me form who would go after a man if he steals anything from me and send him to jail? And what can be my highest idea of forgiveness? Nothing beyond myself. Which of you can jump out of your own bodies? Which of you can jump out of your own minds? Not one of you. What idea of divine love can you form except what you actually live? What we have never experienced we can form no idea of. So all my best attempts of forming an idea of God would fail in every case. And here are plain facts, and not idealism— actual facts of love, of mercy, of purity, of which I can have no conception even. What wonder that I should fall at the feet of these men and worship them as God? And what else can anyone do? I should like to see the man who can do anything else, however much he may talk. Talking is not actuality. Talking about God and the Impersonal, and this and that, is all very good; but these man-Gods are the real Gods of all nations and all races. These divine men have been worshipped and will be worshipped so long as man is man. Therein is our faith, therein is our hope, of a reality.[24]

Emancipation from all grossness and littleness, liberation from "I" and believing that everything is the efflorescence of nature are the fundamental steps to the concept of realising religion for which man must strive for manifestation of the Self by means of Vairagya— non-attachment. This will lead to man to be blessed with the invaluable and ever desirable prize for man— Samadhi. From the standpoint of Yoga philosophy, Vivekananda highlights this poignant relationship between man and religion as follows:

We have first to understand what the Purusha, the Self, is and what the qualities are. According to Yoga philosophy, the whole of nature consists of three qualities or forces; one is called Tamas, another Rajas, and the third Sattva. These three qualities manifest themselves in the physical world as darkness or inactivity, attraction or repulsion, and equilibrium of the two. Everything that is in nature, all manifestations, are combinations and recombinations of these three forces. Nature has been divided into various categories by the Sankhyas; the Self of man is beyond all these, beyond nature. It is effulgent, pure, and perfect. Whatever of intelligence we see in natures but the reflection of this Self upon nature. Nature itself is insentient. You must remember that the word nature also includes the mind; mind is in nature; thought is in nature; from thought, down to the grossest form of matter, everything is in nature, the manifestation of nature. This nature has covered the Self of man, and when nature takes away the covering, the Self appears in Its own glory.[25]

The true religion of man is manifested in cultivating the spirit of inherent power of spirituality. It is a religion that seeks the pleasure that is within through the Self that ensures perfect calmness. It is the real universe that is within. It is infinite and perennial. To rise above all attractions of the external world which is like a fish basket with a foul smell and to endlessly try to live like a Sattvika, an introspective one for the glory of the Self are the essential ends-in-view of man as a true follower of religion par excellence. Vivekananda makes us aware of this fundamental vision of man and religion:

Stand upon the Self, then only can we truly love the world. Take a very, very high stand; knowing out universal nature, we must look with perfect calmness upon all the panorama of the world. It is but baby's play, and we know that, so cannot be disturbed by it. If the mind is pleased with praise, it will be displeased with blame. All pleasures of the senses or even of the mind are evanescent, but within ourselves is the one true unrelated pleasure, dependent upon nothing. It is perfectly free, it is bliss. The more our bliss is within, the more spiritual we are. The pleasure of the Self is what the world calls religion.

The internal universe, the real, *is infinitely greater than the external, which is only a shadowy projection of the true one. The world is neither true nor untrue, it is the shadow of truth. "Imagination is the gilded shadow of truth", says the poet.*

We enter into creation, and then for us it becomes living. Things are dead in themselves; only we give them life, and then, like fools, we turn around and are afraid of them, or enjoy them. But be not like certain fisher-women, who, caught in a storm on their way home from market, took refuge in the house of a florist. They were lodged for the night in a room next to the garden where the air was full of the fragrance of flowers. In vain did they try to rest, until one of their number suggested that they wet their fishy baskets and place them near their heads. Then they all fell into a sound sleep.[26]

The religion of man as Vivekananda time and again reminds us is the religion of love. We are the creators of God. Everyone of us has God within ourselves. We are God. As such, we must love Him. This should be the universal philosophy of God as love and vice versa. This would always make us prepared to love God that is within man and cannot remain apart from man.

That everyone of us is a great lover of God, we must accept the truth that we must worship that God is existent within ourselves. We cannot but accept the truth that each one of us is a Svayambhu, and there is no scope for learning the religion of love except loving all as the manifestation of All Love, All Worship—God. It is Atman absolutely fearless, free and devoted to All Love within man.

As an incomparable exponent of man and religion in terms of love, Vivekananda characteristically remarks:

Never ask that foolish question, what good will it do to the world? Let the world go. Love and ask nothing; love and look for nothing further. Love and forget all the "isms". Drink the cup of love and become mad. Say "Thine, O Thine for ever O Lord!" and plunge in, forgetting all else. The very idea of God is love. Seeing a cat loving her kittens stand and pray. God has become manifest there; literally believe this. Repeat "I am Thine, I am Thine"; for we can see God everywhere. Do not seek for Him, just see Him.

* * * * * * * *

The Absolute cannot be worshipped, so we must worship a manifestation, such a one as has our nature. Jesus had our nature; he became the Christ; so can we, and so must we. Christ and Buddha were the names of a state to be attained; Jesus and Gautama were the persons to manifest it. "Mother" is the first and highest manifestation, next the Christs and Buddhas. We make our own environment, and we strike the fetters off. The Atman is the fearless. When we pray to a God outside, it is good, only we do not know what to do. When we know the Self, we understand. The highest expression of love is unification.[27]

To realise religion, man must realise perfection. For this, man must realise and manifest the divinity already in him. This calls for an unending endeavour to crystallise and re-crystallise his behavioural expressions verbal or non-verbal, good or bad, natural or artificial, habitual or accidental. To be truly justified to religion, man must exercise the three stages of manifestation viz. sub-conscious, conscious and super-conscious states of mind. Until and unless these states are totally fool-proof, man cannot realise the Self in the light of totality of vision. Again, if realisation necessitates re-thinking and re-exercising all the mental states, it obviously calls forth overhauling of all the endeavour in the ends-in-view of clarity, precision, purity, simplicity, spontaneity and poignancy of vision for religion par excellence and ascent. As Vivekananda significantly observes:

> *If a thing happens once, it can happen again. If any human being has ever realised perfection, we too can do so. If we cannot become perfect here and now, we never can in any state or heaven or condition we may imagine. If Jesus Christ was not perfect, then the religion bearing his name falls to the ground. If he was perfect, then we too can become perfect. The perfect man does not reason or "know", as we count "knowing", for all our knowledge is mere comparison, and there is no comparison, no classification, possible in the Absolute. Instinct is less liable to error than reason, but reason is higher and leads to intuition, which is higher still. Knowledge is the parent of intuition, which like instinct, is also unerring, but on a higher plane. There are three grades of manifestation in living beings: (1) sub-conscious— mechanical, unerring; (2) conscious— knowing, erring and (3) super-conscious— intuitional, unerring; and these are illustrated in an animal, man and God. For the man who has become perfect, nothing remains but to apply his understanding. He lives only to help the world, desiring nothing for himself. What distinguishes is negative—the positive is ever wider and wider. What we have in common is the widest of all, and that is "Being".*[28]

The study of man and religion becomes more inclusive, more intense, more meaningful and more adventurous in the realisation of the fact that there are many religions and their different methods. In fact, there should be as many religions because each individual should have a religion of his or her own. This will facilitate a wider canvas of realisation of religion from diverse dimensions. This properly signifies the purpose of religion. The Vedanta philosophy welcomes the different methods of working with religion to be truly one's very own as well of of others. In the poignant words of Vivekananda:

> *If there were only one method to arrive at truth, it would be death for everyone else who is not similarly constituted. Therefore, the methods should be various. Vedanta understands that and wants to lay before the world different methods through which we can work. Take up any one you like; and if one does not suit you, another may. From this standpoint we see how glorious it is that there are so many religions in the world, how good it is that there are so many teachers and prophets, instead of there being only one, as many persons would like to have it.*
>
> * * * * * * * *
>
> *How much better it is, even on the physical plane, to have the opportunity of so many various things spread before us, so that we may choose any one we like, the one which suits us best! So it is with the world of religions. It is a most glorious dispensation of the Lord that there are so many religions in the world; and would to God that that these would increase every day, until every man had a religion unto himself!*[29]

When would we fully translate Vivekananda's viewpoints on man and religion in the light of the above into reality?

1. Swami Vivekananda: *The Complete Works of Swami Vivekananda*, Advaita Ashrama, Kolkata, Mayavati Memorial Edition, 1989, Vol. IV, p. 358.
2. *Ibid.*, Vol.VII, pp. 421-422.
3. *Ibid.*, pp. 82-83.
4. *Ibid.*, Vol. IV, pp. 203-204.
5. *Ibid.*, Vol. VII, pp. 420-421.
6. *Ibid.*, Vol. IV, pp. 215-216.
7. *Ibid., pp.* 216-217.
8. *Ibid.*, Vol. VII, pp. 12-13.
9. *Ibid.*, Vol. IV, pp. 190-191.
10. *Ibid.*, Vol. VII, pp. 30-31.
11. *Ibid.*, Vol. VI. pp. 81-82.
12. *Ibid.*, p. 46.
13. *Ibid.*, Vol. IV, pp. 164-165.
14. *Ibid.*, pp. 356-357.
15. *Ibid.*, Vol. I, pp. 317-318.
16. *Ibid.*, Vol. VIII, pp. 32-33.
17. *Ibid.*, p. 169.
18. *Ibid.*, Vol. VII, pp. 85-86.
19. *Ibid.*, Vol. I, pp. 374-375.
20. *Ibid.*, Vol. VII, pp. 64-65.
21. *Ibid.*, Vol. IV, pp. 247-248.
22. *Ibid.*, Vol. I, pp. 257-258.
23. *Ibid.*, Vol. IV, p. 209.
24. *Ibid.*, pp. 124-125.
25. *Ibid.*, Vol. I, pp. 209-210..
26. *Ibid.*, Vol. VII, pp. 11-12.
27. *Ibid.*, pp. 29-30.
28. *Ibid.*, Vol. VIII, pp. 17-18.
29. *Ibid.*, Vol.VI, pp. 16-17.

Man and Humanism: Vivekananda's Perspectives

One of the most essential components of the essence of man is that he must be a humanist. This directs our attention towards a few fundamental attributes that consolidate and strengthen the foundation of humanism. First, man must actualise the vision of being 'men' in a man and vice versa. It will then welcome the concept of man as a truly social being. It will also encourage and stimulate the vision of the Universal Brotherhood of Man. Second, man with his broadened vision and widened approach to cohesion and harmony of humane consciousness will translate the truth of *vasudhaiva kutumvakam*—the whole universe is one single Family of Man. Third, with all differences and disunities— apparent and, therefore, insignificant— man is the champion of positive humanism. He knows and respects the identity of an individual from diverse points of view, be it with reference to creed, colour, caste, culture or civilisation whatsoever and howsoever. He ignites the warmth of humane relationship even under trying and challenging circumstances. He welcomes diverse thoughts and visions, principles and practices because all these welcome a fusion of human advancement. He adorns all forms of cultural development because these expose a furtherance of humane visions. Thus, the world of man becomes a wonderful panorama of human progress and culture.

Man is restless by nature. Humanism cannot avert this fact. At the same time, he is always in quest of the new and the excellent, the marvellous and the poignant because these altogether contribute a lot to the march for humanism. To sit idly and dream for what is not, to care for the inane and endear the ukase of inertness, and to nurture and enrich indiscipline are never considered to be a prudent man's cup of tea. Rare is the man who is totally blind to goodness. In holding the head high, man builds the paradise out of his timeless and tireless endeavour crystallised in transparency and transfer of humane viewpoints and thought-patterns.

A harbinger par excellence of humanism, Swami Vivekananda eyes humanism as the inseparable identity of man. Sans humanism is sans manhood, sans divinity. Indeed, it is the religion of all religions of man, the Divine Being.

Vivekananda gives a clarion call to man to be readily prepared for and fulfil the great mission of fullness of humanism: "Arise, awake and stop not till the goal is reached." What prompts man to be devoted to his divine? Self is to be bold enough to honour his own pristine and catholic identity in order to translate it into vibrant reality. There is neither any room for nurturing slovenliness nor is there any time for toying with human power and excellence. The promise of each and every man to unfold and enrich the spirit of humanism cannot at all be ignored. It ought to be given a universal habitation and a name anew and afresh with the ever changing and startlingly accelerating progress of humanism.

The challenges of man for advancement of humanism are legion. Vivekananda makes us alert of the fact that there is no short cut to the excellence of man in any direction. Rather is it arduous and persevering, strenuous and painstaking. Admittedly, man ought to adore the unknown and challenging, adventurous and thrilling avenues of the ends-in-view of humanism. It requires boldness and readiness of the mind and the heart to embrace all eventualities even under adverse conditions. "Revile none" as Vivekananda reminds us should be our guideline for exercising positive humanism. Transcendence of truth that crystallises our senses is the need of the hour. When he speaks on Rishihood, this spirit of humanism finds its serene efflorescence:

> *The essentials are eternal, the non-essentials have value only for a certain time; and if after a time they are not replaced by something essential, they are positively dangerous. I do not mean that you should stand up and revile all your old customs and institutions. Certainly not; you must not revile even the most evil one of them. Revile none. Even those customs that are now appearing to be positive evils, have been positively life-giving in times past; and if we have to remove these, we must not do so with curses, but with blessings and gratitude for the glorious work these customs have done for the preservation of our race. And we must also remember that the leaders of our*

societies have never been either generals or kings, but Rishis. And who are the Rishis? The Rishi as he is called in the Upanishads is not an ordinary man, but a Mantra-drashta. He is a man who sees religion, to whom religion is not merely book-learning, not argumentation, nor speculation, nor much talking, but actual realisation, a coming face to face with truths which transcends the senses. This is Rishihood, and that Rishihood does not belong to any age, or time, or even to sects or caste. Vatsayana says, truth must be realised; and we have to remember that you, and I, and every one of us will be called upon to become Rishis; and we must have faith in ourselves; we must become world-movers, for everything is in us. We must see Religion face to face, experience it, and thus solve our doubts about it; and then standing up in the glorious light of Rishihood, each one of us will be a giant; and every word falling from our lips will carry behind it the infinite sanction of security; and before us evil will vanish by itself without the necessity of cursing any one, without the necessity of abusing any one, without the necessity of fighting any one in the world.[1]

For a revival and re-exercise of Rishihood, man must prove his worth as man. He must visualise God in every one irrespective of caste, gender or any other insignificant points of difference. He must leave the pride of authoritarianism and come down to the level of the ignorant and the outcast, the lowly and the lost. He must prove that his heart goes out for the well-being of others and sacrifice all petty desires like name and fame, popularity and superiority. The quest for bringing light to every one everywhere must be his most important end-in-view of life and action, performance and contemplation. As Vivekananda vibrantly asserts:

Look upon every man, woman, and every one as God. You cannot help anyone, you can only serve: serve the children of the Lord, serve the Lord Himself, if you have the privilege. If the Lord grants that you can help any one of His children, blessed you are; do not think too much of yourselves. Blessed you are that that privilege was given to you when others had it not. Do it only as a worship. I should see God in the poor, and it is for my salvation that I go and worship them. The poor and the miserable are for our salvation, so that we may serve the Lord, coming in the shape of the diseased, coming in the shape of the lunatic, the leper, and the sinner! Bold are my words; and let me repeat that it is the greatest privilege in our life that we are allowed to serve the Lord in all these shapes. Give up the idea that by ruling over others you can do any good to them. But you can do just as much as you can in the case of the plant; you can supply the growing seed with the materials for the making up of its body, bringing to it the earth, the water, the air, that it wants. It will take all that it wants by its own nature, it will assimilate and grow by its own nature.

> *Bring all light into the world. Light, bring light! Let light come unto every one; the task will not be finished till every one has reached the Lord. Bring light to the poor; and bring more light to the rich, for they require it more than the poor. Bring light to the ignorant, and more light to the educated, for the vanities of the education of our time are tremendous! Thus bring light to all and leave the rest unto the Lord, for in the words of the same Lord, "To work you have the right and not to the fruits thereof."*[2]

That we are infinite beings ever upholding the torch of humanism should be the motto of our life. We should not belittle ourselves by making a difference between the high and the low, the rich and the poor and so on because the infinite spirit in every one of us eliminates all these apparent differences. The march of man always presupposes the march of truth, and all true religion stands for the march of humanity. There lies the spirit of man and humanism. In elucidating this truth Vivekananda elegantly observes:

> *If one thing is true, its negation is false. How can contradictory opinions be true at the same time? This is the question which I intend to answer. But I will first ask you: Are all the religions of the world really contradictory? I do not mean the external forms in which great thoughts are clad. I do not mean the different buildings, languages, rituals, books, etc., employed in various religions, but I mean the internal soul of every religion. Every religion has a soul behind it, and that soul may differ from the soul of another religion; but are they contradictory? Do they contradict or supplement each other?— that is the question. I took up the question when I was quite a boy, and have been studying it all my life. Thinking that my conclusion may be of some help to you, I place it before you. I believe that they are not contradictory; they are supplementary. Each religion, as it were,*

takes up one part of the great universal truth, and spends its whole force in embodying and typifying that part of the great truth. It is, therefore, addition, not exclusion. That is the idea. System after system arises, each one embodying a great idea, and ideals must be added to ideals. And this is the march of humanity. Man never progresses from error to truth, but from truth to truth, from lesser truth to higher truth— but it is never from error to truth. The child may develop more than the father, but was the father inane? The child is the father plus something else. If your present state of knowledge is much greater than it was when you were a child, would you look down upon that stage now? Will you look back and call it inanity? Why, your present stage is the knowledge of the child plus some-thing more.

** ** ** **

We are viewing truth, getting as much of it as these circumstances will permit, colouring the truth with our own heart, understanding it with our own intellect, and grasping it with our own mind. We can know as much of truth as it is related to us, as much of it as we are able to receive. This makes the difference between man and man, and occasions sometimes even contradictory ideas; yet we all belong to the same great universal truth.[3]

The role of man in the march of humanism must be open-ended and free from all doubts and ambiguities. This necessitates a state of mind balanced and crystallised to be free from all constraints like pessimism, desolation and disappointment that eat up the vitality of excellence and ascent. Man must know the highest truth which cannot be had unless there is the intense and sincere exercise of freedom. As Vivekananda advises:

Our sole concern is to know the highest truth. Our goal is the loftiest. We have said big words to ourselves—absolute realisation and all that. Let us measure up to the words. Let us worship the spirit in spirit, standing on spirit. Let the foundation be spirit, the middle spirit, the culmination spirit. There will be no world anywhere. Let it go and whirl into space— who cares? Stand thou in the spirit! That is the goal. We know we cannot reach it yet. Never mind. Do not despair, and do not drag the ideal down. The important thing is: how much less you think of

> *the body, of yourself as matter—as dead, dull, insentient matter; how much more you think of yourself as shining immortal being. The more you think of yourself as shining immortal spirit, the more eager you will be to be absolutely free of matter, body, and senses. This is the intense desire to be free.*[4]

Humanism stands for a positive approach to life in the natural and spontaneous exercise of freedom. Self-consciousness is the true indicator in realising the actual position to be in tune with the infinite spirit inherent in every human being. Am I in the right direction towards the destiny of man? Do I respond to the great vision of man enjoying the freedom of the self and declaring in an open mind: I am what I am? Do I believe that I am never under any bondage? Unless a positive approach to humanism in terms of freedom is existent, man loses his real identity.

With the exercise of freedom as a vibrant component of humanism, there must be the fighting spirit in man. Vivekananda explains this in the light of the 'awakening of the soul' from every kind of bondage, be it that of nature or that of the mind, to prove the fact that freedom leads to success and grandeur that is innate within every man:

> *Man begins to struggle and fight against nature. He makes many mistakes, he suffers. But eventually he conquers nature and realises his freedom. When he is free, nature becomes his slave.*
>
> *The awakening of the soul to its bondage and its effort to stand up and assert itself—this is called life. Success in this struggle is called evolution. The eventual triumph, when all the slavery is blown away, is called salvation, Nirvana, freedom. Everything in the universe is struggling for liberty. When I am bound by nature, by name and form, by time, space, and causality, I do not know what I am truly. But even in this bondage my real Self is not completely lost. I strain against the bonds; one by one they break, and I become conscious of my innate grandeur. Then comes complete liberation. I attain to the clearest and fullest consciousness of myself— I know that I am the infinite spirit, the master of nature, not its slave.*[5]

The perfect revelation of man is the end-in-view for which he eternally strives in and through the exercise of freedom. To make a real fusion between God and man in the light of purity and extinction of body, mind and imagination as day-to-day affairs of life and prove that man is the apex of of the only world that stands for the Self, the Bliss Absolute are the most significant hallmarks of humanism. Vivekananda characteristically draws our attention to the most prized identity of man in terms of freedom and humanism:

> *The man who discovers a spiritual truth is what we call "inspired", and what he brings to the world is revelation. But revelation too is eternal and is not to be crystallised as final and then blindly followed. Revelation may come to any man who has fitted himself to receive it. Perfect purity is the most essential thing, for only "the pure in heart shall see God". Man is the highest being that exists and this is the greatest world, for here can man realise freedom. The highest concept we can have of God is man. Every attribute we give Him also belongs to man, only in a lesser degree. When we rise higher and want to get out of this concept of God, we have to get out of the body, out of mind and imagination, and leave this world out of sight. When we rise to be the absolute, we are no longer in the world— all is Subject, without object. Man is the apex of the only "world" we can ever know. Those who have attained "sameness" or perfection, are said to be "living in God". All hatred is "killing the self by the self"; therefore, love is the law of life. To rise to this is to be perfect; but the more "perfect" we are, the less work can we do. The Sattvika see and know that all this world is mere child's play and do not trouble themselves about that. We are not too much disturbed when we see two puppies fighting and biting each other. We know it is not a serious matter. The perfect one knows that this world is Maya. Life is called Samsara—it is the result of the conflicting forces acting upon us. Materialism says, "The voice of freedom is a delusion." Idealism says, "The voice that tells of bondage is but a dream." Vedanta says, "We are free and not free at the same time." That means that we are never free on the earthly plane, but ever free on the spiritual side. The Self is beyond both freedom and bondage. We* are *Brahman, we* are *immortal knowledge beyond the senses, we* are *Bliss Absolute.*[6]

The concept of humanism in terms of man becomes ambiguous or blurred in detaching man from God. The religion of man becomes confusing in such an undesirable detachment. The most accessible idea of God as man and vice versa is to study the life and teachings of the Avataras of God who are successful in visualising God through human manifestations. As we are arrested by the weaknesses of humanity and dwarfing of transcendence and transparency, we are bound to worship God as man, which would show us the way to become free souls—jivanmukta—for realisation of God in ourselves, the highest glory of man. Vivekananda has distinctly elucidated as follows:

> *Higher and nobler than all ordinary ones are another set of teachers, the Avataras of Ishvara, in the world. They can transmit spirituality with a touch, even with a mere wish. The lowest and the most degraded characters become in one second saints at their command. They are the Teachers of all teachers, the highest manifestations of God through man. We cannot see God except through them. We cannot help worshipping them; and indeed they are the only ones whom we are bound to worship.*
>
> *No man can see God except through these human manifestations. If we try to see God otherwise, we make for ourselves a hideous creature of Him and believe the caricature to be no worse than the original. There is a story of an ignorant man who was asked to make an image of the God Shiva, and who, after days of hard struggle, manufactured only the image of a monkey. So whenever we try to think of God as He is in His absolute perfection, we invariably meet with the most miserable failure, because as long as we are men, we cannot conceive Him as anything higher than man. The time will come when we shall transcend our human nature and know Him as He is; but as long as we are men, we must worship Him in man and as man. Talk as you may, try as you may, you cannot think of God except as a man. You may deliver great intellectual discourses on God and on all things under the sun, become great rationalists and prove to your satisfaction that all these accounts of the Avataras of God as men are nonsense. But let us come for a moment to practical common sense. What is there behind this kind of remarkable intellect? Zero, nothing, simply so much froth. When next you hear a man delivering a great intellectual lecture against this worship of the Avataras of God, get hold of him and ask what*

his idea of God is, what he understands by "omnipotence", "omnipresence", and all similar terms, beyond the spelling of the words. He really means nothing by them; he cannot formulate as their meaning any idea unaffected by his own human nature; he is no better off in this matter than the man in the street who has not read a single book. That man in the street, however, is quiet and does not disturb the peace of the world, while this big talker creates disturbance and misery among mankind. Religion is, after all, realisation, and we must make the sharpest distinction between talk and intuitive experience. What we experience in the depths of our souls is realisation. Nothing indeed is so uncommon as common sense in regard to this matter.[7]

Not only realisation but also devotion and dedication are the pathways for man in understanding and appreciating himself as a Divine Being. It is this divinity manifested in man which truly stands for religion of the highest order. The concept of humanism in terms of man explaining God as Brahman encapsulates man altogether. This not only glorifies the identity of man but also heightens the vision of man. He becomes aware of the fact that all his happiness and misery, joy and sorrow, success and failure are the outcome of his own role and never that of anyone else. Vivekananda explains this in terms of defining Brahman:

What is this Brahman? He is eternal, eternally pure, eternally awake, the almighty, the all-knowing, the all-merciful, the omnipresent, the formless, the partless. He creates this universe. If he is always creating and holding up this universe, two difficulties arise. We see that there is partiality in the universe. One person is born happy, and another unhappy; one is rich, and another is poor; this shows partiality. Then there is cruelty also, for here the very condition of life is death. One animal tears another to pieces, and every man tries to get the better of his own brother. This competition, cruelty, horror, and sighs rending hearts day and night is the state of things in this world of ours. If this be the creation of a God, that God is worse than cruel, worse than any devil that man ever imagined. Ay! says the Vedanta, it is not the fault of God that this partiality exists, that this competition exists. Who makes it? We ourselves. There is a cloud shedding its rain on all fields alike. But it is only the field that is well cultivated, which gets the advantage of the shower; another field, which has not been tilled or taken care of cannot get that advantage. It is not the fault of the cloud. The mercy of God is eternal and unchangeable; it is we that make the differentiation.[8]

Moreover, Vivekananda explains these diverse differences between man and man from the standpoint of the law of Karma:

If life began but yesterday, it must end tomorrow, and annihilation is the result. Life must have been existing. It does not now require much acumen to see that, for all the sciences of modern times have been coming round to our help, illustrating from the material world the principles embodied in our scriptures. You know it already that each one of us is the effect of the infinite past; the child is ushered into the world not as something flashing from the hands of nature, as poets delight so much to depict, but he has the burden of an infinite past; for good or evil he comes to work out his own past deeds. That makes the differentiation. This is the law of Karma. Each one of us is the maker of his own fate. This law knocks on the head at once all doctrines of predestination and fate and gives us the only means of reconciliation between God and man. We, we, and none else, are responsible for what we suffer. We are the effects, and we are the causes. We are free therefore. If I am unhappy, it has been my own making, and that very thing shows that I can be happy if I will. The human will stands beyond all circumstance. Before it—the strong, gigantic, infinite will and freedom in man—all the powers, even of nature, must bow down, succumb, and become its servants. This is the result of the law of Karma.[9]

To honour the human will is to idealise and glorify humanism. Man then becomes the architect of his own fate in the true spirit of man. His religion then becomes his very own. This extends the vision of man to be worthy of his own responsibilities because he is a thinking, rational and conscious being who is prepared to glorify his religion in terms of the glory of the humankind. So his vision becomes altruistic in welcoming all sects, all religions that show diverse avenues of the march of man. As Vivekananda clearly points out:

In every country, probably, if the statistics are taken, you would find that religions are sometimes progressing and sometimes going back. Sects are multiplying all the time. If the claims of a religion that it has all the truth and God has given it all this truth in a certain book were true, why are there so many sects? Fifty years do not pass because there are twenty sects founded upon the same book. If God has put all the truth in certain books, He does not give us those books in order that we may quarrel over texts. That seems to be the fact. Why is it? Even if a book were given by God which contained all the truth about religion, it would not serve the purpose because nobody could understand the book. Take the Bible, for instance, and all the sects that exist among Christians; each one puts its own interpretation upon the same text, and each says that it alone understands the text and all the rest are wrong. So with every religion. There are many sects among the Mohammedans and among the Buddhists, and hundreds among the Hindus. Now, I bring these facts before you in order to show you that any attempt to bring all humanity to one method of thinking in spiritual things has been a failure and always will be a failure. Every man that starts a theory, even at the present day, finds that if he goes twenty miles away from his followers, they will make twenty sects. You see that happening all the time. You cannot make all conform to the same ideas: that is a fact, and I thank God that it is so. I am not against any sect. I am glad that sects exist, and I only wish they may go on multiplying more and more. Why? Simply because of this: If you and I and all who are present here were to think exactly the same thoughts, there would be no thoughts for us to think. We know that two or more forces must come into collusion in order to produce motion. It is the clash of thought, the differentiation of thought, that awakes thought. Now, if we thought all alike, we would be like Egyptian mummies in a museum looking vacantly at one another's faces—no more than that! Whirls and eddies occur only in a rushing, living stream. There are no whirlpools in stagnant, dead water. When religions are dead, there will be no more sects; it will be the perfect peace and harmony of the grave. But so long as mankind thinks, there will be sects. Variation is the sign of life, and it must be there. I pray that they may multiply so that at last there will be as many sects as human beings, and each one will have his own method, his individual method of thought in religion.[10]

The fusion of man and religion in terms of humanism as Vivekananda upholds is the most significant march of man. It has created a history of its own in the sphere of religion , sectarianism, and, above all, humanism that speaks forth the spirit of altruism. When we think of universal religion or universal brotherhood of man, the ultimate end-in-view is to honour and uphold truth so that the distinct vision of humanism adorns every religion.

That each religion is on the march of the real realisation of the spirit of humanism is universally true. In an address delivered in the Universalist Church, Pasadena, California, on January 28, 1900, Vivekananda remarks:

> *My idea, therefore, is that all these religions are different forces in the economy of God, working for the good of mankind; and that not one can become dead, not one can be killed. Just as you cannot kill any force in nature, so you cannot kill any one of these spiritual forces. You have seen that each religion is living. From time to time it may retrograde or go forward. At one time, it may be shorn of a good many of its trappings; at another time it may be covered with all sorts of trappings; but all the same, the soul is ever there, it can never be lost. The ideal which every religion represents is never lost, and so every religion is intelligently on the march.*
>
> *And that universal religion about which philosophers and others have dreamed in every country already exists. It is here. As the universal brotherhood of man is already existing, so also is universal religion. Which of you, that have travelled far and wide, have not found brothers and sisters in every nation? I have found them all over the world. Brotherhood already exists; only there are numbers of persons who fail to see this and only upset it by crying for new brotherhoods. Universal religion, too, is already existing. If the priests and other people that have taken upon themselves the task of preaching different religions simply cease preaching for a few moments, we shall see it is there. They are disturbing it all the time, because it is to their interest. You see that priests in every country are very conservative. Why is it so? There are very few priests who lead the people; most of them are led by the people and are their slaves and servants. If you say it is dry, they say it is so; if you*

say it is black, they say it is black. If the people advance, the priests must advance. They cannot be behind. So, before blaming the priests— it is the fashion to blame the priest—you ought to blame yourselves. You only get what you deserve. What would be the fate of a priest who wants to give you new and advanced ideas and lead you forward? His children would probably starve, and he would be clad in rags. He is governed by the same worldly laws as you are. "If you go on," he says, "let us march." Of course, there are exceptional souls, not cowed down by public opinion. They see the truth and truth alone they value. Truth has got hold of them, has got possession of them, as it were, and they cannot but march ahead.[11]

How to be on the right track of humanism? How to be prepared for making life a citadel for the Brahman? Here is Vivekananda's incomparable words of advice to one of his disciples:

Day and night think and meditate on Brahman, meditate with great one-pointedness of mind. And during the time of awakening to outward life, either do some work for the sake of others or repeat in your mind, 'Let good happen to Jivas and the world!' 'Let the mind of all flow in the direction of the Brahman!' even by such continuous current of thought the world will be benefited. Nothing good in the world becomes fruitless, be it work or thought.[12]

An unparalleled exponent of vibrant and dynamic humanism, Vivekananda makes a clarion call to join the 'worship of the living present'. Lost is the time in weakness and indolence. Lost, too, is the time to prove the real worth of man and humanism. Let every one of us pay sincere attention to the eternal apostle of humanism and ascent of man:

The dead never return; the past night does not reappear; a spent-up tidal wave does not rise anew; neither does man inhabit the same body over again. So from the worship of the dead past, O man, we invite you to the worship of the living present; from the regretful brooding over bygones, we invite you to the activities of the present; from the waste of energy in retracing lost and demolished pathways, we call you back to broad new-laid highways lying very near. He that is wise, let him understand.

Of that power, which at the very first impulse has roused distant echoes from all the four corners of the globe, conceive in your mind the manifestation in its fullness; and discarding all misgivings, weaknesses, and the jealous characteristic of enslaved peoples, come and help in the turning of this mighty wheel of new dispensation![13]

The clarion call for dynamism as Vivekananda gives has its infinite appeal to be vibrant in contemplation and action for the success of living and thrilling humanism. He inspires man to understand and appreciate, work and actualise the divinity already in him. He also reminds man of the great saying: Thou art That.

In his poem, "The Song of the Sannyasin" composed at the Thousand Island Park, New York, in July, 1895, Vivekananda boldly asserts to eliminate all bondage and dismal darkness, and glorify Atman and truth which build the strong foundation spiritual humanism:

Strike off thy fetters! Bonds that bind thee down,
Of shining gold, or darker, baser ore;
Love, hate— good, bad— and all the dual throng,
Know, slave is slave, caressed or whipped, not free;
For fetters, though of gold, are not less strong to bind;
Then off with them, Sannyasin bold! Say—
"Om Tat Sat, Om!"

Let darkness go; the will-o'-the-wisp that leads
With blinking light to pile more gloom on gloom.
This thirst for life, for ever quench; it drags
From birth to death, and death to birth, the soul.
He conquers all who conquers self. Know this
And never yield, Sannyasin bold! Say—
"Om Tat Sat, Om!"

"Who sows must reap," they say, "and cause must bring
The sure effect; good, good; bad, bad; and none
Escape the law. But whoso wears a form
Must wear the chain." Too true; but far beyond
Both name and form is Atman, ever free.
Know thou art That, Sannyasin bold! Say—
"Om Tat Sat, Om!"

They know not truth who dream such vacant dreams
As father, mother, children, wife, and friend.
The sexless Self! whose father He? whose child?
Whose friend, whose foe is He who is but One?
The Self is all in all, none else exists;
And thou art hat, Sannyasin bold! Say—
"Om Tat Sat, Om!"[14]

To become an atheist is to be prepared for understanding true religion and to understand true religion is to march on the way of humanism. Mere argumentation never solves the issue of anything. There must be a sound foundation of arguments which enrich both religion and humanism because these two are not in essence different but are complementary to each other. When we speak about concentration, this idea of religion in terms of humanism becomes clear and objective, specific and natural. Thus the vision of God as a matter of religion becomes clear and specific in terms of man in tune with concentration. As Vivekananda poignantly observes:

Perception is our only real knowledge or religion. Talking about it for ages will never make us know our soul. There is no difference between theories and atheism. In fact, the atheist is the truer man. Every step I take in the light is mine for ever. When you go to a country and see it, then it is yours. We have each to see for ourselves; teachers can only "bring the food", we must eat it to be nourished. Argument can never prove God save as a logical conclusion.

It is impossible to find God outside of ourselves. Our own souls contribute all the divinity that is outside of us. We are the greatest temple. The objectification is only a faint imitation of what we see within ourselves.

Concentration of the powers of the mind is our only instrument to help us see God. If you know one soul (your own), you know all souls, past, present, and to come. The will concentrates the mind, certain things excite and control this will, such as reason, love, devotion, breathing. The concentrated mind is a lamp that shows us every corner of the soul.[15]

The concept of the religion of One leading to the path of becoming many and vice versa is the nursery of the flowers of humanism. It spreads its petals in the form of altruism where man knows the real worth as man and tries to translate it in reality as best as possible. From consciousness to the plane beyond the senses which denotes superconsciousness and the return to the root is an eternal sojourn where man finds religion as the 'moon of realisation' for fullness. That realisation offers us the spirit of perceiving God in every human being. In the invaluable words of Vivekananda:

> *God is the perception of every being: He is all there to be perceived. That which says "I" is Brahman, but although we, day and night, perceive Him, we do not know that we are perceiving Him. As soon as we become aware of this truth, all misery goes; so we must get knowledge of the truth. Reach unity; no more duality will come. But knowledge does not come by sacrifice, but by seeking, worshipping, knowing the Atman.*
>
> ** ** ** **
>
> *The realist asks, "How does the nihilist get any idea of identity?" How does the revolving light appear a circle? A point of rest alone explains motion. The nihilist can never explain the genesis of the delusion that there is a background; neither can the idealist explain how the One becomes the many. The only explanation must come from beyond the sense-plane; we must rise to the superconscious, to a state entirely beyond sense-perception. That metaphysical power is the further instrument that the idealist alone can use. He can experience the Absolute; the man Vivekananda can resolve himself into the Absolute and then come back to the man again. For him, then the problem is solved and secondarily for others, for he can show the way to others. Thus religion begins where philosophy ends. The "good of the world" will be that what is now superconsciousness for us will in ages to come be the conscious for all. Religion is therefore the highest work the world has; and because man has unconsciously felt this, he has clung through all the ages to the idea of religion.*
>
> *Religion, the great milch cow, has given many kicks, but never mind, it gives a great deal of milk. The milkman does not mind the kick of the cow which gives much milk. Religion is the greatest child to be born, the great "moon of realisation"; let us feed it and help it grow, and it will become a giant.*[16]

As a practical humanist, Vivekananda identifies man as the embodiment of Brahman. This is not all. He extends the horizon of Brahman to actualise goodness in the world. Whatever role man plays in the world is to be primarily directed towards elimination of the ego which is the first lesson for genuine humanism. Let us forget the desire of the little "I" and endlessly strive for realisation of the great "I" which is perennial and deathless, purest and most perfect.

Vivekananda wants man to be absolutely selfless, Jivanmukta, absolutely successful in extinction of personality:

> *In the realisation of Brahman, the personal "I" and all sense of the world is lost. The Light does not know the darkness, because it has no existence in the light; so Brahman is all. While we recognise a God, it is really only the Self that we have separated from ourselves and worship as outside of us ; but all the time it is our own true Self, the one and only God. The nature of the brute is to remain where he is, of man to seek good and avoid evil, of God to neither seek nor avoid, but just to be blissful eternally. Let us be Gods, let us make our hearts like an ocean, to go beyond all the trifles of the world and see it only as a picture. We can then enjoy it without being in any way affected by it. Why look for good in the world, what can we find there? The best it has to offer is only as if children playing in a mud puddle found a few glass beads. They lose them again and have to begin the search anew. Infinite strength is religion and God. We are only souls if we are free, there is immortality only if we are free, there is God only if He is free.*
>
> *Until we give up the world manufactured by the ego, never can we enter the Kingdom of Heaven. None ever did, none ever will. To give up the world is to utterly forget the ego, to know it not at all, living in the body but not being ruled by it. This rascal ego must be obliterated. Power to help mankind is with the silent ones who only live and love and withdraw their own personality entirely. They never say "me' or "mine', they are only blessed in being the instruments to help others. They are wholly identified with God, asking nothing and not* consciously *doing anything. They are the true Jivanmuktas— the absolutely selfless, their little personality thoroughly blown away, ambition non-existent. They are all principle, with no personality. The*

> *more we sink the "little self", the more God comes. Let us get rid of the little "I" and let only the great "I" live in us. Our best work and our greatest influence is when we are without a thought of self. It is the "desireless" who bring great results to pass. Bless men when they revile you. Think how much good they are doing by helping to stamp out the false ego. Hold fast to the real Self, think only pure thoughts, and you will accomplish more than a regiment of mere preachers.*[17]

The humanistic quest for divinity by means of the harmony of matter and mind as Vivekananda idealises is the only pointer to the progress of man. It is the quest for which man must unendingly strive. Only then the mental and the material world will no longer be different but one through perfect fusion. Our action in life will only then be steered towards the spirit of oneness which is the avenue of successful efflorescence of the truth of spiritual humanism.

The fusion of the material and the mental world as the most fascinating and wonderful manifestation of spiritual humanism as Vivekananda points out is very significant:

> *The majority of philosophies in every country, especially in the West, have started with the assumption that these two, matter and mind, are contradictory existences; but in the long run we shall find that they converge towards each other and in the end unite and form an infinite whole. So it is not that by this analysis I mean a higher or lower standpoint with regard to the subject I do not mean that those who want to search after truth through external nature are wrong, nor that those who want to search after truth through internal nature are higher. These are the two modes of procedure. Both of them must live; both of them must be studied; and in the end we shall find that they meet. We shall see that neither is the body antagonistic to the mind, nor the mind to the body, although we find, many persons who think that this body is nothing. In old times, every country was full of people who thought that this body is only a disease, a sin, or something of that kind. Later on, however, we see how, as it was taught in the Vedas, this body melts into the mind, and the mind into the body.*

** ** ** **

It is the finding of a unity towards which we are all going. Every action of our lives— the most material, the grossest as well the finest, the highest, the most spiritual— is like tending towards this one ideal, the finding of unity. A man is single. He marries. Apparently it may be a selfish act, but at the same time, the impulsion, the motive power, is to find that unity. He has children, he has friends, he loves his country, he loves the world, and ends by loving the whole universe. Irresistibly we are impelled towards that perfection which consists in finding the unity, killing this little self and making ourselves broader and broader. This is the goal, the end towards which the universe is rushing. Every atom is trying to go and join itself to the next atom. Atoms after atoms combine, making huge balls, the earths, the suns, the moons, the stars, the planets. They, in their turn, are trying to rush towards each other, and, at last, we know that the whole universe, mental and material, will be fused into one.[18]

The search for humanism as a prayer to God is also an efflorescence of humanism exercised in humility and pure submission. It is love both humanistic and divine at the same time. Thus the relationship between man and God is pure and simple based and bonded by the thread of love devoid of any interest. It is to prove the fact that God and man unite in the essence and excellence of love.

In his address at the Parliament of Religions on 15th September, 1893, Vivekananda has reminded us of the great teaching of Lord Krishna 'to live in this world like a lotus leaf' submitting 'his heart to God and his hands to work':

It is good to love God for hope of reward in this or the next world, but it is better to love God for love's sake, and the prayer goes: "Lord, I do not want wealth, nor children, nor learning. If it be Thy will, I shall go from birth to birth, but grant me this, that I may love Thee without the hope of reward—love unselfishly for love's sake." One of the disciples of Krishna, the then Emperor of India, was driven from the kingdom by his enemies and had to take shelter with his queen in a forest in the Himalayas, and there one day the queen asked him how it was that he, the most virtuous of men, should suffer so much misery. Yudhishthira answered, "Behold, my queen, the Himalayas, how grand and beautiful they are; I love them. They do not give me anything, but my nature is to love the grand, the beautiful, therefore I love them. Similarly, I love the Lord. He is the source of all beauty, of all sublimity. He is the only object to be loved; my nature is to love Him, and therefore I love. I do not pray for anything; I do not ask for anything. Let Him place me wherever He likes. I must love Him for love's sake. I cannot trade in love."[19]

The harmony of man and religion is indeed the harmony of the All Serene and humanity. For this, we pay due respect to the great messages of all the great thinkers and preachers of humanity. As the nature of man is to embrace and endear personal religion, it becomes easier to understand and appreciate them in terms of their personal role than in and through sacrifice of individual process of thinking. But the ultimate end-in-view is to strengthen and stabilise the harmony of all religions contributing endlessly to the advancement of man and humanism. In the address at the Shakespeare Club, Pasadena, California on February 3, 1900, Vivekananda splendidly elucidates:

Man has an idea that there can be only one religion, that there can be only one Prophet, and that there can be only one Incarnation; but that idea is not true. By studying the lives of all these great Messengers, we find that each, as it were, was destined to play a part, and a part only; that the harmony consists in the sum total, and not in one note. As in the life of races— no race is born to alone enjoy the world. None dare say no. each race has a part to play in this divine harmony of nations. Each race has its mission to perform, its duty to fulfil. The sum total is the great harmony.

** ** ** **

Most of us are born believers in a personal religion. We talk of principles, we think of theories, and that is all right; but every thought and every movement, every one of our actions, shows that we can only understand the principle when it comes to us through a person. We can grasp an idea only when it comes to us through a materialised ideal person. We can understand the precept only through the example. Would to God that all of us were so developed that we would not require any example, would not require any person. But that we are not; and, naturally, the

> *vast majority of mankind have put their souls at the feet of these extraordinary personalities, the Prophets, the Incarnations of God—Incarnations worshipped by the Christians, by the Buddhists, and by the Hindus. The Mohammedans from the beginning stood against any such worship. They would have nothing to do with worshipping the Prophets or the Messengers, or paying any homage to them; but, practically, instead of one Prophet, thousands upon thousands of saints are being worshipped. We cannot go against facts! We are bound to worship personalities, and it is good. Remember that word from your great Prophet to the query: "Lord, show us the Father", "He that hath seen me hath seen the Father." Which of us can imagine anything except that He is a man? We can only see Him in and through humanity.*[20]

To work for the good of others by remaining disinterested in rewards in return is the essence of true humanism. Man must be worthy of being non-attached all the time under any circumstances. This is positive humanism. In such humanism, man learns to live in the world, come in close association with different influences not for his own interest at all but entirely for the well-being of others. The work he performs is not meant for his own enjoyment at any time because that will be the moratorium for his ascent and excellence as man. He must kill his little self so that with the efflorescence of his power of non-attachment he performs his work in the world with the humanistic spirit of service to all.

In his analysis of the role of man in terms of work as a pointer to the exercise of non-attachment for enlightened and poignant humanism, Vivekananda elegantly exposes:

> *If the world is created for us, we are also created for the world. That this world is created for our enjoyment is the most wicked idea that holds us down. This world is not for our sake. Millions pass out of it every year; the world does not feel it; millions of others are supplied in their place. Just as much as the world is for us, so we also are for the world.*
>
> *To work properly, therefore, you have first to give up the idea of attachment. Secondly, do not mix in the fray, hold yourself as a witness and go on working. My Master used to say, "Look upon your children as a nurse does." The nurse will take your baby*

and fondle it and play with it and behave towards it as gently as if it were her own child; but as soon as you give her notice to quit, she is ready to start off bag and baggage from the house. Everything in the form of attachment is forgotten; it will not give the ordinary nurse the least pang to leave your children and take up other children. Even so are you to be with all that you consider your own. You are the nurse, and if you believe in God, believe that all these things which you consider yours are really His. The greatest weakness always insinuates itself as the greatest good and strength. It is a weakness to think that any one is dependent on me, and that I can do good to another. This belief is the mother of all our attachment, and through this attachment comes all our pain.

** ** ** **

It is sheer nonsense on the part of any man to think that he is born to help the world; it is simply pride, it is selfishness insinuating itself in the form of virtue. When you have trained your mind and your nerves to realise this idea of the world's non-dependence on you or on anybody, there will then be no reaction in the form of pain resulting from work. When you give something to a man and expect nothing— do not even expect the man to be grateful— his ingratitude will not tell upon you, because you never expected anything, never thought you had any right to anything in the way of a return. You gave him what he deserved; his own Karma got it for him; your Karma made you the carrier thereof. Why should you be proud of having given away something? You are the porter that carried the money or other kind of gift, and the world deserved it by its own Karma. Where is then the reason for pride in you? There is nothing very great in what you give to the world. When you have acquired the feeling of non-attachment, there will then be neither good nor evil for you. It is only selfishness that causes the difference between good and evil. It is a very hard thing to understand, but you will come to learn in time that nothing in the universe has power over you until you allow it to exercise such a power. Nothing has power over the Self of man , until the Self becomes a fool and loses independence. So, by non-attachment, you overcome and deny the power of anything to act upon you. It is very easy to say that nothing has the right to act upon you until you allow it to do so; but what is the true sign of the man who really does not allow anything to work upon him, who is neither happy nor unhappy when acted upon by the external world? The sign is that good or ill fortune causes no change in his mind; in all conditions he continues to remain the same.[21]

The mind of man is enriched with diverse experiences. The ores, as it were, of humanism waiting to be transformed into an enamelled coating to present the humankind with the pearls of perfection necessitate nursing of the right kind at the right moment with right approach to sincerity of purpose and dedication. The mind of man must be controlled and chiselled in the fire of experiences so that the problems or the ripples and the waves do not affect concentration. Human intelligence allows probing into the pros and cons of all experiences. How to understand the true nature of the mind? How should man as a positive contributor to humanism deal with it? Here are Vivekananda's poignant perspectives:

The real man is behind the mind; the mind is the instrument in his hands; it is his intelligence that is percolating through the mind. It is only when you stand behind the mind that it becomes intelligent. When man gives it up, it falls to pieces and is nothing. Thus you understand what is meant by Chitta. It is the mind-stuff, and Vrittis are the waves and ripples rising in it when external causes impinge on it. These Vrittis are our universe.

The bottom of a lake we cannot see, because its surface is covered with ripples. It is only possible for us to catch a glimpse of of the bottom, when the ripples have subsided, and the water is calm. If the water is muddy or is agitated all the time, the bottom will not be seen. If it is clear, and there are no waves, we shall see the bottom. The bottom of the lake is our own true Self; the lake is the Chitta and the waves the Vrittis. Again, the mind is in three states, one of which is darkness, called Tamas, found in brutes and idiots; it only acts to injure. No other idea comes into that state of mind. Then there is the active state of mind, Rajas, whose chief motives are power and enjoyment. "I will be powerful and rule others." Then there is the state called Sattva, serenity, calmness, in which the waves cease, and the water of the mind-lake becomes clear. It is not inactive, but rather intensively active. It is the greatest manifestation of power to be calm. It is easy to be active. Let the reins go, and the horses will run away with you. Anyone can do that, but he who can stop the plunging horses is the strong man. Which requires the greater strength, letting go, or restraining? The calm man is not the man who is dull. You must not mistake Sattva for dullness or laziness. The calm man is the one who has control over the mind waves. Activity is the manifestation of inferior strength, calmness, the superior.[22]

To make a perfect cohesion between human love and All Love is the apex of man and humanism. Unless man is totally devoted to this end-in-view and unendingly strive for manifestation of divinity already in him, the lotus land of humanism will remain a myth.

Meanwhile, let us listen to Vivekananda's serene words expressed in his poem "To a Friend":

Let go your vain reliance on knowledge,
Let go your prayers, offerings, and strength,
For Love selfless is the only resource;—
Lo, the insects teach, embracing the flame!
The base insect's blind, by beauty charmed,
Thy soul is drunken with the wine of Love;
O thou Lover true, cast into the fire
All thy dross of self, thy mean selfishness.[23]

Are we listening to the apostle of humanism?

1. Swami Vivekananda: *The Complete Works of Swami Vibekananda*, Advaita Ashrama, Kolkata, Mayavati Memorial Edition, 1989, Vol. III, pp. 174-175.
2. *Ibid.*, pp. 246-247.
3. *Ibid.*, Vol. II, pp. 365-366.
4. *Ibid.*, Vol. VIII, p. 120.
5. *Ibid.*, p. 249.
6. *Ibid.*, pp. 34-35.
7. *Ibid.*, Vol. III, pp. 53-54.
8. *Ibid.*, pp. 123-124.
9. *Ibid.*, pp. 124-125.
10. *Ibid.*, Vol. II, pp. 362-364.
11. *Ibid.*, pp. 366-367.
12. *Ibid.*, Vol. VII, p. 237.
13. *Ibid.*, Vol. VI. p. 186.
14. *Ibid.*, Vol. IV, p. 393.
15. *Ibid.*, Vol. VII, pp. 59-60.
16. *Ibid.*, pp. 43-44.
17. *Ibid.*, Vol. VIII, pp. 30-32.
18. *Ibid.*, Vol. VI, pp. 4-5.
19. *Ibid.*, Vol. I, p. 12.
20. *Ibid.*, Vol. IV, pp. 121-122.
21. *Ibid.*, Vol. I, pp. 88-90.
22. *Ibid.*, p. 202.
23. *Ibid.*,Vol. IV, p. 495-496.

Man and Values: Vivekananda's Pointers

Man's identity is in idealising and translating values in every walk of life. His very becoming is turned into being and the beyond of it from mere becoming. That he stands apart from other living creatures is his continuous and sustained endeavour in achieving fullness and perfection already inherent but not yet manifested.

An incomparable and unparalleled thinker and propagator of accelerating the inherent potentialities of values in man, Swami Vivekananda draws our attention to take care of and intensify eternal values for excellence and ascent. He does not believe in assistance and dependence on others because these would definitely tell upon the growth and development of man as an independent and living identity who knows, and knows very well, how to be true to self-knowledge and self-dependence in order to be justified to values at every stage of involvement and ascent.

Vivekananda reminds us of the fact that the values under which freedom is nurtured, be it right or wrong, encompass a great truth that we adore and renew values even when freedom is misdirected and the nature of man becomes gullible. Thus values call forth unity and variety in terms of freedom exercised under trying circumstances. Vivekananda splendidly elucidates this as follows:

> *That at which all marvel, that at which we call evil, is His worship too. This too is a part of freedom. Nay, I will be terrible even and tell you that, when you are doing evil, the impulse behind is also that freedom. It may have been misguided and misled, but it was there; and there cannot be any life or any impulse unless that freedom be behind it. Freedom breathes in the throb of the universe. Unless there is unity at the universal heart, we cannot understand variety. Such is the conception of the Lord in the Upanishads. Sometimes it rises even higher, presenting to us an ideal before which at first we stand aghast—that we are in essence one with God. He who is the colouring in the wings of the butterfly, and the blossoming of the rose-bud, is*

the power that is in the plant and in the butterfly. He who gives us life is the power within us. Out of His fire comes life, and the direst death is also His power. He whose shadow is death, His shadow is immortality also. Take a still higher conception. See how we are flying like hunted hares from all that is terrible, and like them, hiding our heads and thinking we are safe. See how the whole world is flying from everything terrible. Once when I was in Varanasi, I was passing through a place where there was a large tank of water on one side and a high wall on the other. It was in the grounds where there were many monkeys. The monkeys of Varanasi are huge brutes and are sometimes surly. They now took it into their heads not to allow me to pass through their street, so they howled and shrieked and clutched at my feet as I passed. As they pressed closer, I began to run, but the faster I ran, the faster came the monkeys and they began to bite at me. It seemed impossible to escape, but just then I met a stranger who called out to me, "Face the brutes." I turned and faced the monkeys, and they fell back and finally fled. That is a lesson for all life—face the terrible, face it boldly. Like the monkeys, the hardships of life fall back when we cease to flee before them.[1]

One of the most essential components of values in life is self-renunciation. This leads us to purity and poignancy, grandeur and decency in life to be worth living for self-advancement and self-ascent. For this, non-attachment acts as one of the finest components in tune with Karma-Yoga. Vivekananda characteristically unfolds its nature and how to exercise it:

Non-attachment does not mean anything that we may do in relation to our external body, it is all in the mind. The binding link of "I and mine" is in the mind. If we have not this link with the body and with the things of the senses, we are non-attached, wherever and whatever we may be. A man may be on a throne and perfectly non-attached; another man may be in rags and still very much attached. First we have to attain this state of non-attachment and then to work incessantly. Karma-Yoga gives us the method that will help us in giving up all attachment, though it is indeed very hard.

Here are the two ways of giving up all attachment. The one is for those who do not believe in God, or in any outside help. They are left to their own devices; they have simply to work with their own will, with the powers of their mind and discrimination, saying, "I must be non-attached". For those who believe in God there is another way, which is much less difficult. They give up the fruits of work unto the Lord; they work and are never attached to the results. Whatever they see, feel, hear, or do, is for Him. For whatever good work we may do, let us not claim any praise or benefit. It is the Lord's; give up the fruits unto Him. Let us stand aside and think that we are only servants obeying the Lord, our Master, and that every impulse for action comes from Him every moment. Whatever thou worshippest, whatever thou perceivest, whatever thou doest, give up all unto Him, and be at rest. Let us be at peace, perfect peace, with ourselves, and give up our whole body and mind and everything as an eternal sacrifice unto the Lord. Instead of the sacrifice of pouring oblations into the fire, perform this one great sacrifice day and night— the sacrifice of your little self. "In search of wealth in this world, Thou art the only wealth I have found; I sacrifice myself unto Thee. In search of some one to be loved, Thou art the only one I have found; I sacrifice myself unto Thee." Let us repeat this day and night, and say, "Nothing for me; no matter whether the thing is good, bad, or indifferent; I do not care for it; I sacrifice all unto Thee." Day and night let us renounce our seeming self until it becomes a habit with us to do so, until it gets into the blood, the nerves, and the brain, and the whole body is every moment obedient to this idea of self-renunciation. Go then into the midst of the battlefield, with the roaring cannon and the din of war, and you will find yourself to be free and at peace.[2]

With elimination of the little self in every one of us by means of exercise of purity, renunciation or non-attachment, we ennoble and enrich ourselves. This enrichment is just to remove the iron cask by transforming it into a glass cask— a mirror of the inner self for higher and higher reflection until the cask itself is eliminated. Vivekananda adroitly explains this point:

All knowledge is of the reflected, as we can only see our face in a mirror. No one will ever know his own Self or God; but we are that own Self, we are God.

In Nirvana you are when you are not. Buddha said, "You are best, you are real, when you are not"— when the little self is gone.

The Light Divine within is obscured in most people, it is like a lamp in a cask of iron, no gleam of light can shine through. Gradually, by purity, and unselfishness we can make the obscuring medium less and less dense, until at last it becomes as transparent as glass. Shri Ramakrishna was like the iron cask transformed into a glass cask through which can be seen the inner light as it is. We are all on the way to become the cask of glass and even higher and higher reflections. As long as there is a "cask" at all, we must think through material means. No impatient can ever succeed.[3]

Man and values are entirely based on this ever accelerating and quality-reflecting transparency. Whenever as men we are entrusted with our duties, the prime target on our part so far as transparency is concerned is to be devoted to values associated with our duties. If we are successful in accomplishing our duties without paying any attention to self-interest but by cultivation of values through devotion and dedication for excellence of performance, we would be on the right track of the ascent of man. Vivekananda significantly points out how one should stick to one's duties and responsibilities in an unattached, sincere and steadfast manner in order to attain the zenith of success:

The great lesson to learn is that I am not the standard by which the whole universe is to be judged; each man is to be judged by his own idea, each race by its own standard and ideal, each custom of each country by its own reasoning and conditions. American customs are the result of the environment in which the Americans live, and Indian customs are the result of the environment in which the Indians are; and so of China, Japan, England, and every other country.

We all find ourselves in the position for which we are fit, each ball finds its own hole; and if one has some capacity above another, the world will find that out too, in this universal adjusting that goes on. So it is no use to grumble. There may be a rich man who is wicked, yet there must be in that man certain qualities that made him rich; and if any other man has the same qualities, he will also become rich. What is the use of fighting and complaining? That will not help us to better things. He who grumbles at the little thing that has fallen to his lot to do will grumble at everything. Always grumbling, he will lead a miserable life, and everything will be a failure. But that man who does his duty as he goes, putting his shoulder to the wheel, will see the light, and higher and higher duties will fall to his share.[4]

To be a man of values is never to be fanatic. Man and fanaticism are antithetic from the standpoint of values. A fanatic is always devoid of the values of love and sympathy. Vivekananda inspires us to cultivate the values of love and sympathy by totally eliminating hatred and apathy to man. Even those who are fanatics should be endeared with love and sympathy:

My experience comes to this, that it is rather wise to avoid all sorts of fanatical reforms. This world is slowly going on; let it go slowly. Why are you in a hurry? Sleep well and keep your nerves in good order; eat right food, and have sympathy with the world. Fanatics only make hatred. Do you mean to say that the temperance fanatic loves these poor people who become drunkards? A fanatic is a fanatic simply because he expects to get something for himself in return. As soon as the battle is over, he goes for the spoil. When you come out of the company of fanatics, you may learn how really to love and sympathise. And the more you attain of love and sympathy, the less will be your power to condemn these poor creatures; rather you will sympathise with their faults. It will possible for you to sympathise with the drunkard and to know that he is also a man like yourself. You will then try to understand the many circumstances that are dragging him down, and feel that if you had been in his place, you would perhaps have committed suicide.[5]

The value of non-attachment is one of the finest and most desirable values that man should cultivate. It indicates the identity of man as the true servant of God who is in every living creature. Perfect non-attachment, as Vivekananda points out, is to exercise and disseminate the attitude of perfect reverence. The relation between God and man in terms of values is to ascertain the fact that God allows us to do a work in a disinterested and non-attached manner. If we can prove our worth to work in that manner, we would be justified in visualising Him in everyone everywhere.

To be selfish in attitude is to belie and denounce the value of non-attachment. It becomes the folly of man. As Vivekananda refers to the 'highest of mankind' as the most ideal exponents of the value of non-attachment in terms of Karma-Yoga:

> *Help the Lord! There is a proverb in our language, "Shall we teach the Architect of the universe how to build?" So those are the highest of mankind who do not work. The next time you see these silly phrases about the world and how we must help God and do this and that for Him, remember this. Do not think such thoughts; they are too selfish. All the work you do is subjective, is done for your own benefit. God has not fallen into a ditch for you and me to help Him out by building a hospital or something of that sort. He* allows *you to work. He allows you to exercise your muscles in this great gymnasium, not in order to help Him but that you may help yourself. Do you think even an ant will die for want of your help? Most arrant blasphemy! The world does not need you at all. The world goes on, you are like a drop in the ocean. A leaf does not move, the wind does not blow without Him. Blessed are we that we are given the privilege of working for Him, not of helping Him. Cut out this word "help" from your mind. You cannot help; it is blaspheming. You are here yourself at His pleasure. Do you mean to say, you help Him? You worship. When you give a morsel of food to the dog, you worship the dog as God. God is in that dog. He is the dog. He is all and in all. We are allowed to worship Him. Stand in that reverent attitude to the whole universe, and then will come perfect non-attachment. This should be your duty. This is the proper attitude of work. This is the secret taught by Karma-Yoga.*[6]

The ascent of man in visualising the All Serene in everyone irrespective of caste, creed, religion or any other apparent differences is to revere the most essential value of all— the Kingdom of God is in man. When Vivekananda speaks about *Naranarayana*, man as the embodiment of God, he highlights this invaluable truth.

The highest consciousness that God is in good as well as in evil signifies one of the most cherished values for which man eternally strives. Vivekananda has idealised and translated this value in man. In explaining this to one of his disciples, he strongly asserts:

> *You see, there are, in reality, no such different things as good and evil. They are mere conventional terms. The same thing we call bad , and again another time we call good, according to the way we make use of it. Take for example this lamplight; because of its burning, we are able to see and do various works of utility; this is one mode of using the light. Again, if you put fingers in it, they will be burnt; that is another mode of using the same light. So we should know that a thing becomes good or bad according to the way we use it. Similarly with virtue and vice. Broadly speaking, the proper use of any of the faculties of our mind and body is termed virtue, and its improper application or waste is called vice.*[7]

That the neglect of the body indicates the absence of the value of goodness is one of the most characteristic teachings of Vivekananda. Referring to the great saying of the Katha Upanishad that the Self cannot be attained by the weak, he points out to one of his disciples:

> *Well, do you consider yourselves as men? You have got only a bit of rationality— that's all. How will you struggle with the mind unless the physique be strong? Do you deserve to be called men any longer— the highest evolution in the world? What have you got besides eating, sleeping, and satisfying the creature-comforts? Thank your stars that you have not developed into quadrupeds yet! Shri Ramakrishna used to say, "He is the man who is conscious of his dignity". You are but standing witnesses to the lowest class of insect-like existence of which the scripture speaks, that they simply undergo the round of births and deaths without being allowed to go to any of the higher spheres! You are simply living a life of jealousy among yourselves and are objects of hatred in the eyes of the foreigner. You are animals, therefore I recommend you to struggle. Leave aside theories and all that. Just reflect calmly on your own everyday acts and dealings and find out whether you are not a species of beings intermediate between the animal and human planes of existence! First build up your physique. Then you can only get control over the mind.*[8]

The value of toleration is the true identification of man. He does not allow impatience to overpower his spirit of tolerance which makes a happy bridge of understanding between man and man irrespective of many apparent differences. Vivekananda points out the fact that the Vedanta teaches this value of tolerance and observes how one can be a true Vedantist by propagating the spirit of universal brotherhood of man:

> *If one man is slower than another, we need not be impatient, we need not curse him, or revile him. When our eyes are opened and the heart is purified, the work of the same divine influence, the unfolding of the same divinity in every human heart, will become manifest; and then alone we shall be in a position to claim the brotherhood of man.*
>
> *When a man has reached the highest, when he sees neither man nor woman, neither sect nor creed, nor colour, nor birth, nor any of these differentiations, but goes beyond and finds that divinity which is the real man behind every human being— then alone he has reached the universal brotherhood, and that man alone is a Vedantist.*[9]

The concept of good and evil in terms of man and values is more often than not misunderstood. This is simply because we fail to accept both evil and good as the natural outcome of human life. At the same time, we also fail to appreciate anything beyond good and evil and the striving for the best remains absent from our quest for values. Thus our assessment of man becomes erroneous.

Vivekananda points out an altogether splendid avenue of efflorescence of individuality which is far above the so-called value of good and evil. Disseminating the view that everything is the reflection of the Atman, he poignantly observes:

> *"This earth is so blissful, so helpful to every being; and all beings are so helpful to this earth: all these are manifestations of that Self-Effulgent One, the Atman." All that is bliss, even in the lowest sense, is but the reflection of Him. All that is good is His reflection, and when that reflection is a shadow, it is called evil. There are no two Gods. When He is less manifested, it is called darkness, evil; and when He is more manifested, it is called light. That is all. Good and evil are only a question of degree: more manifested or less manifested. Just take the example*

of our own lives. How many things we see in our childhood which we think to be good, but which really are evil, and how many things seem to be evil which are good! How the ideas change! How an idea goes up and up! What we thought very good at one time we do not think so good now. So good and evil are but suppositions, and do not exist. The difference is only in degree. It is all a manifestation of that Atman; He is being manifested in everything; only, if the manifestation is very thick we call it evil; and when it is very thin, we call it good. It is the best, when all covering goes away. So everything that is in the universe is to be meditated upon in that sense alone, that we can see it as all good, because it is the best. There is evil and there is good; and the apex, the centre, is the Reality. He is neither evil nor good; He is the best. The best can be only one, the good can be many, and the evil many. There will be degrees of variation between the good and the evil, but the best is only one, and that best, when seen through thin coverings, we call different sorts of good, and when through thick covers, we call evil. Good and evil are different forms of superstition. They have gone through all sorts of dualistic delusion, and all sorts of ideas, and the words have sunk into the hearts of human beings, terrorising men and women and living there as terrible tyrants. They make us become tigers. All the hatred with which we hate others is caused by these foolish ideas which we have inhibited since our childhood—good and evil. Our judgement of humanity becomes entirely false; we make this beautiful earth a hell; but as soon as we can give up good and evil, it becomes a heaven.[10]

The value that Vivekananda highlights in religion is all-endearing all-pervasiveness. No religion is insignificant. No religion is greater than the other ones in terms of values. What counts more and is appositely appreciated is in the practice and pursuit of poignancy it carries forth for the ascent of man as a connoisseur of values. Religion as such is very often misunderstood and misinterpreted. One of the fundamental reasons for misunderstandings and misinterpretations is that the religion of religions remains unknown and despite being in the endeavour of being known, remains utterly underestimated in the whirlpool of sham superiority. Besides this, the values inculcated by any religion are often assessed under erroneous and dubious scanner. When the values of any religion are not honoured in the right perspective of advancement, religion turns into something else than religion and becomes a favourable food for nursing fanaticism.

Vivekananda's concern for religion for promotion of values is to make every possible adventure and inroads to manifestation of inherent divinity. He pays highest adoration and devotion to religion essentially because the values of religion are identification and exercise of the divinity already in man. How to be initiated in the true spirit of the value of religion? Here is an exquisite and matchless interpretation in terms of the synthesis of values in the religion of Mohammedanism:

> *The fact that all the old religions are living today proved that they must have kept that mission intact; in spite of all their mistakes, in spite of all difficulties, in spite of all quarrels, in spite of all the incrustation of forms and figures, the heart of every one of them is sound— it is a throbbing, beating, living heart. They have not lost, any one of them, the great mission they came for. And it is splendid to study that mission. Take Mohammedanism, for instance. Christian people hate no religion in the world so much as Mohammedanism. They think it is the very worst form of religion that ever existed. As soon as a man becomes a Mohammedan, the whole of Islam receives him as a brother with open arms, without making any distinction, which no other religion does. If one of your American Indians becomes a Mohammedan, the Sultan of Turkey would have no objection to dine with him. If he has brains, no position is barred to him. In this country, I have never yet seen a church where the white man and the negro can kneel side by side to pray. Just think of that; Islam makes its followers all equal— so, that, you see, is the peculiar excellence of Mohammedanism. In many places in the Koran you find very sensual ideas of life. Never mind, what Mohammedanism comes to preach to the world is the practical brotherhood of all belonging to their faith. That is the essential part of the Mohammedan religion; and all the other ideas about heaven and of life etc., are not Mohammedanism. They are accretions.*[11]

The new vision of man in terms of self-identity as a specific component of morality as Vivekananda points out is the liberation of the soul. That man is infinite and the struggle for reaching the infinite is endless can be most appropriately evaluated in terms of the values of the quest for freedom.This is why the vision of enriching self-identity by means of finding out the best means of true liberation of the soul becomes the touchstone of the ascent of man.

Vivekananda clarifies the the infinite nature of man in appreciating the values of freedom of the soul very significantly:

> *The goal of the soul among all the different sects in India seems to be the same. There is one idea with all, and that is liberation. Man is infinite; and this limitation in which he exists now is not his nature. But through these limitations he is struggling upward and forward until he reaches the infinite, the unlimited, his birthright, his nature. All these combinations and recombinations and manifestations that we see round us are not the aim or the goal, but merely by the way and in passing. These combinations as earths and suns, moons and stars, right and wrong, good and bad, our laughter and our tears, our joys and sorrows, are to enable us are to gain experience through which the soul manifests its perfect nature and throws off limitation. No more, then, is it bound by laws either of internal or of external nature. It has gone beyond all law, beyond all limitation, beyond all nature. Nature has come under the control of the soul, not the soul under the the control of nature, as it thinks it is now. That is the one goal that the soul has; and all the succeeding steps through which it is manifesting, all the successive experiences through which it is passing in order to attain to that goal—freedom— are represented as its births. The soul is, as it were, taking up a lower body and trying to express itself through that. It finds that to be insufficient,throws it aside, and a higher one is taken up. Through that it struggles to express itself. That also is found to be insufficient, is rejected, and a higher one comes; so on and on until a body is found through which the soul manifests its highest aspirations. Then the soul becomes free.*[12]

The freedom of the soul as man values above everything shows the way to the true ascent of man. It is the most prized identity of man to to be true to the soul. The existence of the soul, the unlimited one, cannot live in a limited space, in the body of a man—a fact that is apparent. But that becomes possible only when we understand that man, the limited one, revolves round that soul. Only then we can understand the limitless existence and value of the soul.

Vivekananda clarifies the value of the unlimited soul and ever precious soul by means of referring to a very simple and fascinating explanation:

> *It is meaningless nonsense to say that the soul lives in a body. How can the unlimited live in a limited space? But as a man having a book in his hands reads one page and turns it over, goes to the next page, reads that, turns it over, and so on, yet it is the book that is being turned over, the pages that are revolving, and not he— he is where he is always— even so with regard to the soul. The whole nature is that book which the soul is reading. Each life, as it were, is one page of that book; and that read, it is turned over, and so on and so on, until the whole of the book is finished, and the soul becomes perfect, having got all the experiences of nature. Yet at the same time it never moved, nor came, nor went; it was only gathering experiences. But it appears to us that we are moving. The earth is moving, yet we think that the sun is moving instead of the earth, which we know to be a mistake, a delusion of the senses. So is also that delusion that we are born and that we die, that we come or that we go. We neither come nor go, nor have we been born. For where is the soul to go? There is no place for it to go. Where is it not already?*[13]

Commonalities eat up all the genuineness and vitalities of man in terms of values. The inherent spirit in each of us must as Vivekananda inspires us, rise up, roar and uphold the values that truth transpires. Otherwise, man becomes a slave to mechanical and dull life aping all the time by sacrificing individual freedom of thought and expression. Truth also suffers under the pressure of devaluation of values, and falsehood gets the upper hand in an opposition-free ambience of treason. What, then, should be the role of man so far as restoration and enrichment of values are concerned? Here is Vivekananda's vibrant answer:

> *Each one of us is thinking in his own way, but his natural course has been obstructed all the time and is still being obstructed. If the sword is not used directly, other means will be used. Just hear what one of the best preachers in New York says: he preaches*

that the Filipinos should be conquered because that is the only way to teach Christianity to them! They are already Catholics, but he wants to make them Presbyterians, and for this, he is ready to lay all this terrible sin of bloodshed upon his race. How terrible! And this man is one of the greatest preachers of this country, one of the best informed men. Think of the state of the world when a man like that is not ashamed to stand up and utter such arrant nonsense; and think of the state of the world when an audience cheers him! Is this civilisation? It is the old blood-thirstiness of the tiger, the cannibal, the savage, coming out once more under new names, new circumstances. What else can it be? If the state of things is such now, think of the horrors through which the world passed in olden times, when every sect was trying by every means in its power to tear to pieces the other sects. History shows that. The tiger in us is only asleep; it is not dead. When opportunities come, it jumps up and, as of old, uses its claws and fangs. Apart from the sword, apart from material weapons, there are weapons still more terrible— contempt, social hatred, and social ostracism. Now, these are the most terrible of all inflictions that are hurled against persons who do not think exactly in the same way as we do. And why should everybody think as we do? I do not see any reason. If I am a rational man, I should be glad they do not think just as I do. I do not want to live in a grave-like land; I want to be a man in a world of men. Thinking beings must differ; difference is the first sign of thought. If I am a thoughtful man, certainly I ought to like to live amongst thoughtful persons where there are differences of opinion.[14]

Indeed, variety is one of the most fundamental components of values in man. If there is no point of difference between man and man, it indicates that we bid farewell to individual process and exercise of thinking which ultimately leads to burial of rationality and innovative spirit of man. At the same time, we invite indolence as the inevitable mark of progress and civilisation of humankind. This is simply devaluation of values.

While speaking on the ideal of religion, Vivekananda has splendidly spelt out the importance of nursing unity in variety as a compulsory and positive force of man and values. In his words:

Unity in variety is the plan of the universe. We are all men, and yet we are all distinct from one another. As a part of humanity I am one with you, and as Mr So-and-so I am different from you. As a man you are separate from the woman; as a human being you are one with the woman. As a man you are separate from the animal, but as living beings, man, woman, animal, and plant are all one; and as existence, you are one with the whole universe. That universal existence is God, the ultimate Unity in the universe. In Him we are all one. At the same time, in manifestation, the differences must always remain. In our work, in our energies, as they are being manifested outside, these differences must always remain. We find then that if by the idea of a universal religion it is meant that one set of doctrines should be believed in by all mankind, it is wholly impossible. It can never be, there can never be a time when all faces will be the same. Again, if we expect that there will be one universal mythology, that is also impossible; it cannot be. Neither can there be one universal ritual. Such a state of things can never come into existence; if it ever did, the world would be destroyed, because variety is the first principle of life. What makes us formed beings? Differentiation. Perfect balance would be our destruction. Suppose the amount of heat in this room, the tendency of which is towards equal and perfect diffusion, gets that kind of diffusion, then for all practical purposes that heat will cease to be. What makes motion possible in this universe? Lost balance. The unity of sameness can come only when this universe is destroyed, otherwise such a thing is impossible. Not only so, it would be dangerous to have it. We must not wish that all of us should think alike, as the Egyptian mummies in a museum, looking at each other without a thought to think. It is this difference, this differentiation, this losing of the balance between us, which is the very soul of our progress, the soul of all thought. This must always be.[15]

The value of right thinking leads to consciousness which, with the elimination of ego, leads to super-consciousness or Samadhi. When we remain unconscious, we are not in a position to learn or know the exact position of our very being. The sum total of our knowledge only indicates that we arrive at the same position of our knowledge whose value rests on consciousness in our state of egoism.

But when the state of the Samadhi is achieved there is total elimination of egoism which indicates the state of super-conscious the highest value that man should ceaselessly strive for.

Vivekananda clearly explains the concept and value of Samadhi in terms of man and knowledge as follows:

> *Just as unconscious work is beneath consciousness, so there is another work which is above consciousness, and which also is not accompanied with the feeling of egoism. The feeling of egoism is only on the middle plane. When the mind is above or below that line, there is no feeling of "I", and yet the mind works. When the mind goes beyond this line of self-consciousness, it is called Samadhi or super-consciousness. How, for instance, do we know that a man in Samadhi has not gone below consciousness, has not degenerated instead of going higher? In both cases the works are unaccompanied with egoism. The answer is, by the effects, by the results of the work, we know that which is below, and that which is above. When a man goes into deep sleep, he enters a plane beneath consciousness. He works the body all the time, he breathes, he moves the body, perhaps, in his sleep, without any accompanying feeling of ego; he is unconscious, and when he returns from his sleep, he is the same man who went into it. The sum total of the knowledge which he had before he went into the sleep remains the same; it does not increase at all. No enlightenment comes. But when a man goes into Samadhi, if he goes into it a fool, he comes out a sage.*
>
> *What makes the difference? From one state a man comes out the very same man that he went in, and from another state the man comes out enlightened, a sage, a prophet, a saint, his whole character changed, his life changed, illuminated. These are the two effects. Now the effects being different, the causes must be different. As this illumination with which a man comes back from Samadhi is much higher than can be got by reasoning in a conscious state, it must, therefore, be super-consciousness, and Samadhi is called the super-conscious state.*[16]

The value of transference from consciousness to super-consciousness is one of the best indicators of man's excellence and ascent. For this reasoning as one of the most significant values must be crystallised in terms of truth, and, at the same time, the involvement so required ought to be backed by decency and magnanimity.

What, then, should be our role in the exercise of reason? Here is Vivekananda's characteristic suggestion:

> *On reason we must have to lay our foundation, we must follow reason as far as it leads, and when reason fails, reason itself will show us the way to the highest plane. When you hear a man say, "I am inspired", and then talk irrationally, reject it. Why? Because these three states—instinct, reason, and super-consciousness, or the unconscious, conscious, and super-conscious states— belong to one and the same mind. There are not three minds in one man, but one state of it develops into the others. Instinct develops into reason, and reason into the transcendental consciousness; therefore, not one of the states contradicts the others. Real inspiration never contradicts reason, but fulfils it. Just as you find the great prophet saying, "I come not to destroy but to fulfil," so inspiration always comes to fulfil reason, and is in harmony with it.*[17]

To value reason as Vivekananda observes in the light of transparency is to value it in terms of human relationship best suited to excellence and ascent. It is the stepping stone of nurturing idealism. "The real desire for the ideal", as he characterises in terms of the soul, takes one to a spiritual height never before thought and experimented in best introducing the philosophy of man. In his words:

> *We know we have to give up money and all other things when we die, and yet, see the amount of energy we can put forth on them. But we, the same human beings, should we not put forth a thousandfold more strength and energy to acquire that which never fades, but which remains to us for ever? For this is the one great friend, our own good deeds, our own spiritual excellence, that follows us beyond the grave. Everything else is left behind here with the body.*
>
> *That is the one great first step—the real desire for the ideal. Everything comes easy after that. That the Indian mind found out; there, in India, men go to any length to find truth. But here, in the West, the difficulty is that everything is made so easy. It is not truth, but development, that is the great aim. The struggle is the great lesson. Mind you, the great benefit in this life is struggle. It is through that we pass. If there is any road to Heaven,*

it is through Hell. Through Hell to Heaven is always the way. When the soul has wrestled with circumstance and has met death, a thousand times death on the way, but nothing daunted has struggled forward again and again and yet again— then the soul comes out as a giant and laughs at the ideal he has been struggling for, because he finds how much greater is he than the ideal. I am the end, my own Self, and nothing else, for what is there to compare to my own Self? Can a bag of gold be the ideal of my Soul? Certainly not! My Soul is the highest ideal that I can have. Realising my own real nature is the one goal of my life.[18]

The value of self-realisation as Vivekananda observes in terms of the Soul becomes more explicit and unparalleled in realising the external and internal natures not differently but in unison of identity. In the same way, the real value of matter and mind can be best identified not in isolation but in fusion.

Vivekananda's vision of the philosophy of man and values clarifies the real position of matter and mind which are not different but one and the same. Therefore, materialism and spiritualism are synthesised in man in the exercise of manifestation. As he characteristically elucidates:

The external and internal natures are not two different things; they are really one. Nature is the sum total of all phenomena. "Nature" means all that is, all that move. We make a tremendous distinction between matter and mind; we think that the mind is entirely different from matter. Actually, they are but one nature, half of which is continually acting on the other half. Matter is pressing upon the mind in the form of various sensations. These sensations are nothing but force. The force from the outside evokes the force within. From the will to respond to or get away from the outer force, the inner force becomes what we call thought.

Both matter and mind are really nothing but forces; and if you analyse them far enough, you will find that at root they are one. The very fact that the external force can somehow evoke the internal force shows that somewhere they join each other— they must be continuous and, therefore, basically the same force. When you get to the root of things, they become simple and general. Since the same force appears in one form as matter and in another form as mind, there is no reason to think matter and mind are different. Mind is changed into matter, matter is changed into mind. Thought force becomes nerve force, muscular force; muscular and nerve force become thought force. Nature is all this force, whether expressed as matter or mind.[19]

The value of religion lies in altruism. It is a continuous striving for assertion of the all round goodness of one and all and total negation of the little self. It cares for all the values that promotes the advancement of man and the world in every direction and eliminates littleness and selfishness with strict soul consciousness and discipline at every step towards excellence and ascent.

In fact, the value of extinction of personality is the true value of the religion of man. Vivekananda clarifies this point most adroitly:

Through practice comes Yoga, through Yoga comes knowledge, through knowledge love, and through love bliss.

"Me and mine" is a superstition; we have lived in it so long that it is well-nigh impossible to shake it off. Still we must get rid of it if we would rise to the highest. We must be bright and cheerful, long faces do not make religion. Religion should be the most joyful thing in the world, because it is the best. Asceticism cannot make us holy. Why should a man who loves God and who is pure be sorrowful? He should be like a happy child, be truly a child of God. The essential thing in religion is making the heart pure; the Kingdom of Heaven is within us, but only the pure in heart can see the King. While we think of the world, it is only the world for us; but let us come to it with the feeling that the world is God, and we shall have God. This should be our thought towards everyone and everything—parents, children, husbands, wives, friends, and enemies. Think how it would change the whole universe for us if we could consciously fill it with God! See nothing but God, all sorrow, all struggle, all pain would be for ever lost to us![20]

The new religion of values is the realisation of the self in terms of others who must be one's own, very own. Then the little self evaporates and the Self within comes out with ever shining brilliance. In this exercise of the value of religion we distinctly realise that we are what our true realisation of the Self within the self really means and works selflessly.

That the value of religion is not religiosity but realisation of being is the essence of religion. It is genuine and practical religion, the religion that contains the worth for which it stands in the advancement of man. How to be truly religious? How to be justified to the real value of religion? Here is Vivekananda's most in-depth and practical answer:

> *To be religious, you have to throw books overboard. The less you read of books, the better for you; do one thing at a time. It is a tendency in Western countries, in these modern times, to make a hotchpotch of the brain; all sorts of unassimilated ideas run riot in the brain and form a chaos without ever obtaining a chance to settle down and crystallise into a definite shape. In many cases it becomes a sort of disease, but this is not religion. Then some want a sensation. Tell them about ghosts and people coming from the North Pole or any other remote place, with wings or in any other form, and they are invisibly present and watching over them, and make them feel uncanny, then they are satisfied and go home; but within twenty-four hours they are ready for a fresh sensation. This is what some call religion. This is the way to the lunatic asylum, and not to religion. The Lord is not to be reached by the weak, and all these weird things tend to weakness. Therefore go not near them; they only make people weak, bring disorder to the brain, weaken the mind, demoralise the soul, and a hopeless muddle is the result. You must bear on mind that religion does not consist in talk, or doctrines, or books, but in realisation; it is not learning, but* being. *Everybody knows, "Do not steal", but what of it? That man has really known who has not stolen. Everybody knows, "Do not injure others", but of what value is it? Those who have not done so have realised it, they know it and have built their character on it. Religion is realising; and I will call you a worshipper of God when you have become able to realise the Idea. Before that it is the spelling of the word, and no more. It is this power of realisation that makes religion. No amount of doctrines or philosophies or ethical books, that you may have stuffed into your brain, will matter much, only what you* are *and what you have* realised. *So we have to realise religion, and this realisation of religion is a long process. When men hear of something very high and wonderful, they all think they will get that, and never stop for a moment to*

consider that they will have to work their way up to it; they all want to jump there. If it is the highest, we are for it. We never stop to consider whether we have the power, and the result is that we do not do anything. You cannot take a man with a pitchfork and push him up there; we all have to work up gradually.[21]

The quest for truth as a value of all values man makes rests on the fact that he is the embodiment of All True emancipated from the dark spells of Maya and ignorance, hatred and bondage. Man cannot remain isolated from the value of vastness that beckons—the real adventure unending, ever struggling, ever free. As Vivekananda poignantly pronounces:

Truth never comes where lust and fame and greed
Of gain reside. No man who thinks of woman
As his wife can never perfect be;
Nor he who owns the least of things, nor he
Whom anger chains, can ever pass thro' Maya's gates.
So, give these up, Sannyasin bold! Say—
"Om Tat Sat, Om!"

Have thou no home. What home can hold thee, friend?
The sky is thy roof, the grass thy bed; and food
What chance may bring, well cooked or ill, judge not.
No food or drink can taint that noble Self
Which knows Itself. Like rolling river free
Thou ever be, Sannyasin bold! Say—
"Om Tat Sat, Om!"

Few only know the truth. The rest will hate
And laugh at thee, great one; but pay no heed.
Go thou, the free, from place to place, and help
Them out of darkness, Maya's veil. Without
The fear of pain or search for pleasure, go
Beyond them both, Sannyasin bold! Say—
"Om Tat Sat, Om!"[22]

Are we devoted and dedicated to the vision of values as above?

1. Swami Vivekananda: *The Complete Works of Swami Vivekananda,* Advaita Ashrama, Kolkata, Mayavati Memorial Edition, 1989, Vol. I, pp. 338-339.
2. *Ibid.*, pp. 101-102.
3. *Ibid.*, Vol. VII, p. 21.
4. *Ibid.*, Vol. V, pp. 241-242.
5. *Ibid.*, pp. 243-244.
6. *Ibid.*, pp. 245-246.
7. *Ibid.*, p. 337.
8. *Ibid.*, Vol. VII, p.155.
9. *Ibid.*, Vol. I, pp. 391-392.
10. *Ibid.*, Vol. II, pp. 420-421.
11. *Ibid.* pp. 371-372.
12. *Ibid.*, Vol. VI, pp. 22-23.
13. *Ibid.*, pp. 23- 24.
14. *Ibid.*, Vol. II, pp. 364-365.
15. *Ibid.*, pp. 381-382.
16. *Ibid.*, Vol. I, pp. 180-181.
17. *Ibid.*, p. 185.
18. *Ibid.*, pp. 252-253.
19. *Ibid.*, pp. 245-246.
20. *Ibid.*, pp. 7-8.
21. *Ibid.*, Vol. IV, pp. 34-36.
22. *Ibid.*, pp. 394-395.

Man and Spirituality: Vivekananda's Quest for Excellence

Spirituality is the essence of man for excellence and ascent. It indicates the path towards self-abnegation and seeks the only identity in altruism. It makes the real platform of man for introspection. Man identifies joy and sorrow, freedom and bondage, laughter and tears from an altogether different canvas where he remains over and above the self and unendingly strives for quality and excellence, ascent and poignance derived from the best exercise of the inner being. It is the realisation of the inner being which is far apart and above becoming.

The efflorescence of spirituality in man is natural and spontaneous, and never artificial and mechanical. As such, in the exercise of spirituality no two persons are one and the same. It remains unique and unparalleled, incomparable and individual. There may be a group of people devoted to the exercise of spirituality, but what is most interesting and characteristic is that they maintain originality of mission and vision, ends-in-view and evaluation in every endeavour of spiritual accomplishment. Over and above, the focal point of interest in idealising and formulating the true concept of spirituality is goodness and excellence, advancement and brilliance.

The essence of spontaneity that spirituality unfolds is always unique. As Swami Vivekananda reminds us:

> *You think that because you talk a little more polished language you are superior to the man in the street. Remember that when you are thinking this, you are not going towards freedom, but are forging a fresh chain for your feet. And, above all, if the pride of spirituality enters into you, woe unto you. It is the most awful bondage that ever existed. Neither can wealth nor any other bondage of the human heart bind the soul so much as this. "I am purer than others", is the most awful idea that can enter into the human heart. In what sense are you pure? The God in you is the God in all. If you have not known this, you have*

known nothing. How can there be difference? It is all one. Every being is the temple of the Most High; if you can see that, good, if not, spirituality has yet to come to you.[1]

Spirituality, indeed, is the highest component in the excellence and ascent of man. Apparently, it might not be as prominent as intellectual and physical help for the march of man because it requires depth of vision and purity and poignance of imagination but ultimately it stands out incomparable and unparalleled in the efflorescence of man. It leads us to the zenith of consciousness and the beyond.

In the secret of work, we often fail to realise the truth as above in which spirituality is enriched. We prioritise intellectual and physical help and spiritual development remains far beyond the orbit of human advancement. That spiritual help is the highest help for the march of man can hardly be ignored. As Vivekananda categorically observes:

> *It is only with the knowledge of the spirit that the faculty of want is annihilated for ever; so helping man spiritually is the highest help that can be given to him. He who gives man spiritual knowledge is the highest benefactor of mankind and as such we always find that those who were the most powerful of men who helped man in his spiritual needs, because spirituality is the true basis of all our activities in life. A spiritually strong and sound man will be strong in every other respect, if he so wishes. Until there is spiritual strength in man even physical needs cannot be well satisfied. Next to spiritual comes intellectual help. The gift of knowledge is a far higher gift than that of food and clothes; it is even higher than giving life to a man, because the real life of man consists of knowledge. Ignorance is death, knowledge is life. Life is of very little value, if it is a life in the dark, groping through ignorance and misery. Next in order comes, of course, helping a man physically. Therefore, in considering the question of helping others, we must always strive not to commit the mistake of thinking that physical help is the only help that can be given. It is not only the last but the least because it cannot bring about permanent satisfaction. The misery that I feel when I am hungry is satisfied by eating, but hunger returns; my misery can cease only when I am satisfied beyond*

all want. Then hunger will not make me miserable; no distress, no sorrow will be able to move me. So, that help which tends to make us strong spiritually is the highest, next to it comes intellectual help, and after that physical help.[2]

The cultivation of spirituality should start right from childhood. Every child must be given spiritual education because it is the most potent force for imparting the education of the being and the beyond. This is the only means of introducing positive religion from childhood by means of exercise of freedom through spirituality. Vivekananda categorically remarks:

Impress upon your children that true religion is positive and not negative, that it does not consist in merely refraining from evil, but in a persistent performance of noble deeds. True religion comes not from the teaching of men or the reading of books; it is the awakening of the spirit within us, consequent upon pure and heroic action. Every child born into the world brings within it a certain accumulated experience from previous incarnations; and the impress of this experience is seen in the structure of its mind and body. But the feeling of independence which possesses us all shows there is something in us besides mind and body. The soul that reigns within is independent and creates the desire for freedom. If we are not free, how can we hope to make the world better? We hold that human progress is the result of the action of the human spirit. What the world is, and what we ourselves are, are the fruits of the freedom of the spirit.[3]

The education of man begins with the education of spirituality. It is that education which makes a cohesion between He and we. It is that education of spirituality that the Impersonal is manifested in every individual. Therefore, man is never isolated from the Impersonal Being who is none but himself. This also leads to that education of spirituality by which man understands the spirit of oneness— the oneness of the universe. This education of spirituality in terms of oneness of the universe provides man with infinite strength which brings about a revolutionary change. In the words of Vivekananda:

Every one is but a manifestation of that Impersonal, the basis of all being, and misery consists in thinking of ourselves as different from this Infinite, Impersonal Being; and liberation consists in knowing our unity with this wonderful Impersonality.

** ** ** **

It is only through the idea of the Impersonal God that you can have any system of ethics. In every nation the truth has been preached from the most ancient times—love your fellow-beings as yourselves— I mean, love human beings as yourselves. In India it has been preached, "love all beings as yourselves"; we make no distinction between men and animals. But no reason was forthcoming, no one knew why it would be good to love other beings as ourselves. And the reason, why, is there in the idea of the Impersonal God; you understand it when you learn that the whole world is one— the oneness of the universe— the solidarity of all life— that in hurting any one I am hurting myself, in loving any one I am loving myself. Hence we understand why it is that we ought not to hurt others. The reason for ethics, therefore, can only be had from this ideal of the Impersonal God. Then there is the question of the position of the Personal God in it. I understand the wonderful flow of love that comes from the idea of a Personal God, I thoroughly appreciate the power and potency of Bhakti on men to suit the needs of different times. What we now want in our country, however, is not so much of weeping, but a little strength. What a mine of strength is this Impersonal God, when all superstitions have been thrown overboard, and man stands on his feet with the knowledge— I am the Impersonal Being in the world! What can make me afraid? I care not even for nature's laws. Death is a joke to me.[4]

The lesson of spirituality as above should start in man right from childhood. This will make every child to be a lover of purity and freedom, strong and all-conquering. This will also enable every child independent, self-conscious, self-conquering and self-supportive for learning 'the glory of the soul' which is the essence of spirituality. As Vivekananda strongly advocates:

Whatever you think, that you will be. If you think yourselves weak, weak you will be; if you think yourselves strong, strong you will be; if you think yourselves impure, impure you will be; if you think yourselves pure, pure you will be. This teaches us not to think ourselves weak, but as strong, omnipotent, omniscient. No matter that I have not expressed it yet, it is in me. All knowledge is in me, all power, all purity, and all freedom.

Why cannot I express this knowledge? Because I do not believe in it, and it must and will come out. This is what the idea of the Impersonal teaches. Make your children strong from their very childhood; teach them not weakness, nor forms, but make them strong; let them stand on their feet— bold, all-conquering, all-suffering; and first of all, let them learn of the glory of the soul. That you get alone in the Vedanta— and there alone. It has ideas of love and worship and other things which we have in other religions, and more besides; but this idea of the soul is the life-giving thought, the most wonderful. There and there alone is the great thought that is going to revolutionise the world and reconcile the knowledge of the material world with religion.[5]

The new role of the fusion between education and spirituality must welcome a regeneration of spiritual consciousness among the teachers and the taught. What is very important in the education of spirituality is the endless pursuit of quickening of impulse. This alone would lead to the desirable exercise of higher thoughts leading to the understanding and appreciation of the true nature of the soul. As a matter of fact, what is education but an unending quest for knowing the essence of spirituality translated in the natural and spontaneous exercise of inwardness?

For a new dawn of education for spiritual awareness and vice versa, what we think and know should definitely undergo a constant scanning through transfer and transcendence of the essence of spirituality. In that case, books will hardly serve our purpose. Vivekananda adroitly elucidates this point and welcomes religion as a positive and allied tool:

Whatever we are now is the result of our acts and thoughts in the past; and whatever we shall be in the future will be the result of what we think and do now. But this, the shaping of our own destinies, does not preclude our receiving help from outside; nay, in the vast majority of cases such help is absolutely necessary. When it comes, the higher powers and possibilities of the soul are quickened, spiritual life is awakened, growth is animated, and man becomes holy and perfect in the end.

This quickening impulse cannot be derived from books. The soul can only receive impulses from another soul, and from nothing else. We may study books all our lives, we may become very intellectual, but in the end we find that we have not developed at all spiritually. It is not true that a high order of intellectual development always goes hand in hand with a proportionate development of the spiritual side in Man. In studying books we are sometimes deluded into thinking that thereby we are being spiritually helped; but if we analyse the effect of the study of books on ourselves, we shall find that at the utmost it is only our intellect that derives profit from such studies, and not our inner spirit. This inadequacy of books to quicken spiritual growth is the reason why, although almost every one can speak most wonderfully on spiritual matters, when it comes to action and the living of a truly spiritual life, we find ourselves so awfully deficient. To quicken the spirit, the impulse must come from another soul.

The person from whose soul such impulse comes is called the Guru— the teacher; and the person to whose soul the impulse is conveyed is called the Shishya— the student. To convey such an impulse to any soul, in the first place, the soul from which it proceeds must possess the power of transmitting it, as it were, to another; and in the second place, the soul to which it is transmitted must be fit to receive it. The seed must be a living seed, and the field must be ready ploughed; and when both these conditions are fulfilled, a wonderful growth of genuine religion takes place. "The true preacher of religion has to be of wonderful capabilities, and clever shall his hearer be"— ashcharyang vakta kushalohasya lavdha; *and when both of these are really wonderful and extraordinary, then will a splendid spiritual awakening result, and not otherwise. Such alone are the real teachers, and such alone are also the real students, the real aspirants. All others are only playing with spirituality. They have just a little curiosity awakened, just a little intellectual aspiration kindled in them, but are merely standing on the outward fringe of the horizon of religion. There is no doubt some value even in that, as it may in course of time result in the awakening of a real thirst for religion; and it is a mysterious law of nature that as soon as the field is ready, the seed* must *and does come; as soon as the soul earnestly desires to have religion, the transmitter of the religious force* must *and does appear to help that soul. When the power that attracts the light of religion in the receiving soul is full and strong, the power which answers to that attraction and sends in light does come as a matter of course.*[6]

The education of spirituality in man necessitates the cultivation of *ojas,* the highest of all human energies. This education enables him to to be true to chastity, one of the greatest components contributing to the culture of spirituality. It is the innermost energy in man aspiring for fullness and efflorescence of spirituality. The Yogis are devoted to this because this leads to being a spiritual visionary. Indeed, it makes a harmonious blending of intellect and spirituality.

Vivekananda emphasises on the culture of *ojas* which normally lies dormant in every human being. The education of the cultivation of spirituality is assured in exercising this inner force in man. As he explicitly points out:

> *The Yogis claim that of all the energies that are in the human body the highest is what they call "Ojas". Now this ojas is stored up in the brain, and the more ojas is in a man's head, the more powerful he is, the more intellectual, the more spiritually strong. One man may speak beautiful language and beautiful thoughts, but they do not impress people; another man speaks neither beautiful language nor beautiful thoughts, yet his words charm. Every movement of his is powerful. That is the power of Ojas.*
>
> *Now in every man there is more or less of this Ojas stored up. All the forces that are working in the body in their highest become Ojas. You must remember that it is only a question of transformation. The same force which is working outside as electricity or magnetism will become changed into inner force; the same forces that are working as muscular energy will be changed into Ojas. The Yogis say that that part of the human energy which is expressed as sex energy, in sexual thought, when checked and controlled, easily becomes changed into Ojas, and as the Muladhara guides these, the Yogi pays particular attention to that centre. He tries to take up all his sexual energy and convert it into Ojas. It is only the chaste man or woman who can make the Ojas rise and store it in the brain; that is why chastity has always considered the highest virtue. A man feels*

that if he is unchaste, spirituality goes away, he loses mental vigour and moral stamina. That is why in all the religious orders in the world which have produced spiritual giants you will always find absolute chastity insisted upon.[7]

Vivekananda reminds us of the fact that the study of man in the light of God leads us to excellence in spirituality. Man's quest for goodness must be enriched with spirituality; otherwise, goodness loses its essence and luminousness, cadence and poignance. All our pitfalls and inconsistencies acting as deterrents to goodness await an ardent pursuit to goodness in the light of spirituality.

The surest means for man to eradicate evil and welcome goodness is to devote to spiritual excellence. The more refined his endeavour on this point is, the more is the possibility of marching ahead towards the apposite direction of ascent towards spiritual marvels. As Vivekananda characteristically observes:

Man is an infinite circle whose circumference is nowhere, but the centre is located in one spot; and God is an infinite circle whose circumference is nowhere, but whose centre is everywhere. He works through all hands, sees through all eyes, walks on all feet, breathes through all bodies, lives in all life, speaks through every mouth, and thinks through every brain. Man cannot become like God and acquire control over the whole universe if he multiplies infinitely his centre of self-consciousness. Consciousness, therefore, is the chief thing to understand. Let us say that here is an infinite line amid darkness. We do not see the line, but on it there is one luminous point which moves on. As it moves along the line, it lights up its different parts in succession, and all that is left behind becomes dark again. Our consciousness may well be likened to this luminous point. Its past experiences have been replaced by the present, or have become subconscious. We are not aware of their presence in us; but there they are, unconsciously influencing our body and mind. Every movement that is now being made without the help of consciousness was previously conscious. Sufficient impetus has been given to it to work of itself.

The great error in all ethical systems, without exception, has been the failure of teaching the means by which man could refrain from doing the evil. All the systems of ethics teach, "Do not steal" very good; but why does a man steal? Because all stealing, robbing and other evil actions, as a rule, have become automatic. The systematic robber, thief, liar, unjust man and woman, are all these in spite of themselves! It is really a tremendous psychological problem. We should look upon man in the most charitable light. It is not so easy to be good. What are you but mere machines until you are free? Should you be proud because you are good? Certainly not. You are good because you cannot help it. Another is bad because he cannot help it. If you were in this position, who knows what you would have been? The woman in the street, or the thief in the jail, is the Christ that is being sacrificed that you may be a good man. Such is the law of balance. All the thieves and the murderers, all the unjust, the weakest, the wickedest, the devils, they all are my Christ! I owe a worship to the God Christ and to the demon Christ! That is my doctrine, I cannot help it. My salutation goes to the feet of the good, the saintly, and to the feet of the wicked and the devilish! They are all my teachers, all are my spiritual fathers, all are my Saviours.[8]

The education of spirituality with which man ought to be enlightened is the lesson of self-divinity. It is the lesson of *Tat Tvam Asi*—That Thou art. This is the supreme truth, the supreme identity of man. This eliminates all fear and futility, care and anxiety, and leads man to become the owner of the Kingdom of fullness and freedom.

Vivekananda explains the fact as above in the light of introducing the role of the Self of man:

The Self is the illuminator, and the mind is the instrument in its hands, and through that instrument. It gets hold of the external instrument, and thus comes perception. The external instruments get hold of the impressions and carry them to the organs, for you must remember always, that the eyes and ears are only receivers — it is the internal organs, the brain centres, which act. In Sanskrit these centres are called Indriyas, and they carry sensations to the mind, and the mind presents them further back to another state of the mind, which in Sanskrit is called Chitta, and there they are organised into will, and all these present them to the King of kings inside, the Ruler on His throne, the Self of man. He then sees and gives His orders. Then the mind immediately acts on the organs, and the organs on the external body. The real Perceiver, the real Ruler, the Governor, the Creator, the Manipulator of all this, is the Self of man.

> *We see, then, that the Self of man is not the body, neither is It thought. It cannot be a compound. Why not? Because everything that is a compound can be seen or imagined. That which we cannot imagine or perceive, which we cannot bind together, is not force or matter, cause or effect, and cannot be a compound. The domain of compounds is only so far as our mental universe, our thought universe extends. Beyond this it does not hold good; it is as far as law reigns, and if there is anything beyond law, it cannot be a compound at all. The Self of man being beyond the law of causation, is not a compound. It is ever free and is the Ruler of everything that is within law. It will never die, because death means going back to the component parts, and that which was never a compound can never die. It is sheer nonsense to say It dies.*[9]

In the light of the above, Vivekananda further extends and clarifies our vision of the Self. It is the all pervading, eternal, free, all powerful entity of One Being. It neither fears birth nor death, nor anxiety, nor happiness, nor sorrow. It is ever victorious. As Vivekananda categorically asserts and inspires us with the spiritual vision and grandeur of One Self:

> *You are the omniscient, omnipresent being of the universe. But of such beings can there be many? Can there be a hundred thousand millions of omnipresent beings? Certainly not. Then, what becomes of us all? You are only one, there is only one such Self, and that One Self is you. Standing behind this little nature is what we call the Soul. There is only One Being, One Existence, the ever-blessed, the omnipresent, the omniscient, the birthless, the deathless. "Through His control the sky expands, through His control the air breathes, through His control the sun shines, and through His control all live. He is the Reality in nature, He is the Soul of your soul, nay, more, you are He, you are one with Him." wherever there are two, there is fear, there is danger, there is conflict, there is strife. When it is all One, who is there to hate, who is there to struggle with? When it is all He, with whom can you fight? This explains the true nature of life; this explains the*

true nature of being. This is perfection, and this is God. As long as you see the many, you are under delusion. "In this world of many he who sees the One, in this ever-changing world he who sees Him who never changes, as the Soul of his own soul, as his own Self, he is free, he is blessed, he has reached the goal." Therefore know that thou art He; thou art the God of this universe, "Tat Tvam Asi" (That thou art). All these various ideas that I am a man or a woman, or sick or healthy, or strong or weak, or that I hate or I love, or have a little power, are but hallucinations. Away with them! What makes you weak? What makes you fear? You are the One Being in the universe. What frightens you? Stand up then and be free.[10]

Vivekananda's vibrant vision of spirituality with which he glorifies man as One Being heightens the spirit of human consciousness. That consciousness indicates a greater truth, a better existence and a truer reality of man: he is divinely spiritual. The education of spirituality in this light of promise and poignance prepares man to ardently become 'a messenger of Light'. In the soul-stirring words of Vivekananda:

I should better like that each one of you became a Prophet of this real New Testament, which is made up of all the Old Testaments. Take all the old messages, supplement them with your own realisations, and become a Prophet unto others. Each one of these Teachers has been great; each has left something for us; they have been our Gods. We salute them, we are their servants; and, all the same, we salute ourselves; for if they have been Prophets and Children of God, we also are the same. They reached their perfection, and we are going to attain ours now. Remember the words of Jesus. "The Kingdom of Heaven is at hand!" This very moment let every one of us make a staunch resolution: "I will become a Prophet, I will become a messenger of Light, I will become "a Child of God, nay, I will become a God!"[11]

The new concept spirituality in the light of education welcomes the truth of the eternity of the Atman through the education of the eternity of the soul. So it is necessary to know the difference between the gross body and the spiritual body in relation to the soul which is eternal. This will broaden our vision of spirituality in all transparency. Vivekananda explains this fact in a very simplified way:

The soul must also be eternal. Why? In the first place we see that the soul is not matter. It is neither a gross body, nor a fine body, which we call mind or thought. It is neither a physical body, nor what in Christianity is called a spiritual body. It is the gross body and the spiritual body that are liable to change. The gross body is liable to change almost every minute and dies, but the spiritual body endures through long periods, until one becomes free, when it also falls away. When a man becomes free, the spiritual body disperses. The gross body disintegrates every time a man dies. The soul not being made of any particles must be indestructible. What do we mean by destruction? Destruction is disintegration of the materials out of which anything is composed. If this glass is broken into pieces, the materials will disintegrate, and that will be the destruction of the glass. Disintegration of particles is what we mean by destruction. It naturally follows that nothing that is not composed of particles can be destroyed, can ever be disintegrated. The soul is not composed of any materials. It is unity indivisible. Therefore, it must be indestructible. For the same reasons it must also be without any beginning. So the soul is without any beginning and end.[12]

Vivekananda also extends the vision of spirituality with the concept of God as an inseparable part of the soul. The study of the cause-effect relationship between God and the universe ultimately leading to the truth that the soul is the part of God and vice versa consolidates our education in terms of spirituality. The infinity of soul and God as unchangeable makes the learning of spirituality very serene and poignant.

By means of referring to a very day-to-day experience, Vivekananda comes to this logical and valid conclusion that the concept of God becomes really very clear and explicit from the study of cause-effect relationship between the soul and God:

God being the cause of the projection, the continuance, and the dissolution of the universe, the cause must be present to produce the effect. Not only so, the cause becomes the effect. Glass is produced out of certain materials and certain forces used by the manufacturer. In the glass there are those forces plus the materials. The forces used have become the force of adhesion, and if that force goes, the glass will fall to pieces; the materials also are undoubtedly in the glass. Only their form is changed. The cause has become the effect. Wherever you see an effect you can always analyse it into a cause, the cause manifests itself as the effect. It follows, if God is the cause of the universe, and the universe is the effect, that God has become the universe. If souls are the effect, and God the cause, God has become the souls. Each soul, therefore, is a part of God. "As from a mass of fire an infinite number of sparks fly, even so from the Eternal One all this universe of souls has come out."[13]

What, then, should be the best endeavour on our part to have the most significant and worthwhile spiritual education? How should we strive for having the essence and excellence in spiritual ascent? Here is Vivekananda's eternally telling and vibrant answer:

Do not talk of the wickedness of the world and all its sins. Weep that you are bound to see wickedness yet. Weep that you are bound to see sin everywhere, and if you want to help the world, do not condemn it. Do not weaken it more. For what is sin and what is misery, and what are all these, but the results of weakness? The world is made weaker and weaker every day by such teachings. Men are taught from childhood that they are weak and sinners. Teach them that they are all glorious children of immortality, even those who are the weakest in manifestation. Let positive, strong, helpful thought enter into their brains from very childhood. Lay yourselves open to these thoughts, and not to weakening and paralysing ones. Say to your own minds, "I am He, I am He". Let it ring day and night in your minds like a song, and at the point of death declare, "I am He." That is the Truth; the infinite strength of the world is yours. Drive out the superstition that has covered your minds. Let us be brave. Know the Truth and practise the Truth. The goal may be distant, but awake, arise, and stop not till the goal is reached.[14]

The message of spirituality is unity. It is unity of thought and action, contemplation and realisation leading to the infinite discovery of man the ever unknown but never lost in abstraction and inconsistencies, silence and ambiguity. In making such a discovery by means of inwardness and excellence, man must strive very hard to realise that elimination of the self in order to be blessed with the more enlightened soul is the most positive approach to tread on the right track of spirituality. His business is to turn his little "I" into the great "You" and devote all his thoughts and actions for better and more refined fusion between the two.

Unity for every action in tune with unity of minds leads man towards spirituality. Nevertheless, it is an unending process, but the quest must be an ardent and positive one to uphold the great vision of man the ever unknown , the ever spiritual and the ever positive in the efflorescence of the lotus land, as it were, of inward excellence. Vivekananda vibrantly shows us the way:

> *It is the finding of a unity towards which we are all going. Every action of our lives— the most material, the grossest as well as the finest, the highest, the most spiritual— is alike tending towards this one ideal, the finding of unity. A man is single. He marries. Apparently it may be a selfish act, but at the same time, the impulsion, the motive power, is to find that unity. He has children, he has friends, he loves his country, he loves the world, and ends by loving the whole universe. Irresistibly we are impelled towards that perfection which consists in finding the unity, killing this little self and making ourselves broader and broader. This is the goal, the end towards which the universe is rushing. Every atom is trying to go and join itself to the next atom. Atoms after atoms combine, making huge balls, the earths, the suns, the moons, the stars, the planets. They, in their turn, are trying to rush towards each other, and, at last, we know that the whole universe, mental and material, will be fused into one.*
>
> *The process that is going on in the cosmos on a large scale, is the same as that going on in the microcosm on a smaller scale. Just as the universe has its existence in separation, in distinction, and all the while is rushing towards unity, non-separation, so in our little worlds, each soul is born, as it were, cut off from the rest of the world. The more ignorant, the more enlightened the soul, the more it thinks that it is separate from the rest of the universe. The more ignorant the person, the more he thinks, he will die or will be born, and so forth— ideas that are an expression of this separateness. But we find that, as knowledge comes, man grows, morality is evolved, and the idea of non-separateness begins. Whither men understand it or not, they are impelled by*

that power behind to become unselfish. That is the foundation of all morality. It is the quintessence of all ethics, preached in any language, or in any religion, or by any prophet in the world. "Be thou unselfish", "Not 'I', but 'thou'"— that is the background of all ethical codes. And what is meant by this is the recognition of non-individuality— that you are a part of me, and I of you; the recognition that in hurting you I hurt myself, and in helping you I help myself; the recognition that there cannot possibly be death for me when you live. When one worm lives in this universe, how can I die? For my life is the life of that worm. At the same time it will teach us that we cannot leave one of our fellow-beings without helping him, that in his good consists my good.[15]

The symphony of aesthetics and spirituality which is vital to excellence and ascent is the true identity of man. For this enviable identity man must have faith in God which inevitably leads to truth and morality from a new angle of spiritual attainment. To restore truth and faith is to kindle the lamp of spirituality already in man. Vivekananda explicitly unfolds this vision of spirituality:

All great teachers have taught, "Resist not evil," that non-resistance is the highest moral ideal. We all know that, if a certain number of us attempted to put that maxim fully into practice, the whole socio fabric would fall to pieces, the wicked would take possession of our properties and our lives, and would do whatever they liked with us. Even if only one day of such resistance were practised, it would lead to disaster. Yet, intuitively, in our heart of hearts we feel the truth of the teaching "Resist not evil." This seems to us to be the highest ideal; yet to teach this doctrine only would be equivalent to condemning a vast portion of mankind. Not only so, it would be making men feel that they were always doing wrong, and cause in them scruples of conscience in all their actions; it would weaken them, and that constant self-disapproval would breed more vice than any other weakness would. To the man who has begun to hate himself the gate to degeneration has already opened; and the same is true of a nation.

Our first duty is not to hate ourselves, because to advance we must have faith in ourselves first and then in God. Therefore,

> *the only alternative remaining to us is to recognise that duty and morality vary under different circumstances; not that the man who resists evil is doing what is always and in itself wrong, but that in the different circumstances in which he is placed it may become even his duty to resist evil.*[16]

A radical and iconoclastic spiritual thinker, Vivekananda refines the vision of man in spirituality and vice versa. He unfolds truth as it actually means and delivers it from the standpoint of the march of man in search of spirituality. He heightens and glorifies man because the latter alone knows how to translate the concept of the infinite and the unknown, reality and existence in terms of spiritual advancement. He also ennobles man who alone can prove that the whole world is nothing but the reflection of One Eternal Being, the spiritual one, the Atman.

As a profound exponent of spirituality, Vivekananda elucidates the role of man in the light of Advaita philosophy. He wards off all forms of superstitions from which man suffers and heralds the glory of the Atman, the Self:

> *We are like little, weak plants, always wanting a support. How many times I have been asked for a "comfortable religion!" Very few men ask for the truth, fewer still dare to learn the truth, and fewest of all dare to follow it in all its practical bearings. It is not their fault; it is all weakness of the brain. Any new thought, especially of a high kind, creates a disturbance, tries to make a new channel, as it were, in the brain matter, and that unhinges the system, throws men off their balance. They are used to certain surroundings, and have to overcome a huge mass of ancient superstitions, ancestral superstition, class superstition, city superstition, country superstition, and behind all, the vast mass of superstition that is innate in every human being. Yet there are a few brave souls in the world who dare to conceive the truth, who dare to take it up, and who dare to follow it to the end.*[17]

The truth for which man strives is the essence of spirituality. It is the truth that shows him the avenue of realisation of freedom in the true sense of the term. It is truth, again, that shows him the avenue of realisation of the 'one real Self'. Unless man arrives at this truth, spirituality becomes an abstraction. Therefore, the Self in the self becomes the identity of the spiritual man. And the spiritual man alone is the embodiment of 'one real Self'.

Vivekananda significantly upholds spirituality in the light of the above. He wants man to project according to his own freedom of thought and action till, through continuous crystallisation of freedom by self-realisation, the aura of spirituality flashes in eternal splendour of extinction of personality and extends welcome to the Innermost One:

> *The God of heaven becomes the God in nature, and the God in nature becomes the God who is nature, and the God who is nature becomes the God within this temple of the body, and the God dwelling in the temple of the body at last becomes the temple itself, becomes the soul and man— and there it reaches the last word it can teach. He whom the sages have been seeking in all these places is in our own hearts; the voice that you heard was right, says the Vedanta, but the direction you gave to the voice was wrong. That ideal of freedom that you perceived was correct, but you projected it outside yourself, and that was your mistake. Bring it nearer and nearer, until you find that it was all the time within you, it was the Self of your own self. That freedom was your own nature, and this Maya never bound you. Nature never has power over you. Like a frightened child you were dreaming that it was throttling you, and the release from this fear is the goal; not only to see it intellectually, but to perceive it, actualise it, much more definitely than we perceive the world. Then we shall know that we are free. Then, and then alone, will all difficulties vanish, then will all the perplexities of heart be smoothed away, all crookedness made straight, then will vanish the delusion of manifoldness and nature; and Maya, instead of being a horrible, hopeless dream, as it is now, will become beautiful, and this earth, instead of being a prison-house, will become our playground; and even dangers and difficulties, even all sufferings, will become deified and show us their real nature, will show us that behind everything, as the substance of everything, He is standing, and that He is the one real Self.*[18]

The study of man in terms of spirituality is more often than not confusing to us. This is due to the fact that we fail to accept the existence of another body within the body as such, which never dies. It is called "the spiritual body" as St Paul names it or "the seed of the new body" as Vivekananda calls it. To know the real Self, the inner mind, the mind beyond, looks forward to the endless endeavour of man.

Elucidating the real nature of the mind in relation to the Self, Vivekananda clarifies the vision of man in quest of spirituality:

> *When a man dies, the body dies; but a little bit of the mind, the seed, is left when all else is shattered; and this is the seed of the new body called by St Paul "the spiritual body". This theory of the materiality of the mind accords with all modern theories. The idiot is lacking in intelligence because his mind-stuff is injured. Intelligence cannot be in matter nor can it be produced by any combinations of matter. Where then is intelligence? It is behind matter; it is the Jiva, the real Self, working through the instrument of matter. Transmission of force is not possible without matter, and as the Jiva cannot travel alone, some part of the mind is left as a transmitting medium when all else is shattered by death.*
>
> ** ** ** **
>
> *What is true of the external mind must also apply to the internal world. Mind also wants to know itself, but this Self can only be known through the medium of the mind and is, like the wall, unknown. This self we may call Y, and the statement would then be , Y plus mind is the inner self. Kant was the first to arrive at this analysis of mind, but it was long ago stated in the Vedas. We have thus, as it were, mind standing between X and Y and reacting on both.*[19]

The quest excellence in spirituality is a matter of inner refinement, and that refinement must guarantee refinement of culture. It is superior culture that always bears the stamp of catholicity of vision. And this catholicity of vision is another name for refinement of culture that leads us towards spiritual excellence.

The culture of oneness of the world that serves as a significant component of exercise of spirituality is in reality an absence of difference between the material and the spiritual or between the mental and spiritual entities of man. Man becomes a true worshipper of culture only when he makes a fusion, thereby arriving at a definite and desirable idea of culture by dint of assimilating realisation of the Absolute Reality. This also leads spirituality towards excellence and paves the avenue of the beyond.

The man in quest of spirituality, therefore, devotes more to excellence in the exercise of culture that is a harmonious blending of transparency and transfer, prudence and poignance. It is the unending quest for the truth that places man as real and infinite simultaneously and spontaneously. It is the real culture of man. Pointing out the life of man, Vivekananda elucidates this point very characteristically:

> *Life is only a vibration. That which vibrates this ocean of ether, vibrates you. Just as in a lake, various strata of ice of various degrees of solidity are formed, or as in an ocean of vapour there are various degrees of density, so is this universe an ocean of matter. This is an ocean of ether in which we find the sun, moon, stars, and ourselves— in different states of solidity; but the continuity is not broken; it is the same throughout.*
>
> *Now, when we study metaphysics, we come to know the world is one, not that the spiritual, the material, the mental, and the world of energies are separate. It is all one, but seen from different planes of vision. When you think of yourself as a body, you forget that you are a mind, and when you think of yourself as a mind, you will forget the body. There is only one thing, that you are; you can see it either as matter or body— or you can see it as mind or spirit. Birth, life, and death are but old superstitions. None was ever born, none will ever die; one changes one's position— that is all. I am sorry to see in the West how much they make of death: always trying to catch a little life. "Give us life after death! Give us life!" They are so happy if anybody tells them that they are going to live afterwards! How can I ever doubt such a thing! How can I imagine that I am dead! Try to think of yourself as dead, and you will see that you are present to see your own dead body. Life is such a wonderful reality that you cannot for a moment forget it. You may as well doubt that you exist. This is the first fact of consciousness— I am. Who can imagine a state of things which never existed? It is the most self-evident of all truths. So, the idea of immortality is inherent in man. How can one discuss a subject that is unimaginable? Why should we want to discuss the* pros *and* cons *of a subject that is self-evident?*
>
> *The whole universe, therefore, is a unit, from whatever standpoint you view it. Just now, to us, this universe is a unit of*

Prana and Akasha, force and matter. And mind you, like all other basic principles, this is also self-contradictory. For what is force? – that which moves matter. And what is matter? – that which is moved by force. It is a see-saw! Some of the fundamentals of our reasoning are most curious, in spite of our boast of science and knowledge. "It is a headache without a head", as the Sanskrit proverb says. This state of things is called Maya. It has neither existence nor non-existence. You cannot call it existence, because that only exists which is beyond time and space, which is self-existence. Yet this world satisfies to a certain degree our idea of existence. Therefore, it has apparent existence.

But there is a real existence in and through everything; and that reality, as it were, is caught in the meshes of time, space, and causation. There is the real man, the infinite, the beginningless, the endless, the ever-blessed, the ever-free. He has been caught in the meshes of time, space, and causation. So has everything in this world.[20]

The realisation of man in terms of culture is that he is a spirit, and nothing but spirit. This realisation is his spiritual identity, his religion crystallised in spirituality. This is the only way to honour and heighten religion par excellence for spiritual culture. In the words of Vivekananda:

Our actions are not of the soul and can therefore be impure. It is our spirit that becomes perfect and holy. There is no resting place for the soul. It has no material qualities. Man assumes the perfect state when he realises he is a spirit. Religion is the manifestation of the soul nature. The deeper they see is what makes one holier than another. Worship is feeling the holiness of God. Our religion does not believe in missions and teaches that man should love God for love's sake and his neighbour in spite of himself. The people of the West struggle too hard; repose is a factor of civilisation. We do not lay our infirmities to God. There is a tendency toward a union of religions.[21]

The culture of man is to be true to spirituality, and to be true to spirituality is to be a master in winning over every situation under any position. It is a test of his identity in terms of altruism. If he succeeds in the test , it means he is blessed with the blessings of culture. If, on the other hand, he fails, it indicates that he must redefine his culture and renew his spiritual mission and vision in terms of more crystallised sensibilities derived from transparent objectives and selfless involvements.

Referring to the Upanishads, Vivekananda explains the role of man in terms of the culture of spirituality in a very simplified way:

> *I have found the most curious fact. You have a certain idea and you do not want to have it, and you think of something else, and the idea you want to suppress is entirely suppressed. What is that idea? I saw it come out in fifteen minutes. It came out and staggered me. It was strong, and it came in such a violent and terrible fashion [that] I thought here was a mad man. And when it was over, all that had happened [was a suppression of the previous emotion]. What came out? It was my own bad impression which had to be worked out. ... "Nature will have her way. What can suppression do?" That is a terrible statement in the Gita it seems it may be a vain struggle after all. You may have a hundred thousand [urges competing] at the same time. You may repress [them], but the moment the spring rebounds, the whole thing is there again.*
>
> *[But there is hope]. If you are powerful enough, you can divide your consciousness into twenty parts all at the same time. I am changing my psychology. Mind grows. That is what the Yogis say. There is one passion and it rouses another, and the first one dies. If you are angry, and then happy, the next moment the anger passes away. Out of that anger you manufactured the next state. These states are always interchangeable. Eternal happiness and misery are a child's dream. The Upanishads point out that the goal of man is neither misery nor happiness, but we have to be master of that out of which these are manufactured. We must be masters of the situation at its very root, as it were.*[22]

To control the mind is to enter into the altar, as it were, of culture. As soon as one enters into the altar of culture, one enjoys the warmth and blessings of spirituality. Then calmness comes and restlessness bids farewell. Then goodness prevails and evil is forgotten. But for this exercise of the culture of spirituality, one must ardently exercise two things—one is faith, and the other, quietude.

Prior to exercising faith and quietude, man must be tolerant. This component serves as the key point of culture and spiritual depth of vision. Vivekananda elucidates the relation between the spiritual ascent of man in terms of the exercise of these components that enrich culture:

> *No spiritual knowledge is possible so long as the mind is restless and out of control. The disciple has to learn to control the mind. Yes, it is the function of the mind to think, but it must not think if the disciple does not want it to; it must stop thinking when he commands it to. To qualify as a disciple, this state of the mind is very necessary.*
>
> *Also, the disciple must have great power of endurance. Life seems comfortable; and you find the mind behaves well when everything is going well with you. But if something goes wrong, your mind loses its balance. That is not good. Bear all evil and misery without one murmur of hurt, without one thought of unhappiness, resistance, remedy, or retaliation. That is true endurance; and that you must acquire.*
>
> *Good and evil there always are in the world. Many forget there is any evil— at least they try to forget; and when evil comes upon them, they are overwhelmed bu it and feel bitter. There are others who deny that there is any evil at all and consider everything good. That also is a weakness; that also proceeds from a fear of evil. If something is evil-smelling, why sprinkle it with rose-water and call it fragrant? Yes, there are good and evil in the world—God has put evil in the world. But you do not have to whitewash Him. Why there is evil is none of your business. Please have faith and keep quiet.*[23]

The essence of culture is the dawn of spirituality. It is that culture which takes every affair of life in the spirit of endurance. Endurance and concentration as pointers to the path of spirituality go hand in hand. They are inseparable in the light of spiritual efflorescence.

Referring to the incomparable and extraordinary spiritual power of Shri Ramkrishna, and the eternal emblem of endurance as the culture of spirituality of Jesus Christ, Vivekananda inspires us to uphold and practise the spirit of endurance as the spiritual culture to rise above physical life, give up all illusion and dedicate ourselves wholeheartedly to the service of the All Good:

> *He (Shri Ramakrishna) refused to think of body and illness. His mind was continually conscious of God; it was dedicated to Him utterly. He would not use it for any other purpose.*

This craving for health, wealth, long life, and the like— the so-called good— is nothing but an illusion. To devote the mind to them in order to secure them only strengthens the delusion. We have these dreams and illusions in life, and we want to have more of them in the life to come, in heaven. More and more illusion. Resist not evil. Face it! You are higher than evil.

There is this misery in the world— it has to be suffered by someone. You cannot act without making evil for somebody. And when you seek worldly good, you only avoid an evil which must be suffered by somebody else. Everyone is trying to put it on somebody else's shoulders. The disciple says, "Let the miseries of the world come on me; I shall endure them all. Let others go free."

Remember the man on the cross. He could have brought legions of angels to victory; but he did not resist. He pitied those who crucified him. He endured every humiliation and suffering. He took the burden of all upon himself: "Come unto me, all ye that labour and are heavy laden, and I will give you rest." Such is true endurance. How very high he was above this life, so high that we cannot understand it, we slaves! No sooner does a man slap me in the face than my hand hits back: bang, it goes! How can I understand the greatness and blessedness of the Glorified One? How can I see the glory of it?[24]

What, then, should be the role of man in terms of exercising spirituality? How should man be the most successful follower of spiritual essence and values? Should he be trapped in the web of worldliness, or should he continually strive for that spirituality that stands for renunciation— the lotus land of unworldliness?

India has from time immemorial nurtured the culture of spirituality where man becomes glorious through pursuit of renunciation or unworldliness. It is the culture that believes and acts upon 'the spiritualisation of the human race' as Vivekananda reminds us. He advances a step further in making a harmonious relationship between spirituality and assimilation of man irrespective of caste, creed, colour, race, religion etc. whatsoever and howsoever. In explaining India's message to the world through the Vedanta, he poignantly observes:

Ay, a glorious destiny, my brethren, for as far back as the days of the Upanishads we have thrown the challenge to the world: Na prajaya dhanena tyagenaike amritatvamanasuh— *"Not by progeny, not by wealth, but by renunciation immortality is reached." Race after race has taken the challenge up and tried their utmost to solve the world-riddle on the plane of desires. They have all failed in the past—the old ones have become extinct under the weight of wickedness and misery, which lust for power and gold brings in its train, and the new ones are tottering to their fall. The question has yet to be decided whether peace will survive or war; whether patience will survive or non-forbearance; whether goodness will survive or wickedness; whether muscle will survive or brain; whether worldliness will survive or spirituality. We have solved our problem ages ago, and held on to it through good or evil fortune, and mean to hold on to it till the end of time. Our solution is unworldliness— renunciation. This is the theme of Indian life-work, the burden of her eternal songs, the backbone of her existence, the foundation of her being, the* raison d'etre *of her very existence— the spiritualisation of the human race. In this her life-course she has never deviated, whether the Tartar ruled or the Turk, whether the Mogul ruled or the English.*

And I challenge anybody to show one single period of her national life when India was lacking in spiritual giants capable of moving the world. But her work is spiritual, and that cannot be done with blasts of war-trumpets or the march of cohorts. Her influence has always fallen upon the world like that of the gentle dew, unheard and scarcely marked, yet bringing into bloom the fairest flowers of the earth. This influence, being in its nature gentle, would have to wait for a fortunate combination of circumstances, to go out of the country into other lands, though it never ceased to work within the limits of its native land. As such, every educated person knows that whenever the empire-building Tartar or Persian or Greek or Arab brought this land in contact with the outside world, a mass of spiritual influence has immediately flooded the world from here. The very same circumstances have presented themselves once more before us. The English high roads over land and sea and the wonderful power manifested by the inhabitants of that little island have once more brought India in contact with the rest of the world,

> *and the same work has already begun. Mark my words, this is but the small beginning, big things are to follow; what the result of the present work outside India will be I cannot exactly state, but this I know for certain that millions, I say deliberately, millions in every civilised land are waiting for the message that will save them from the hideous abyss of materialism into which modern money-worship is driving them headlong, and many of the leaders of the new social movements have already discovered that Vedanta in its highest form can alone spiritualise their social aspirations.*[25]

Are we the true followers of Swami Vivekananda, the spiritual visionary in theory and practice par excellence?

1. Swami Vivekananda: *The Complete Works of Swami Vivekananda,* Advaita Ashrama, Calcutta, Mayavati Memorial Edition,1989, Vol. I, p. 429.
2. *Ibid.,* pp. 52-53.
3. *Ibid.,* Vol. IV, p. 190.
4. *Ibid., Vol.* III, pp. 129-130.
5. *Ibid.,* pp. 130-131.
6. *Ibid.,* pp. 45-46.
7. *Ibid.,* Vol. I, pp.169-170.
8. *Ibid.,* Vol. II, pp. 33-34.
9. *Ibid.,* pp. 233-234.
10. *Ibid.,* pp. 235-236.
11. *Ibid.,* Vol. IV, p. 134.
12. *Ibid.,* Vol. II, p. 428.
13. *Ibid.,* p. 429.
14. *Ibid.,* p. 87.
15. *Ibid.,* Vol. VI, pp. 4-6.
16. *Ibid.,* Vol. I, pp. 37-38.
17. *Ibid.,* Vol. II, p. 248.
18. *Ibid.,* pp. 128-129.
19. *Ibid.,* Vol. VI, pp. 42-43.
20. *Ibid.,* Vol. II, pp. 31-32.
21. *Ibid.,* pp. 478-479.
22. *Ibid.,* Vol. I, pp. 451-452.
23. *Ibid.,* Vol. VIII, p. 110.
24. *Ibid.,* p. 111.
25. *Ibid.,* Vol. IV, pp. 314-316.

Man and Aesthetics: Vivekananda's Essence of Elegance

Aesthetics is the core of efflorescence of man. It denotes man's identity for whatever signifies best and worthiest at every moment and from every direction. It also denotes the best path of fullness in Truth, Goodness and Beauty which are the essence of refinement intrinsic, extrinsic or otherwise for which man strives unendingly.

An unparalleled visionary of aesthetic ascent of man, Swami Vivekananda has always highlighted aesthetics in terms of the divine glory of man. This clearly stresses on man the ever divine with all endeavour directed towards greater and higher excellence till the lotus land of aesthetics is abloom with purity and solemnity, cadence and catholicity of sacrifice and service. Like a serene psycho-social visionary, he refines his social thoughts and experiments in terms of eternal kinship with the whole world where Truth stands as the hallmark of socio-aesthetics. The "I" in every man then becomes the genuine representative of "We" of the society near or far, small or big, with the promise and poignance of aesthetic grandeur. As he puts it:

> *The individual's life is the life of the whole, the individual's happiness is the happiness of the whole; apart from the whole, the individual's existence is inconceivable— this is an eternal truth and is the bed-rock on which the universe is built. To move slowly towards the finite whole, bearing a constant feeling of intense sympathy and sameness with it, being happy with its happiness and being distressed in its affliction, is the individual's sole duty. Not only is it his duty, but in its transgression is his death, while compliance with this great truth leads to life immortal. This is the law of nature, and who can throw dust into her ever-watchful eyes? None can hoodwink society and deceive it for any length of time. However much there may have accumulated heaps of refuse and mud on the surface of society —still, at the bottom of those heaps the life-breath of society is ever to be found pulsating in the vibrations*

> *of universal love and self-denying compassion for all. Society is like the earth that patiently bears incessant molestations; but she wakes up one day, however long that may be in coming, and the force of the shaking tremors of that awakening hurls off to a distance the accumulated dirt of self-seeking meanness piled up during millions of patient and silent years!*
>
> *We ignore this sublime truth; and though we suffer a thousand times for our folly, yet, in our absurd foolishness, impelled by the brute in us, we do not believe in it. We try to deceive, but a thousand times we find we are deceived ourselves, and yet we do not desist! Mad that we are, we imagine we can impose on nature! With our short-sighted vision we think ministering to the self at any cost as the be-all and end-all of life.*[1]

For a real quest for Truth as one of the most important components of aesthetics, Vivekananda inspires us to to be warriors against any form of evil. It might so happen that in waging a war against evil in order to bring forth the victory of Truth we would have to embrace defeat, but that does not mean a failure. Nor does it indicate the triumph of truth over evil outright because the value of truth is never-ending and ever challenging in order to be blessed with greater truth. A unique exponent of One Soul, One Existence and *Atman*, man is, as Vivekananda upholds, the epitome of aesthetic humanism:

> *"Know the truth and be free in a moment." All the darkness will then vanish. When man has seen himself as one with the Infinite Being of the universe, when all separateness is ceased, when all men and women, all gods and angels, all animals and plants, and the whole universe have melted into that Oneness, then all fear disappears. Can I hurt myself? Can I kill myself? Can I injure myself? Whom to fear? Can you fear yourself? Then will all sorrow disappear. What can cause me sorrow? I am the One Existence of the universe. Then all jealousies will disappear; of whom to be jealous? Of myself? Then all bad feelings disappear. Against whom can I have bad feeling? Against myself? There is none in the universe but I.*[2]

To be a master of oneself is to be in a position to control good and evil. To be as such is to know the real identity of man. Unless man explores his own identity in terms of the wonder of good and evil, the aesthetics of fullness becomes a myth. How to honour the Infinite Being? What are the minimum essentials for following the path of self-consciousness leading to self-ascent and excellence? Here are Vivekananda's invaluable practical pointers:

> *This is a world of good and evil. Wherever there is good, evil follows, but beyond and behind all these manifestations, all these contradictions, the Vedanta finds out that Unity. It says, "Give up what is evil and give up what is good." What remains then? Behind good and evil stands something which is yours, the real you, beyond every evil, and beyond every good too, and it is that which is manifesting itself as good and bad. Know that first, and then and then alone you will be a true optimist, and not before; for then you will be able to control everything. Control these manifestations and you will be at liberty to manifest the real "you". First be master of yourself, stand up and be free, go beyond the pale of these laws, for these laws do not absolutely govern you, they are only part of your being. First find out that you are not the slave of nature, never were and never will be; that this nature, infinite as you may think it, is only finite, a drop in the ocean, and your Soul is the ocean; you are beyond the stars, the sun, and the moon. They are like mere bubbles compared with your infinite being. Know that, and you will control both good and evil. Then alone the whole vision will change and you will stand up and say, "How beautiful is good and how wonderful is evil!"*
>
> *That is what the Vedanta teaches. It does not propose any slipshod remedy by covering wounds with gold leaf and the more the wound festers, putting on more gold leaf. This life is a hard fact; work your way through it boldly, though it may be adamantine; no matter, the soul is stronger. It lays no responsibility on little gods; for you are the makers of your own fortunes. You make yourselves suffer, you make good and evil, and it is you who put your hands before your eyes and say it is dark. Take your hands away and see the light; you are effulgent, you are perfect already, from the very beginning.*[3]

To be a man who believes and accordingly acts as one sincere to be perfect is the quintessence of Vivekananda's philosophy of aesthetics. He gives highest priority and honour to every man irrespective of power and position, action and inaction. He also emphasises on the irresistible will force of everyone under any circumstances to prove his incomparable worth as a human being because he is divine and loves to be as one ought to be to realise and translate Truth, Beauty and Goodness.

Simultaneously, Vivekananda also reminds us of the aesthetic truth of perfection, which we very often forget to realise:

> *However we may try, there cannot be any action which is perfectly pure or any which is perfectly impure, taking purity or impurity in the sense of injury or non-injury. We cannot breathe or live without injuring others, and every morsel of food that we eat is taken from another's mouth; our very lives are crowding out some other lives. It may be those of men, or animals, or small fungi, but someone somewhere we have to crowd out. That being the case, it naturally follows that perfection can never be attained by work. We may work through all eternity, but there will be no way out of this intricate maze; we may work on and on and on, but there will be no end.*[4]

Bearing earnestly in mind the aesthetics of perfection in terms of our unending action as above, we have no alternative but to find out the means by which we can love the world without having any self-interest. How to be aware of 'the gilded shadow of truth'? How to explore the *real* universe? How would we be aesthetically spiritual and vice versa? Here are Vivekananda's classic pointers:

> *Stand upon the Self, then only can we truly love the world. Take a very, very high stand; knowing out universal nature, we must look with perfect calmness upon all the* panorama *of the world. It is but baby's play, and we know that, so cannot be disturbed by it. If the mind is pleased with praise, it will be displeased with blame. All pleasures of the senses or even of the mind are evanescent; but within ourselves is the one true unrelated pleasure, dependent upon nothing. It is perfectly free, it is bliss.* The more our bliss is within, the more spiritual we are. *The pleasure of the Self is what the world calls religion.*
>
> *The internal universe, the* real, *is infinitely greater than the external, which is only a shadowy projection of the true one. The world is neither true nor untrue, it is the shadow of truth. "Imagination is the gilded shadow of truth", says the poet.*

We enter into creation, and then for us it becomes living. Things are dead in themselves; only we give them life, and then, like fools, we turn around and are afraid of them, or enjoy them. But be not like certain fisher-women, who, caught in a storm on their home from market, took refuge in the house of a florist. They were lodged for the night in a room next to the garden where the air was full of the fragrance of flowers. In vain did they try to rest, until one of their members suggested that they wet their fishy baskets and place them near their heads. Then they all fell into a sound sleep.[5]

Unfolding the real nature of the world in which we live, and the life we should lead aesthetically, Vivekananda further elucidates:

The world is our fish basket, we must not depend upon it for enjoyment. Those who do are the Tamasas or the bound. Then there are the Rajasas or the egotistical, who talk always about "I", "I". They do good work sometimes and may become spiritual. But the highest are the Sattvikas, the introspective, those who live only in the Self. These three qualities, Tamas, Rajas, and Sattva (idleness, activity, and illumination), are in everyone, and different ones predominate at different times.

Creation is not a "making" of something, it is the struggle the equilibrium, as when atoms of cork are thrown to the bottom of a pail of water and rush to rise to the top, singly or in clusters. Life is and must be accompanied by evil. *A little evil is the source of life; the little wickedness that is in the world is very good; for when the balance is regained, the world will end, because sameness and destruction are one. When this world goes, good and evil go with it; but when we can transcend this world, we get rid of both good and evil and have bliss.*[6]

As a practical and aesthetic visionary of man, Vivekananda draws our attention to cultivate freedom of thought and action, reality and contemplation in the in the perfect evaluation of good and evil . For this, our mind should be liberated from all forms of bondage. Unless we are strong in our mind aesthetically, we will fail to prove ourselves as ideal and practical human beings. As Vivekananda suggests in aesthetic elegance:

The world for me, not I for the world. Good and evil are our slaves, not we theirs. It is the nature of the brute to remain where he is (not to progress); it is the nature of man to seek good and avoid evil; it is the nature of God to seek neither, but just to be eternally blissful. Let us be God! Make the heart like an ocean, go beyond all the trifles of the world, be mad with joy even at evil; see the world as a picture and then enjoy its beauty, knowing that nothing affects you. Children finding glass beads in a mud puddle, that is the good of the world.[7]

The aesthetics of man finds a new language and a transparent connotation in Vivekananda's philosophy of man in terms of God and worship. He never belittles man or God from the aesthetic points of view because he never dissociates man from God or vice versa. To him, they are one and the same. And as they are one and the same, man is free, self-existent and one. This makes a revolutionary and radical breakthrough in the aesthetic fusion between man and God and glorifies the victory of man as the best creature with divine essence always looking for fullness in every finer vision and manifestation. In Vivekananda's vibrant words:

Do not say "God". Do not say "Thou". Say "I". The language of [dualism] says, "God, Thou, my Father." The language of [non-dualism] says, "Dearer unto me than I am myself. I would have no name for Thee. The nearest I can use is I. ...

"God is true. The universe is a dream. Blessed am I that I know this moment that I [have been and] shall be free from all eternity. ... that I know that I am worshipping only myself; that no nature, no delusion, had any hold on me. Vanish nature from me, vanish [these] gods; vanish worship; ...vanish superstitions, for I know myself. I am the Infinite. All these— Mrs. So-and-So, Mr. So-and-So, responsibility, happiness, misery— have vanished. I am the Infinite. How can there be death for me, or birth? Whom shall I fear? I am the One. Shall I be afraid of myself? Who is to be afraid of [whom]? I am the one Existence. Nothing else exists. I am everything."

** ** ** **

Go on saying, "I am free". Never mind if the next moment delusion comes and says, "I am bound." De-hypnotise the whole thing.

[This truth] is first to be heard. Hear it first. Think on it day and night. Fill the mind [with it] day and night: "I am It. I am the

Lord of the universe. Never was there any delusion. .." Meditate upon it with all the strength of the mind till you actually see these walls, houses, everything, melt away— [until] body, everything, vanishes. "I will stand alone. I am the One." struggle on! "Who cares!" We want to be free; [we] do not want any powers. Worlds we renounce; heavens we renounce; hells we renounce. What do I care about all these powers, and this and that! What do I care if the mind is controlled or uncontrolled! Let it run on. What of that! I am not the mind. Let it go on!"[8]

The aesthetics of man in terms of the above finds an altogether new platform of ascent and excellence. It calls forth a welcome change of man who alone can say that the birth of God is within his mind. Here are the poignant and revolutionary words of Vivekananda which serve as an unparalleled aesthetic boost for every human being:

Down with all superstitions! Neither teachers nor scriptures nor gods [exist]. Down with temples, with priests, or gods, with incarnations, with God Himself! I am all the God that ever existed! There, stand up philosophers! No fear! Speak no more of God and [the] superstition of the world. Truth alone triumphs, and this is true. I am the Infinite.

** ** ** **

"I am the Soul, the ever free; [I] never bound. Time is in me, not I in time. God was born in my mind.[9]

Elsewhere, in the poem "The Living God", Vivekananda highlights the mystic-cum-aesthetic vision of 'the living God' who resides in man both internally and externally:

He who is in you and outside you,

Who works through all hands,

Who walks on all feet,

Whose body are all ye,

Him worship, and break all other idols!

He who is at once the high and the low,

The sinner and the saint,

Both God and worm,

Him worship— visible, knowable, real, omnipresent,

Break all other idols!
In whom is neither past life-breath
Nor future birth and death,
In whom we always have been
And always shall be one,
Him worship. Break all other idols!
Ye Fools! Who neglect the living God,
And His infinite reflections with which the world is full.
While ye run after imaginary shadows,
That had alone to fight and quarrels,
Him worship, the only visible!
Break all other idols![10]

The intrinsic aesthetic harmony where the mind stuff, mind, sense and sense organs work like a composite unit identifies the Self in every human being. These not only represent the mystic identity of man but also promise and translate the aesthetic efflorescence of Truth, Beauty and Goodness. These also liberate man from egotism and lead towards excellence and enrichment of the finer and nobler vision of fullness.

In "Raja-Yoga", Vivekananda significantly upholds the aesthetic vision of man in the light of the above:

> *Egotism is the identification of the seer with the instrument of seeing.*
>
> *The seer is really the Self, the pure one, the ever holy, the infinite, the immortal. This is the Self of man. And what are the instruments? The Chitta or mind-stuff, the Buddhi or determinative faculty, the Manas or mind, and the Indriyas or sense-organs. These are the instruments for him to see the external world, and the identification of the Self with the instruments is what is called the ignorance of egotism. We say, "I am the mind," "I am thought," "I am angry," or "I am happy". How can we be angry and how can we hate? We should identify ourselves with the Self that cannot change. If It is unchangeable, how can It be one moment happy, and one moment unhappy? It is formless, infinite, omnipresent. What can change It? It is beyond all law. What can affect It? Nothing in the universe can produce an*

effect on It. Yet through ignorance, we identify ourselves with the mind-stuff, and think we feel pleasure or pain.[11]

The aesthetics of realisation of man in terms of the Self is yet to be given its topmost priority. It unveils man who represents Truth, Beauty, Goodness and all other invaluable components of aesthetic excellence. This may be illustrated by taking, for instance, the concept of goodness as an aesthetic exercise by an ever great aesthetic visionary, Mohammed who has translated goodness in the elegance of equality.

Vivekananda hails and honours Mohammed as 'the Prophet of equality, of the brotherhood of man' and directs our attention to this invaluable aesthetic component of goodness:

Mohammed by his life showed that amongst Mohammedans there should be perfect equality and brotherhood. There was no question of race, caste, creed, colour, or sex. The Sultan of Turkey may buy a Negro from the mart of Africa, and bring him in chains to Turkey; but should he become a Mohammedan and have sufficient merit and abilities, he might even marry the daughter of the Sultan. Compare this with the way in which the Negroes and the American Indians are treated in this country! And what do Hindus do? If one of your missionaries chance to touch the food of an orthodox person, he would throw it away. Notwithstanding our grand philosophy, you note our weakness in practice: but there you see the greatness of the Mohammedan beyond other races, showing itself in equality, perfect equality regardless of race or colour.[12]

The march of man waits for the efflorescence of inner goodness already in him. It wants the spirit in every man irrespective of caste or creed, colour or religion, nationality or anything whatsoever to be nursed and caressed, developed and disseminated so that the great Family of Man shines out with all brilliance of altruism. Indeed, Vivekananda pays the highest importance to the ascent and excellence of man because he always upholds the spirit of man as the Divine Spirit of the All Good.

A down-to-earth religious visionary from the aesthetic points of view, Vivekananda draws our attention to the essential needs and priorities of man who must be able to have his own food, health care, and education in a thriving and aesthetically conscious society that cares for cultivation of Truth, Goodness and Beauty in all spheres of life and development. In a letter written to Alasinga Perumal on 19th November 1894 from New York, he writes:

> *Material civilisation, nay, even luxury, is necessary to create work for the poor. Bread! Bread! I do not believe in a God, who cannot give me bread here, giving me eternal bliss in heaven! Pooh! India is to be raised, the poor are to be fed, education is to be spread, and the evil of priest-craft is to be removed. No priest-craft, no social tyranny! More bread, more opportunity for everybody! Our young fools organise meetings to get more power from the English. They only laugh. None deserves liberty who is not ready to give liberty. Suppose the English give over to you all the power. Why, the powers that be then, will hold the people down, and let them not have it. Slaves want power to make slaves.*
>
> *Now, this is to be brought about slowly, and by only insisting on our religion and giving liberty to society. Root up priest-craft from the old religion, and you get the best religion in the world. Do you understand me? Can you make a European society with India's religion? I believe it is possible, and must be.*
>
> ** ** ** **
>
> *Have fire and spread all over. Work, work. Be the servant while leading. Be unselfish, and* never listen to one friend in private accusing another. *Have infinite patience, and success is yours.*[13]

The education of the heart which is the core of aesthetic education is long overdue almost everywhere. The education of intellect has become the *summum bonum* in action and deliberation, practice and pursuit sans purity sans truth. As a result, we are yet to taste the 'butter' as the aesthetic kernel of education. As Vivekananda categorically asserts:

> *If you are not pure, and you know all the sciences in the world, that will not help you at all; you may be buried in all the books you read, but that will not be of much use. It is the heart that reaches the goal. Follow the heart. A pure heart sees beyond the intellect; it gets inspired; it knows things that reason can never know, and whenever there is conflict between the pure heart and*

the intellect, always side with the pure heart, even if you think what your heart is doing is unreasonable. When it is desirous of doing good to others, your brain may tell you that it is not politic to do so, but follow your heart, and you will find that you make less mistakes than by following your intellect. The pure heart is the best mirror for the reflection of truth, so all these disciplines are for the purification of the heart. And as soon as it is pure, all truths flash upon it in a minute; all truth in the universe will manifest in your heart, if you are sufficiently pure.[14]

For the manifestation of truth in the heart, the aesthetics of religion holds the key to success. In the pursuit of religion, whatever work is to be accomplished must be guided by the principle of extinction of personality. That I am doing the work should be preceded by the great aesthetic and religious vision of love that I receive from the "inner light". Only then I can have the aesthetic inroad to understand and appreciate the fact that I do not work but my mind and the body work. As such, the elegance of inner light is of absolute importance in both religion and service to the All Light.

In connection with the above, Vivekananda's viewpoints based on the Karma-Yoga of the *Bhagavad-Gita* is very significant:

To give up work before you know, *leads to misery. Work done for the Self gives no bondage. Neither desire pleasure nor fear pain from work. It is the mind and the body that work. Tell yourself this unceasingly and realise it. Try not to know that you work.*

Do all as a sacrifice or offering to the Lord. Be in the world, but not of it, like the lotus leaf whose roots are in the mud but which remains always pure. Let your love go to all, whatever they do to you. A blind man cannot see colour, so how can we see evil unless it is in us? We compare what we see outside with what we find in ourselves and pronounce judgment accordingly. If we are pure, we cannot see impurity. It may exist but not for us. See only God in every man, woman and child; see it by the antarjyotis, *"inner light", and seeing that, we can see naught else. Do not want this world, because what you desire you get. Seek the Lord and the Lord only. The more power there is, the more bondage, the more fear. How much more afraid and miserable are we than the ant! Get out of it all and come to the Lord.*[15]

To learn the aesthetic lesson of love and friendship without making any sort of difference between man and man and without having any particular attachment or desire whatsoever is to cultivate the values of extinction of personality. Vivekananda inspires us to cultivate that aesthetic spirit with devotion and dedication:

> *Learn to help without pitying or feeling that there is any misery. Learn to be the same to enemy and to friend; then when you can do that and no longer have any desire, the goal is attained.*
>
> *Cut down the banyan tree of desire with the axe of non-attachment, and it will vanish utterly. It is all illusion. "He from whom blight and delusion have fallen, he who has conquered the evils of association, he alone is* azad *(free)."*
>
> *To love anyone personally is bondage. Love all alike, then all desires fall off.*
>
> *Time, the "eater of everything", comes, and all has to go. Why try to improve the earth, to paint the butterfly? It all has to go at last. Do not be mere white mice in a treadmill, working always and never accomplishing anything. Every desire is fraught with evil, whether the desire itself be good or evil. It is like a dog jumping for a piece of meat which is ever receding from its reach, and dying a dog's death at last. Do not be like that. Cut off all desire.*[16]

To cut off all desire is to cut off the ego and prepare for self-submission and self-sacrifice. Vivekananda advises us to think for the best of others in order to have the best efflorescence of aesthetic purity and goodness in oneself. In his timeless words:

> *Be perfectly resigned, perfectly unconcerned; then alone can you do any true work. No eyes can see the real forces, we can only see the results. Put out self, lose it, forget it; just let God work, it is His business. We have nothing to do but stand aside and let God work. The more we go away, the more God comes in. get rid of the little "I", and let only the great "I" live.*
>
> *We are what our thoughts have made us; so take care of what you think. Words are secondary. Thoughts live, they travel far. Each thought we think is tinged with our own character, so that for the pure and holy man, even his jests or abuse will have the twist of his own love and purity and do good.*

> *Desire nothing; think of God and look for no return. It is the desireless who bring results. The begging monks carry religion to every man's door; but they think that they do nothing, they claim nothing, their work is unconsciously done. If they should eat of the tree of knowledge, they would become egoists, and all the good they do would fly away. As soon as we say "I", we are humbugged all the time; and we call it "knowable", but it is only going round and round like a bullock tied to a tree. The Lord has hidden Himself best, and His work is best; so he who hides himself best, accomplishes most. Conquer* yourself, *and the whole world is yours.*[17]

The aesthetic avenues of conquering oneself are always adventurous and challenging, marvellous and interesting. The aesthetic spirit of love must be reflected in our devotion to selfless service. How to be christened with disinterested and aesthetic love? Here are Vivekananda's guidelines:

> *Work incessantly, but do not do slave's work. Do you not see how everybody works? Nobody can be altogether at rest. Ninety-nine per cent of mankind work like slaves, and the result is misery; it is all selfish work. Work through freedom! Work through love! The word "love" is very difficult to understand; love never comes until there is freedom. There is no true love possible in the slave. If you buy a slave and tie him down in chains and make him work for you, he will work like a drudge, but there will be no love in him. So when we ourselves work for the things of the world as slaves, there can be no love in us, and our work is not true work. This is true of work done for relatives and friends, and is true of work done for our own selves. Selfish work is slave's work; and here is a test. Every act of love brings happiness; there is no act of love which does not bring peace and blessedness as its reaction. Real, real knowledge, and real love are eternally connected with one another, the three in one: where one of them is, the others also must be; they are the three aspects of the One without a second— Existence-Knowledge-Bliss.*[18]

The aesthetic vision of love in terms of the One embroidered in Existence-Knowledge-Bliss as Vivekananda elucidates goes a long way in idealising and appreciating man the All True. Man in the pursuit of *Sachchidananda* as the essence of aesthetic identity ought to find out and realise the distinction between truth and fiction, reality and mirage . As Vivekananda, in his address delivered before the Graduate Philosophical Society of Harvard University on March 25, 1896, poignantly asserts the role of man in terms of the Advaita philosophy of morality and love:

> *Do not injure another. Love everyone as your own self, because the whole universe is one. In injuring another, I am injuring myself; in loving another, I am loving myself. From this also springs that principle of Advaita morality which has been summed up in one word— self-abnegation. The Advaitist says, this little personalised self is the cause of all my misery. This individualised self, which makes me different from all other beings, brings hatred and jealousy and misery, struggle and all other evils. And when this idea has been got rid of, all struggle will cease, all misery vanish. So this is to be given up. We must always hold ourselves ready, even to give up our lives for the lowest beings. When a man has become ready even to give up his life for a little insect, he has reached the perfection which the Advaitist wants to attain; and at that moment when he has become thus ready, the veil of ignorance falls away from him, and he will feel his own nature. Even in this life, he will feel that he is one with the universe. For a time, as it were, the whole of this phenomenal world will disappear from him, and he will realise what he is. But so long as the Karma of this body remains, he will have to live. This state, when the veil has vanished and yet the body remains for some time, is what the Vedantists call the Jivanmukti, the living freedom. If a man is deluded by a mirage for some time, and one day the mirage disappears— if it comes back again the next day, or at some future time, he will not be deluded. Before the mirage first broke, the man could not distinguish between the reality and the deception. But when it has once broken, as long he has organs and eyes to work with, he will see the image, but will no more be deluded. That fine distinction between the actual world and the mirage he has caught, and the latter cannot delude him any more.*[19]

To be free from delusion in order to be self-controlled is be aesthetic, and to lead one's life aesthetically is to be free from all constraints of the senses. Self-assessment and self-decision well substantiated and enriched by the vision of goodness translated into aesthetic reality of altruism is the hallmark of man's identity. In fact, when man wins over the sense of morbidity and mechanical passivity in life and work, the signs of aesthetic advancement become transparent and real, living and active. Vivekananda adroitly clarifies this point as follows:

> *When you are doing any work, do not think of anything beyond. Do it as worship, as the highest worship, and devote your whole life to it for the time being. Thus, in the story, the Vyadha and the woman did their duty with cheerfulness and whole-heartedness; and the result was that they became illuminated, clearly showing that the right performance of duties of any station in life, without attachment to results, leads us to the highest realisation of the perfection of the soul.*
>
> *It is the worker who is attached to results that grumbles about the nature of the duty which has fallen to his lot; to the unattached worker all duties are equally good, and form efficient instruments with which selfishness and sensuality may be killed, and the freedom of the soul secured. We are all apt to think too highly of ourselves. Our duties are determined by our deserts to a much larger extent than we are willing to grant. Competition rouses envy, and it kills the kindliness of the heart. To the grumbler all duties are distasteful; nothing will ever satisfy him, and his whole life is doomed to prove a failure. Let us work on, doing as we go whatever happens to be our duty, and being ever ready to put our shoulders to the wheel. Then surely shall we see the light!*[20]

'To see the light', as Vivekananda suggests, in the light of aesthetic aura of illumination is to ensure sincere involvement in the culture of values. This also ensures peace of the mind and discipline in action at every endeavour of completion and perfection. But this is not an easy task. Life is an eternal preparation for union with the All Good. In this preparation, the body and the mind must remain free from all evil thoughts which crush all aesthetic values in man.

In explaining the obstructions to Yoga, Vivekananda clearly observes:

> *The obstructions to Yoga are killing, falsehood, etc., whether committed, caused, or approved; either through avarice, or anger, or ignorance; whether slight, middling, or great; and they result*

in infinite ignorance and misery. This is (the method of) thinking the contrary.

If I tell a lie, or cause another to tell one, or approve of another doing so, it is equally sinful. If it is a very mild lie, still it is a lie. Every vicious thought will rebound, every thought of hatred which you may have thought, in a cave even, is stored up, and will one day come back to you with tremendous power in the form of some misery here. If you project hatred and jealousy, they will rebound on you with compound interest. No power can avert them; when once you have put them in motion, you will have to bear them. Remembering this will prevent you from doing wicked things.[21]

Not hatred but love, not jealousy but endearment are the avenues of exercising aesthetic values. It also indicates that the aesthetics of love thus followed and practised leads man to love the All Love. Love that takes place naturally and spontaneously heralds the message of heavenly love full of beauty and grandeur. Even 'wrong love' proves love and submission to the All Love. To exercise true love is to eliminate the little self and to be blessed with the aesthetic blessing 'I am Thou'.

In one of his 'Inspired Talks', Vivekananda encourages us to exercise the aesthetic avenues of love as an absolute entity, a play of the All Love with man:

Give up all evil company, especially at the beginning. Avoid worldly company, that will distract your mind. Give up all "me and mine". *To him who has nothing in the universe the Lord comes. Cut the bondage of all worldly affections; go beyond laziness and all care as to what becomes of you. Never turn back to see the result of what you have done. Give all to the Lord and go on and think not of it. The whole soul pours in a continuous current to God; there is no time to seek money, or name, or fame, no time to think of anything but God; then will come into our hearts that infinite, wonderful bliss of Love. All desires are but beads of glass. Love of God increases every moment and is ever new, to be known only by feeling it. Love is the easiest of all, it waits for no logic, it is natural. We need no demonstration, no proof. Reasoning is limiting something by our own minds. We throw a net and catch something, and then say that we have demonstrated it; but never, never can we catch God in a net.*

*Love should be unlimited. Even when we love wrongly, it is of the true love, of the true bliss; the power is the same, use it as we may. Its very nature is peace and bliss. The murderer when he kisses his baby forgets for an instant all but love. Give up all self, all egotism; get out of anger, lust, give*all *to God. "I am not, but Thou art; the old man is all gone, but Thou remainest." "I am Thou." Blame none; if evil comes, know the Lord is playing with you and be exceeding glad.*[22]

Elsewhere, in a poem entitled "To a Friend", Vivekananda elegantly exposes the aesthetic vision of Love:

Let go your vain reliance on knowledge,
Let go your prayers, offerings, and strength,
For Love selfless is the only resource;—
Lo, the insects teach, embracing the flame!
The base insect's blind, by beauty charmed,
Thy soul is drunken with the wine of Love;
O thou Lover true, cast into the fire
All thy dross of self, thy mean selfishness.
Say— comes happiness e'er to a beggar?
What good being object of charity?
Give away, ne'er turn to ask in return,
Should there be the wealth treasured in thy heart.
Ay, born heir to the Infinite thou art,
Within the heart is the ocean of Love,
"Give", "Give away"— whoever asks return,
His ocean dwindles down to a mere drop.
From highest Brahman to the yonder worm,
And to the very minutest atom,
Everywhere is the same God, the All-Love;
Friend, offer mind,soul, body, at their feet.
These are His manifold forms before thee,
Rejecting them, where seekest thou for God?
Who loves all beings without distinction,
He indeed is worshipping best his God.[23]

The aesthetic vision of love as Vivekananda adroitly spells out also denotes the fact that the world must be looked at from the point of view of the reality as we experience and mould ourselves in terms of goodness which is an inseparable aesthetic force of love. Let us love others not only as our very own but also love in order to encounter the All Love anywhere and everywhere.

Vivekananda highlights the world of love in terms of both optimism and passimism which serve as inspiring experiences of knowing the truth of life and religion of man. He conceptualises religion as the aesthetics of unfolding the truth under varying circumstances. He does not spare reality of the vilest type only to focus on the dawn of truth awaiting apposite avenues of manifestation in contemplation and action. Thus good and evil, right and wrong are to be experiented and crystallised with the spirit of aesthetic calmness and poignance of the mind and the heart as inheritors of the All True and aesthetic religion par excellence in this world, 'a great gymnasium'. In Vivekananda's heart-throbbing viewpoints:

> *Both pessimism and optimism are wrong. Both are taking up the extremes. So long as a man has plenty to eat and drink, and good clothes to wear, he becomes a great optimist; but that very man, when he loses everything, becomes a great peassimist. When a man loses all his money and is very poor, then and then alone, with the greatest force come to him the ideas of brotherhood of humanity. This is the world , and the more I go to different countries and see of this world, and the older I get, the more I am trying to avoid both the extremes of optimism and pessimism. This world is neither good nor evil. It is the Lord's world. It is beyond both good and evil, perfect in itself. His will is going on, showing all these different pictures; and it will go on without beginning and without end. It is a great gymnasium in which you and I, and millions of souls must come and get exercises, and make ourselves strong and perfect. This is what it is for. Not that God could not make a perfect universe; not that He could not help the misery of the world. You remember the story of the young lady and the clergyman, who were looking at the moon through the telescope, and found the moon spots. And the clergyman said, "I am sure they are the spires of some churches." "Nonsense," said the young lady, "I am sure they are the young*

lovers kissing each other." So we are doing with this world. When we are inside, we think we are seeing the inside. According to the plane of existence in which we are, we see the universe. Fire in the kitchen is neither good nor bad. When it cooks a meal for you, you bless the fire, and say, "How good it is!" It would be equally correct and logical to say: This universe is neither good nor evil. The world is the world, and will be always so. If we open ourselves to it in such a manner that the action of the world is beneficial to us, we call it good. If we pit ourselves in the position in which it is painful, we call it evil. So you will always find children, who are innocent and joyful and do not want to injure anyone, are very optimistic. They are dreaming golden dreams. Old men who have all the desires in their hearts and not the means to fulfil them, and especially those who have been thumped and bumped by the world a good deal, are very pessimistic. Religion wants to know the truth. And the first thing it has discovered is that without a knowledge of this truth there will be no life worth living.[24]

The quest for Truth as an aesthetic force necessitates the continuous exercise of finer thoughts and imaginations well backed by 'the symbols of inner light'. It does not require any extraordinary quality for man to exercise for freedom and perfection which are the most essential potential force of the existence of man. What is absolutely required is a steadfast and firm conviction of the Self within the self— the best identity of man the Ever True.

In elucidating the aesthetic identity of man as above, Vivekananda poignantly advises in the fifth lesson of the Raja-Yoga:

Try to keep up the imagination in Yoga, being careful to keep it pure and holy. We all have our peculiarities in the way of imaginative power; follow the way most natural to you; it will be the easiest.

We are the results of all incarnations through Karma: "One lamp lighted from another", says the Buddhist—different lamps, but the same light.

Be cheerful, be brave, bathe daily, have patience, purity, and perseverance, then you will become a Yogi in truth. Never try to hurry, and if the higher powers come, remember that they are but side-paths. Do not let them tempt you from the main road;

> *put them aside and hold fast to your only true aim— God. Seek only the Eternal, finding which we are at rest for ever; having the all, nothing is left to strive for, and we are for ever in free and perfect existence— Existence Absolute, Knowledge Absolute, Bliss Absolute.*[25]

To seek the Eternal in order to realise and translate into action our 'free and perfect existence' as Vivekananda advises is to be in perfect tune with the aesthetic spirit of elegance which is already existent in every one of us. What is of absolute importance in nurturing the aesthetic sprit of elegance is to redefine our thoughts and visions. For that end in view, man must be careful of his own worth in terms of the aesthetic spirit of humanity that really stands for identification of God in man. This fine aesthetic spirit propels the role of man as a worshiper. He then considers work as nothing but worship. This worship teaches him how to be perfectly non-attached, an aesthetic practice for perfection. As Vivekananda admirably and boldly points out:

> *All the work you do is subjective,is done for your own benefit. God has not fallen into a ditch for you and me to help Him out by building a hospital or something of that sort. He* allows *you to work. He allows you to exercise your muscles in this great gymnasium, not in order to help Him but that you may help yourself. Do you think even an ant will die for want of your help? Most errant blasphemy! The world does not need you at all. The world goes on, you are like a drop in the ocean. A leaf does not move, the wind does not blow without Him. Blessed are we that we are given the privilege of working for Him. Cut out the word "help" from your mind. You cannot help; it is blaspheming. You are here yourself at His pleasure. Do you mean to say, you help Him? You worship. When you give a morsel of food to the dog, you worship the dog as God. God is in that dog. He is the dog. He is all and in all. We are allowed to worship Him. Stand in that reverent attitude to the whole universe, and then will come perfect non-attachment. This should be your duty. This is the proper attitude of work.*[26]

The new aesthetic vision of man as the master of his Self is long overdue to be honoured and practised. Man's primary concern as an aesthetic practitioner of goodness and truth is to steadfastly control and manifest the self in the light of the beauty of erudition which shows the avenue of respecting the inherent divinity always awaiting cultivation of catholicity of vision. Therefore, concentration is the right key to success in aesthetic refinement. The only pre-awareness necessary is appropriate selection in intellectual, religious and spiritual contents of advancement in particular. In Kriya-Yoga, which stands for "mortification, study and surrounding fruits of work to God", Vivekananda explains the fundamental points of the aesthetics of human ascent and excellence:

> *The organs are the horses, the mind is the rein, the intellect is the charioteer, the soul is the rider, and the body is the chariot. The master of the household, the King, the Self of man, is sitting in this chariot. If the horses are very strong and do not obey the rein, if the charioteer, the intellect, does not know how to control the horses, then the chariot will come to grief. But if the organs, the horses are well controlled, and if the rein, the mind, is well held in the hands of the charioteer, the intellect, the chariot reaches the goal. What is meant, therefore, by this mortification? Holding the rein firmly while guiding the body and the organs; not letting them do anything they like, but keeping them both under control.* Study. *What is meant by study in this case? No study of novels or story books, but study of those works which teach the liberation of the Soul. Then again this study does not mean controvertial studies at all. The Yogi is supposed to have finished his period of controversy. He has had enough of that, and has become satisfied. He only studies to intensify his convictions. Vada and Siddhanta— these are the two sorts of scriptural knowledge— Vada (the argumentative) and Siddhanta (the decisive). When a man is entirely ignorant he takes up the first of these, the argumentative fighting, and reasoning pro and con; and when he has finished that he takes up the Siddhanta, the decisive, arriving at a conclusion. Simply arriving at the conclusion will not do. It must be intensified. Books are infinite in number, and the time is short; therefore the secret of knowlegde is to take what is essential. Take that and try to live up to it. There is an old Indian legend that if you place a cup of milk and water before a Raja-Hamsa (swan), he will take all the milk and leave the water. In that way we should take what is of value in knowledge, and leave the dross. Intellectual gymnastics are*

necessary at first. We must not go blindly into anything. The Yogi has passed the argumentative state, and has come to a conclusion, which is, like the rocks, is immovable. The only thing he now seeks to do is to intensify that conclusion. Do not argue, he says; if one forces arguments upon you, be silent. Do not answer any argument, bur go away calmly, because arguments only disturb the mind. The only thing necessary is to train the intellect, what is the use of disturbing it for nothing? The intellect is but a weak instrument, and can give us only knowledge limited by the senses. The Yogi wants to go beyond the senses, therefore intelligence is of no use for him. He is certain of this and, therefore, is silent, and does not argue. Every argument throws his mind out of balance, creates a disturbance in the Chitta, and a disturbance is a drawback. Argumentations and searchings of the reason are only by the way. There are much higher things beyond them. The whole life is not for schoolboy fights and debating societies. "Surrendering the fruits of work to God" is to take to ourselves neither credit nor blame, but to give up both to the Lord and be at peace.[27]

Not with arguments but with devotion to purity and perfection through submission to the All True is the aesthetic avenue of emancipation of man. How to control the mind-waves? How to explore and utilise the finer instincts? How to control these instincts so that the finer aesthetics of vision become transparent at any time under any eventualities? Here is Vivekananda's incomparable and unparalleled observation:

Even in the most learned men, who know that this body will go, and who say "never mind, we have had hundreds of bodies, the soul cannot die"— even in them, with all their intellectual convicitions, we still find this clinging on to life. Why is this clinging to life? We have seen that it has become instinctive. In the psychological language of the Yogi it has become a Samskara. The Samskaras, fine and hidden, are sleeping in the Chitta. All this past experience of death, all that which we call instinct, is experience become subconscious. It lives in the Chitta, and is not inactive, but is working underneath.

The Chitta-Vrittis, the mind-waves, which are gross, we can appreciate and feel; they can be more easily controlled, but what about the finer instincts? How can they be controlled? When I am angry, my whole mind becomes a huge wave of anger. I feel it, see it, handle it, can easily manipulate it, can fight with it; but I shall not succeed perfectly in the fight until I can get down below to its causes. A man says something very harsh to me, and I begin to feel that I am getting heated, and he goes on till I am perfectly angry and forget myself, identify myself with anger. When he first began to abuse me, I thought, "I am going to be angry". Anger was one thing, and I was another; but when I became angry, I was anger. These feelings have to be controlled in the germ, the root, in their fine norms, before even we have become conscious that they are acting on us. With the vast majority of mankind the fine states of these passions are not even known—the states in which they emerge from subconsciousness. When a bubble is rising from the bottom of the lake, we do not see it, nor even when it is nearly come to the surface; it is only when it bursts and makes a ripple that we know it is there. We shall only be successful in grappling with the waves when we can get hold of them in their fine causes, and until you can get hold of them, and subdue them before they become gross, there is no hope of conquering any passion perfectly. To control our passions we have to control them at their very roots; then alone shall we be able to burn out their seeds. As fried seeds thrown into the ground will never come up, so these passions will never arise.[28]

The waves of good thoughts side by side with that of the evil ones are not alien to man. He must control the passions of doling out good sense and sensibilities and also control the probable lapses in transparent approaches to what he initially identifies as evil thoughts. Thoughts as thoughts only do not create any vibration in the mind. Unless vibrations are there in the mind, the wavelets of thoughts remain dormant and passive. Then the moratorium of man as an aesthetic thinking being is inevitable.

What man absolutely needs is the cultivation of purity and confidence. These two vital aesthetic components serve as safegurds to our good thoughts that are never afraid of being overpowered by the evil ones. Vivekananda elegantly elucidates this point in terms of the social and humane context:

As vibration continues so thought remains in the form of thought until translated into action. For example, force is latent in the

> *man's arm until he strikes a blow, when he translates it into activity. We are the heirs of good and evil thought. If we make ourselves pure and instruments of good thoughts, these will enter us. The good soul will not be receptive to evil thoughts. Evil thoughts find the best field in evil people; they are like microbes which germinate and increase only when they find a suitable soil. Mere thoughts are like little wavelets; fresh impulses to vibration come to them simultaneously, until at last one great wave seems to stand up and swallow up the rest. These universal thought-waves seem to recur every five hundred years, when invariably the great wave typifies and swallows up the others. It is this which constitutes a prophet. He focuses in his own mind the thought of the age in which he is living and gives it back to mankind in concrete form. Krishna, Buddha, Christ, Mohammed, and Luther may be instanced as the great waves that stood up above their fellows (with a probable lapse of five hundred years between them). Always the wave that is backed by the greatest purity and the noblest character is what breaks upon the world as a movement of social reform. Once again in our day there is a vibration of the waves of thought and the central idea is that of the Immanent God, and this is everywhere cropping up in every form and every sect. In these waves, construction alternates with destruction; yet the construction always makes an end of the work of destruction. Now, as a man dives deeper to reach his spiritual nature, he feels no longer bound by superstition. The majority of sects will be transient, and last only as bubbles because the leaders are not usually men of character. Perfect love, the heart never reacting, this is what builds character. There is no allegiance possible where there is no character in the leader, and perfect purity ensures the most lasting allegiance and confidence.*[29]

The aesthetic vision of man in quest of spirituality par excellence breaks all barriers of reasoning or argument. It ensures human achievement in perfect submission and devotion to the All Good who is beyond space, time and causation. What stands out as the supreme aesthetic and spiritual identity of man is to remain pure and perfect in 'body, mind and speech'. Vivekananda spells out this from the standpoint of Shri Ramakrishna's matchless message:

> *Those who are pure always in body, mind, and speech, who have strong devotion, who discriminate between the real and*

the unreal, who persevere in meditation and contemplation— upon them alone the grace of the Lord descends. The Lord, however, is beyond all natural laws— is not under any rules and regulations, or just as Shri Ramakrishna used to say, He has the child's nature— and that is why we find some failing to get any response even after calling on Him for millions of births, while some one else whom we regard as a sinful or penitent man or a disbeliever, would have illumination in a flash! — On the latter the Lord perhaps lavishes His grace quite unsolicited! You may argue that this man had good merits stored up from previous life, but the mystery is really difficult to understand. Shri Ramakrishna used to say sometimes, "Do rely on Him; be like the dry leaf at the mercy of the wind"; and again he would say, "The wind of His grace is always blowing, what you need to do is to unfurl your sail."[30]

The sailing of the mind in perfect direction towards aesthetic purity and devotion is the way to realisation of the Atman inherent in man. Self-exertion through the aesthetic practice of perseverance is only avenue of encounter with the All Good. In the words of Vivekananda:

Only get your mind to cling to Him as far as you can. For then only the great magic of this world will break of itself. But then, you must persevere. You must take off your mind from lust and lucre, must discriminate always between the real and the unreal— must settle down into the mood of bodilessness with the brooding thought that you are not this body, and must always have the realisation that you are the all-pervading Atman. This persevering practice is called Purushakara (self-exertion as distinguished from grace). By such self-exertion will come true reliance on Him, and that is the goal of human achievement.[31]

The goal of human achievement is unending. Therein lies the charm of living for values to be cultivated in life ceaselessly and ardently. Therein also lies the worth of life selflessly. Begging is not life. It devaluates life. It dwarfs the mission for fulness of life in nurturing eternal values for ascent and excellence.

The desires of life demand careful, cautious and complete crystallisation. It is not an easy procedure. It calls forth a sort of genuine urgency and devotion well backed by self-negation and self-advancement by dint of the exercise of negation of devalued identities. Heaven is within. It does not require any exercise of desire as such. It cares for nothing in everything in a way quite original, natural and spontaneous. Again, what is desirable right now is turned into or spurned as valuable or insignificant through a series of untiring endeavour. What, then, should be role of desire as a symbol or a pointer of values? Vivekananda provides us with the most practical, living, absorbing and inspiring suggestions:

> *Do not pray for little things. If you seek only bodily comforts, where is the difference between men and animals? Think yourselves a little higher than that.*
>
> *So it goes without saying that the first task in becoming a Bhakta is to give up all desires of heaven and other things. The question is how to get rid of these desires. What makes men miserable? Because they are slaves, bound by laws, puppets in the hand of nature, tumbled about like playthings. We are continually taking care of this body that anything can knock down; and so we are living in a constant state of fear. I have read that a deer has to run on e average sixty or seventy miles every day, because it is frightened. We ought to know that we are in a worse plight than the deer. The deer has some rest, but we have none. If the deer gets grass enough it is satisfied, but we are always multiplying our wants. It is a morbid desire with us to multiply our wants. We have become so unhinged and unnatural that nothing natural will satisfy us. We are always grasping after morbid things, must have unnatural excitement—unnatural food, drink, surroundings, and life. As to fear, what are our lives but bundles of fear? The deer has only one class of fear, such as that from tigers, wolves, etc. Man has the whole universe to fear.*
>
> *How are we to free ourselves from this is the question. Utilitarians say, "Don't talk of God and hereafter; we don't know anything of these things, let us live happily in this world." I would be the first to do so if we could, but the world will not allow us. As long as you are a slave of nature, how can you? The more you struggle, the more enveloped you become. You have been devising plans to make you happy, I do not know for how many years, but each year things seem to grow worse. Two hundred years ago in the old world people had few wants; but if their knowledge increased in arithmetical progression, their wants increased in geometrical*

progression. We think that in salvation at least our desires will be fulfilled, so we desire to go to heaven. This eternal, unquenchable thirst! Always wanting something! When a man is a beggar, he wants money. When he has money, he wants other things, society; and after that, something else. Never at rest. How are we to quench this? If we get to heaven, it will only increase desire. If a poor man gets rich, it does not quench his desires, it is only like throwing butter on the fire, increasing its bright flames. Going to heaven means becoming intensely richer, and then desire comes more and more. We read of many human things in heaven in the different Bibles of the world; they are not always very good there; and after all, this desire to go to heaven is a desire after enjoyment. This has to be given up. It is too little, too vulgar a thing for you to think of going to heaven. It is just the same as thinking, I will become a millionaire and lord it over people. There are many of these heavens, but through them you cannot gain the right to enter the gates of religion and love.[32]

To enter the gates of religion and love is one of the most difficult challenges for man. It is a challenge to be perfectly justified to what he contemplates and what he translates into reality by living a life of complete surrender to the All Good and serve every one in and around him. While serving, he must have complete faith in the divinity already in man. He must be strong. He must be brave. He must be prepared for any sacrifice necessary for encounter with the God of Love. Is there any value more desirable than this to be followed and disseminated wholeheartedly?

To shake off all morbidy, all sentiments, all weakness in the form of devaluation of the value of God as love is the prime need of man. That is religion. That is the most abiding value for which every religion is to be endeared, honoured, followed and inspired for the well-being of man. As Vivekananda categorically asserts:

We are now playing with religion. With inspiration we shall begin to have religion. Just as St. Paul says, "For now we see through a glass darkly, but then face to face." but in the present state of the world they are few and far between who attain to that state; yet perhaps at no other period were such false claims made to inspiration, as now. It is said that women have intuitive faculties, while men drag themselves slowly upward by reason. Do not believe it. There are just as many inspired men as women, though women have perhaps more claim to peculiar forms of hysteria and nervousness. You had better die as an unbeliever than be played upon by cheats and jugglers. The power of reasoning was given you for use. Show then that you have used it properly. Doing so, you will be able to take care of higher things.

We must always remember that God is Love. "A fool indeed is he who, living on the banks of the Ganga, seeks to dig a little well for water. A fool indeed is the man who, living near a mine of diamonds, spends his life in searching for beads of glass." god is that mine of diamonds. We are fools indeed to give up God for legends of ghosts or flying hobgoblins. It is a disease, a morbid desire. It degenrates the race, weakens the nerves and the brain, living in incessant morbid fear of hobgoblins, or stimulating the hunger for wonders; all these wild stories about them keep the nerves at an unnatural tension—a slow and sure degeneration of the race. It is degeneration to think of giving up God, purity, holiness, and spirituality, to go after all these nonsense! Reading other men's thoughts! If I must read everyone else's thoughts for five minutes at a time I shall go crazy. Be strong and stand up and seek the God of Love. This is the highest strength. What power is higher than the power of purity? Love and purity govern the world. This Love of God cannot be reached by the weak; therefore, be not weak, either physically, mrntally, morally or spiritually.[33]

The value most desirable for the good of humankind far exceeds the limits of what he thinks and acts. This is why the aesthetics of the good of mankind entirely depends on how best the aesrhetics of love is revealed in our thoughts and actions towards everyone and everything. When love is thus eyed from the standpoint of aesthetics, it allows our thoughts and actions to be more transparent, more objective, more sensitised towards altruism and more divine in the true sense of the term.

The aesthetics of love Vivekananda highlights goes beyond sex, colour, clime, creed, custom, and so on and promotes us to be serene, perfect and poignant. In explaining the five-fold steps of love and delineating on the triangle of love symbolically, he upholds the grand panorama of love in terms of catholicity in aesthetic cadence. In his words:

There are five steps of human love:

1. *The lowest, most commonplace, "peaceful" love, when we look up to our Father for all we want— protection, food, etc.*
2. *The love which makes us want to serve. Man wants to serve God as his master, the longing to serve dominating every other feeling; and we are indifferent whether the master is good or bad, kind or unkind.*
3. *The love of a friend, the love of equals— companions, playmates. Man feels God to be his companion.*
4. *Motherly love. God is looked upon as a child. In India this is considered a higher love than the foregoing, because it has absolutely no element of fear.*
5. *The love of husband and wife; love for love's sake— God the perfect, beloved one.*

It has been beautifully expressed: "Four eyes meet, a change begins to come into two souls; love come in the middle between these two souls and makes them one."

When a man has this last and most perfect form of love, then all desires vanish, forms and doctrines and churches drop away, even the desire for freedom (the end and aim of all religions is freedom from birth and death other things) is given up. The highest love is the love that is sexless, for it is perfect unity that is expressed in the highest love, and sex differentiates bodies. It is therefore only in spirit that union is possible. The less we have of the physical idea, the more perfect will be our love; at last all physical thought will be forgotten, and the two souls will become one. We love, love always. Love comes and penetrates through the forms and sees beyond.

** ** ** **

Love may be symbolised by a triangle. The first angle is, love never begs, never asks for anything; the second, love knows no fear; the third and the apex, love for love's sake. Through the power of love the senses become finer and higher. The perfect love is very rare in human relation, for human love almost always interdependent and mutual. But God's love is a constant stream, nothing can hurt or disturb it. When man loves God as his highest ideal, as no beggar, wanting nothing, then is love carried to the extreme of evolution, and it becomes a great power in the universe. It takes a long time to get to these things, and we have to begin by that which is nearest to our nature; some are born to service, some to be mothers in love.[34]

The fountain of aesthetics naturally and spontaneously flowing in man-God relationship is the perfect ideal of man. But in reality it is either ignored or denied due to unusual and undesirable ambiguities and abstractions and dissociation of identities comes out prominently perhaps only to create a vicious climate for effloresence of truth in religion and humanity which are inseparable. As a matter of fact, whenever there is an attempt for dwarfing the human spirit, religion becomes devoid of truth and loses the eternal warmth of the human spirit.

The aesthetic spirit of realisation of God as man necessitates ardent and serious nurturing and dissemination. In his "Address on Bhakti-Yoga", Vivekananda exquisitely spells out as follows:

When men see Him, they see Him as man, and the animals as animal— each according to his ideal. That is the only way you can see Him; you have to worship Him as man, because there is no other way out of it. Two classes of men do not worship God as man—the human brute who has no religion, and the Paramahamsa (highest Yogi) who has gone beyond humanity, who has thrown off his mind and body and gone beyond the limits of nature. All nature has become his Self. He has neither mind nor body, and can worship God as God, as can a Jesus or a Buddha. They did not worship God as man. The other extreme is the human brute. You know how two extremes look alike. Similar is the case with the extreme of ignorance and the other extreme of knowledge; neither of these worships anybody. The extremely ignorant do not worship God, not being developed enough to feel the need for so doing. Those that have attained the highest knowledge also do not worship God—having realised and become one with God.

** ** ** **

Do not limit God anywhere. Pay all the reverence that you think is due to God, to Christ; that is the only worship we can have. God cannot be worshipped; He is the immanent Being of the universe. It is only to His manifestation as man that we can pray. It would be a very good plan, when Christians pray, to say, "in the name of Christ". Ir would be wise to stop praying to God, and only pray to Christ. God understands human feelings and becomes a man to do good to humanity. "Whenever virtue subsides and immorality prevails, then I come to help mankind", says Krishna. He also says, "Fools, not knowing that I, the Omnipotent and Omnipresent God of the universe, have taken this human form, deride Me and think that cannot be." their minds have been clouded with demoniacal ignorance, so they cannot see in Him the Lord of the universe. These great Incarnations of God are to be worshipped. Not only so, they alone can be worshipped; and on the days of their birth, and on the days when they went out of this world, we ought to pay more particular reverence to them. In worshipping Christ I would rather worship Him just as He desires; on the day of His birth I would rather worship Him by fasting than by feasting—by praying. When these are thought of, these great ones, they manifest themselves in our souls, and they make us like unto them. Our whole nature changes, and we become like them.[35]

The aesthetic nature of man under such a change as stated above is the key to the advancement of man in excellence and ascent. It is a quest for mystic efflorescence which drives man to ascertain and direct all aesthetic endeavour towards the mystic beyonding of consciousness. It teaches him how to be serene and passionless, altruistic and selfless. The quest for this aesthetic vision in the mystic beyonding of man far exceeds beyond good and evil and transcends towards peace and truth to encounter the All Good, All Peaceful and All True.

Why should man make an earnest quest for quality enhancement in and through the exercise of aesthetics in harmony with that of mystic sensibilities? The answer is simple and distinct. It turns out to be a finer and more catholic step in the unison of man and God as a natural occasion in life and work. Moreover, with the control of his senses, he enters into and learns the lesson of renouncement.

Placing before us the history of the aesthetic grandeur of mystic renouncement as revealed in the lives of Buddha, Christ and Krishna, vivekananda unfolds the spirit of renunciation in terms of saying with "flowers and pictures and incense":

> *The history of the world is the history of persons like Buddha and Jesus. The passionless and unattached do most for the world. Oicture Jesus in the slums. He sees beyond the misery. "You, my brethren, are all divine." His work is calm. He removes causes. You will be able to work for the good of the world when you know for a fact that this work is an illusion. The more unconscious this work, the better, because it is then the more superconscious. Our search is not for good or evil; but happiness and good are nearer to truth than their opposites. A man ran a thorn into his finger, and with another thorn took it out. The first thorn is Evil. The second thorn is Good. The Self is that Peace which passeth beyond evil and good. The universe is melting down: man draws nearer to God. For one moment he is real— God. He is re-differentiated— a prophet. Before him, now, theworld trembles. A fool sleeps and wakes a fool— a man unconscious; and superconscious, he returns with infinite power, purity, and love— the God-Man. This is the use of the superconscious state.*
>
> ** ** ** **
>
> *As a lotus-leaf, living in the water yet untouched by it, so should the soul be in the world. This is a battlefield., fight your way out. Life in this world is an attempt to see God. Make your life a manifestation of will strengthened by renunciation.*
>
> *We must learn to control all our brain-centres consciously. The first step is the joy of living. Asceticism is fiendish. To laugh is better than to pray. Sing. Get rid of misery. Do not for heaven's sake infect others with it. Never think God sells a little happiness and a little unhappiness. Surround yourselves with flowers and pictures and incense.*[36]

Self-admission and self-surrender are two characteristic features of the aesthetic mind that develops its serenity for the beyond. Man cannot but be devoted to the efflorescence of these two aesthetic components. These bring forth calmness of mind by means of elimination of all passions and endearment of humility as best as possible.

In a poem entitled "No one to blame" which he wrote on 16th May, 1895, Vivekananda poignantly highlighted the mystico-aesthetic vision of man in quest of ascent and excellence:

Each day my life I make or mar,
Each deed begets its kind,
Good good, bad bad, the tide once set
No one can stop or stem;
No one but me to blame.

I am my own embodied past;
Therein the plan was made;
The will, the thought, to that conform,
To that the outer frame;
No one but me to blame.

Love comes reflected back as love,
Hate breeds more fierce hate,
They mete their measures, lay on me
Through life and death their claim;
No one but me to blame.

I cast off fear and vain remorse,
I feel my Karma's away
I face the ghosts my deeds have raised—
Joy, sorrow, censure, fame;
No one but me to blame.

Good, bad, love, hate, and pleasure, pain
Forever linked go,
I dream of pleasure without pain,
It never, never came;
No one but me to blame.

I give up hate, I give up love,
My thirst for life is gone;
Eternal death is what I want,
Nirvanam goes life's flame;
No one is left to blame.[37]

The education of the intellect which is cultivated to a great extent necessitates a total overhauling in terms of aesthetics. Only then it will be a real platform for exercise and culture of the education of the heart. Now-a-days there is a separation between the brain and the heart. The consequences are really alarming. We do not know how to go beyond intellect because we do not know how to synchronise between intellect and aesthetics. The pristine purity of man wails for freedom to be natural and poignant so that the All True becomes a constant partner to his excellence and ascent.

As a radical aesthetic thinker, Vivekananda emphasises on education of the heart along with education of the intellect. This is the only alternative to understand and appreciate the fact that all knowledge and all perfection are already there within us and it is our obligation to cultivate knowledge and perfection with sincerity and dedication. In this connection, Vivekananda's viewpoints show how to to exercise aesthetic elegance:

> *We may study all the books that are in the world, yet we may not understand a word of religion or of God. We may talk all our lives and yet may not be the better for it; we may be the most intellectual people the world ever saw, and yet we may not come to God at all. On the other hand, have you not seen what irreligious men have been produced from the most intellectual training ? It is one of the evils of your Western civilisation that you are after intellectual education alone, and take no care of the heart. It only makes men ten times more selfish, and that will be your destruction. When there is conflict between the heart and the brain, let the heart be followed, because intellect has only one state, reason, and within that, intellect works, and cannot get beyond. It is the heart that takes one to the highest plane, which intellect can never reach; it goes beyond intellect, and reaches to what is called inspiration. Intellect can never become inspired; only the heart when it is enlightened, becomes inspired. An intellectual, heartless man never becomes an inspired man. It is always the heart that speaks in the man of love; it discovers a greater instrument than intellect can give you, the instrument of inspiration. In a lower state it is a much weaker instrument than intellect. An ignorant man knows nothing, but he is a little emotional by nature. Compare him with a great professor—what wonderful power the latter possesses! But the professor is*

bound by his intellect, but he can be a devil and an intellectual man at the same time; but the man of heart can never be a devil; no man with emotion was ever a devil. Properly cultivated, the heart can be changed, and will go beyond intellect; it will be changed into inspiration. Man will have to go beyond intellect in the end. The knowledge of man, his powers of perception, of reasoning and intellect and heart, all are busy churning this milk of the world.[38]

How to make the best use of knowledge is the key point of the aesthetics of man. For this, he must prepare himself ceaselessly and strenuously. For this, he must undergo training in purity and poignance, perfection and balance of thought and action, analysis and interpretation. This must, as it were, be a prologue to the quest for the "Real Man". In this connection, the classical viewpoints of Vivekananda are remarkable:

It is only the Spirit that is the individual, because it is infinite. No infinity can be divided; infinity cannot be broken into pieces. It is the same one, undivided unit for ever, and this is the individual man, the Real Man. The apparent man is merely a struggle to express, to manifest this individuality which is beyond; and evolution is not in the Spirit. These changes which are going on— the wicked becoming good, the animal becoming man, take them in whatever way you like— are not in the Spirit. They are evolution of nature and manifestation of Spirit. Suppose there is a screen hiding you from me, in which there is a small hole through which I can see some of the faces before me, just a few faces. Now suppose the hole begins to grow larger and larger, and as it does so, more and more of the scene before me reveals itself and when at last the whole screen has disappeared, I stand face to face with you all. You did not change at all in this case; it was the hole that was evolving, and you were gradually manifesting yourselves. So it is with the Spirit. No perfection is going to be attained. You are already free and perfect. What are these ideas of religion and God and searching for the hereafter? Why does man look for a God? Why does man, in every nation, in every state of society, want a perfect ideal somewhere, either in man, in God or elsewhere? Because that idea is within you. It was your own heart beating and you did not know; you were mistaking it for something external. It is the God within your own self that is propelling you to seek for Him, to realise Him. After long searches here and there, in temples and in churches, in earths and in heavens, at last you come back, completing the circle from where you started, to your own soul and find that He for whom you have been seeking all over the world, for whom you have been weeping and praying in churches and temples, on whom you were looking as the mystery of all mysteries shrouded in the clouds, is nearest of the near, is your own Self, the reality of your life, body, and soul. That is your own nature. Assert it, manifest it. Not to become pure, you are pure already. You are not to be perfect, you are that already. Nature is like that screen which is hiding the reality beyond. Every good thought that you think or act upon is simply tearing the veil, as it were; and the purity, the Infinity, the God behind, manifests Itself more and more.[39]

The essence of elegance we seek in the culture of aesthetics must imbibe the spirit of man in continual and unrelenting quest for the All Good, All Pure, All Perfect. Let us be devoted to the aesthetics of goodness, purity and perfection with the eternal words of optimism:

We only get what we deserve. It is a lie when we say, the world is bad and we are good. It can never be so. It is a terrible lie we tell ourselves. This is the first lesson to learn: be determined not to curse anything outside, not to lay the blame upon anyone outside, but be a man. Stand up, lay the blame on yourself. You will find that is always true. Get hold of yourself.

We are to take care of ourselves— that much we can do— and give up attending to others, for a time. Let us perfect the means; the end will take care of itself. For the world can be good and pure, only if our lives are good and pure. It is an effect, and we are the means. Therefore, let us purify ourselves. Let us make ourselves perfect.[40]

To accept pleasure and pain, happiness and misery as positive and strong components of bliss man seeks for poignance and perfection is the pointer to understanding the aesthetic Self which always demands calmness in all perfection. How to raise the Self above all actions and interactions with the changing affairs of life is the great aesthetic challenge. Man must accept that challenge. Unless he accepts it, the aesthetic bliss within will ever remain absent. Let us be forewarned with Vivekananda's invaluable words:

> *Both happiness and misery are chains, the one golden, the other iron; but both are equally strong to bind us and hold us back from realising our true nature. The Atman knows neither happiness nor misery. These are merely "states", and states must ever change. The nature of the soul is bliss and peace unchanging. We have not to get it; we* have *it; let us wash away the dross from our eyes and see it. We must stand ever on the Self and look with perfect calmness upon all the panorama of the world. It is but baby's play and ought never to disturb us. If the mind is pleased by praise, it will be pained by blame. All pleasures of the senses or even of the mind are evanescent, but within ourselves is the one true unrelated pleasure, dependent on nothing outside. "The pleasure of the Self is what the world calls religion." The more our bliss is within, the more spiritual we are. Let us not depend upon the world for pleasure.*[41]

Are we aesthetically alert?

1. Swami Vivekananda, *The Complete Works of Swami Vivekananda*, Advaita Ashrama, Calcutta, Mayavati Memorial Edition, 1989, Vol. IV, pp. 463-464.
2. *Ibid*. Vol. II, pp. 251-252.
3. *Ibid*., pp. 181-182.
4. *Ibid*., Vol. V, pp. 240-241.
5. *Ibid*., Vol. VII, pp. 11-12.
6. *Ibid*., p. 12.
7. *Ibid*., p. 13.
8. *Ibid*., Vol. I, p. 501.
9. *Ibid*., p. 502.
10. *Ibid*., Vol. VIII, p. 169.
11. *Ibid*., Vol. I, pp. 238-239.
12. *Ibid*., Vol. IV, pp. 133-134.
13. *Ibid*., pp. 368-369.
14. *Ibid*., Vol. I, p. 414.
15. *Ibid*., Vol. VII, pp. 63-64.
16. *Ibid*., p. 66.
17. *Ibid*., pp. 14-15.
18. *Ibid*., Vol. I, pp. 57-58
19. *Ibid*., pp. 364-365.
20. *Ibid*., p. 71.
21. *Ibid*., p. 262.
22. *Ibid*., Vol. VII, pp. 10-11.
23. *Ibid*., Vol. IV, pp. 495-496.
24. *Ibid*., pp. 207-208.
25. *Ibid*., Vol. VIII, p. 51.
26. *Ibid*., Vol. V, pp. 245-246.
27. *Ibid*., Vol. I, pp. 235-236.
28. *Ibid*., pp. 241-242.
29. *Ibid*. Vol. VI, pp. 134-135.
30. *Ibid*., pp. 481-482.
31. *Ibid*., p. 482.
32. *Ibid*., Vol. IV, pp. 39-40.
33. *Ibid*., pp. 59-60.

34. *Ibid*., Vol. VI, pp. 142-144.
35. *Ibid*., Vol. IV, pp. 30-32.
36. *Ibid*., Vol. VIII, pp. 226-227.
37. *Ibid*., pp. 175-176.
38. *Ibid*., Vol. I, pp. 412-413.
39. *Ibid*., Vol. II, pp. 81-82.
40. *Ibid*. p. 9.
41. *Ibid*., Vol. VIII, pp. 28-29.

Towards the March of Man: Vivekananda's Dynamic Vision

Unlike any other visionary on the march of man, Swami Vivekananda stands apart as a colossus of optimistic humanism. He directs our attention to the great vision of man as a divine being and inspires us to be bold enough to proclaim the excellence and ascent of man by realising Thou art That. He highlights man as an incomparable messenger of the All Good whom he identifies with the lowly and the lost, the poor and the destitude, the ignorant and the outcast. His religion is the religion of a new order where the worship of God stands for devotion and dedication to man in selfless service. His religion is always a pathbreaker for humanistic spirituality. As a result, he makes rites and rituals in religion as secondary, even unnecessary and redundant for the sake of the manifestation of vibrant reality in the glory of man as the representative of God. He comes down to the level of the poor and wants every one of us to be the servant of each of them: *Daridradeva bhava.*

Vivekananda wants man to be a thinking being—genuine, sincere, serene and dedicated. His concept of man is always evolving, spirited, dynamic, and iconoclastic. He spare no pains in assessing man as the best creation of God. In fact, he places man as a superior spokesman of the divine efflorescence living, inspiring, forceful and transparent. As he vibrantly reminds us:

> *What a mine of strength is in this Impersonal God, where all superstitions have been thrown overboard, and man stands on his feet with the knowledge— I am the Impersonal Being of the world! What can make me afraid? I care not even for nature's laws. Death is a joke ro me. Man stands on the glory of his own soul, the infinite, the eternal, the deathless— that soul which no instruments can pierce, which no air can dry, nor fire burn, no water melt, the infinite, the birthless, the deathless, without beginning and without end, before whose magnitude the suns and moons and all their systems appear like drops in the ocean, before whose glory space melts away into nothingness and time*

vanishes into non-existence. This glorious soul we must believe in. Out of that will come power. Whatever you think, that you will be. If you think yourselves weak, weak you will be; if you think yourselves strong, strong you will be; if you think yourselves impure, impure you will be; if you think yourselves pure, pure you will be. This teaches us not to think ourselves as weak, but as strong, omnipotent, omniscient. No matter that I have not expressed it yet, it is in me. All knowledge is in me, all power, all purity, and all freedom. Why cannot I express this knowledge? Because I do not believe in it. Yet me believe in it, and it nust and will come out. This what the idea of the Impersonal teaches. Make your children strong from their very childhoo; teach them not weakness, nor forms, but make them strong; let them stand on their feet—bold, all-conquering, all-suffering; and first of all, let them learn of the glory of the soul. That you get alone in the Vedanta— and there alone. It has ideas of love and worship and other things which we have in other religions, and more besides; but this idea of the soul is the life-giving thought, the most wonderful.[1]

How to make God personal to man is the hallmark of Vivekananda's philosophy of man. How to bring religion from the high pedestal of philosophy and embrace it as an endearing and inseparable part of humanity are the signals of positive advancement that enlighten humanity. The new Puranas based on these practical aspects of the ascent of man as Vivekananda introduces always keep alive the indomitable spirit of man to evolve and work out a new pathway of all-round progress. In his soul stirring words:

So long as there shall be such a thing as personal and material love, one cannot go behind the teachings of the Puranas. So long as there shall be the human weakness of leaning upon somebody for support, these Puranas, in some form or other, must always exist. You can change their names; you can condemn those that are already existing, but immediately you will be compelled to write another Purana. If there arises amongst us a sage who will not want these old Puranas, we shall find that his disciples, within twenty years of his death, will make of his life another Purana. That will be all the difference.

This is the necessity of the nature of man; for them only there are no Puranas who have gone beyond all human weakness and has become what is really wanted of a Paramahamsa, brave and bold souls, who have gone beyond the bondages of Maya, the necessities even of nature— the triumphant, the conquereors, the gods of the world. The ordinary man cannot do without a personal God to worship; if he does not worship a God in nature, he has to worship either a God in the shape of a wife, or a child, or a father, or a friend, or a teacher, or somebody else; and the necessity is still more upon women than men. The vibration of light may be everywhere; it may be in dark places, sins cats and other animals perceive it, but for us the vibration must be in our plane to become visible. We may talk, therefore, of an Impersonal Being and so forth, but so long as we are ordinary mortals, God can be seen in man alone. Our conception of God and our worship of God are naturally, therefore, human. "This body, indeed, is the greatest temple of God." So we find that men have been worshipped throughout the ages, and although we may condemn or criticise some of the extravagances which naturally follow, we find at once that the heart is sound, that in spite of these extravagances, in spite of this going into extremes, there is an essence, there is a true, firm core, a backbone, to the doctrine that is preached. I am not asking you to swallow without consideration any old stories, or any unscientific jargon. I am not calling upon you to believe in all sorts of Vamachari explanations that, unfortunately, have crept into some of the Puranas, but what I mean is this, thet there is an essence which ought not to be lost, a reason for the existence of the Puranas, and that is the teaching of Bhakti to make religion practical, to bring religion from its high philosophical flights into the evertday lives of our common human beings.[2]

The dynamic vision of man as Vivekananda unfolds through theort and practice of religion opens a new horizon of human consciousness. Thus when we speak about God, it is the reality based on the philosophy of human consciousness that stands out fundamental and supteme. In "Bhakti-Yoga", he significantly spells out:

Bhakti has to float on smoothly with the current of our nature. True is it that we cannot have any idea of the Brahman which is not anthropomorphic, but is it not equally true of everything we know? The greatest psychologist the world has ever known, Bhagavan Kapila, demonstrated ages ago that human consciousness is one of the elements in the make-up of all the objects of our perception and conception, internal as well as external. Beginning with our bodies and going up to Ishvara, we may see that every object of our perception is this consciousness plus something else, whatever that may be; and this unavoidable mixture is what we ordinarily think of as reality. Indeed it is, and ever will be, all of the reality that is possible for the human mind to know. Therefore to say that Ishvara is unreal, because He is anthropomorphic, is sheer nonsense. It is very much like the occidental squibble on idealism and realism, which fearful-looking quarrel has for its foundation a mere play on the word "real". The idea of Ishvara covers all the ground ever denoted and connected by the word real, and Ishvara is as real as anything else in the universe; and after all, the word real means nothing more than what has now been pointed out.[3]

Self-teaching along with self-abnegation and self-restraint, self-discipline and self- excellence are the characteristic components of the advancement of man in endearing and harmonising optimism and pessimism. Indeed self-realisation is one of the greatest challenges of man who alone knows how to make the best fusion between the two. When Vivekananda speaks on Yogas, he wants man to be perfect in every direction—wisdom, devotion, work, dynamism, extinction of personality and the like. In introducing this fact, he elucidates:

We generally find men holding two opinions regarding the world. Some are pessimists and say,"How horrible this world is, how wicked!" Some others are optinists and say, "How beautiful this world is, how wonderful!" To those who have not controlled their own minds, the world is either full of evil or at best a mixture of good and evil; we shall find everything to be in its proper place, to be harmonious. Some men, who begin by saying that the world is a hell, often end by saying that it is a heaven when they succeed in the practice of self-control. If we are genuine Karma-Yogis and wish to train ourselves in that attainment of this state, wherever we may begin we are sure to end in perfect self-abnegation; and as soon as this seeming self-abnegation has gone, the whole world, which at first appears to us to be filled with evil, well appear to be heaven itself and full of blessedness. Its very atmosphere will be blessed; every human face there will be god. Such is the end and aim of Karma-Yoga, and such is its perfection in practical life.

Our various Yogas do not conflict with each other; each of them leads us to the same goal and makes us perfect. Only each has to be strenuously practised. The whole secret is in practising. First you have to hear, then think, and then practise. This is true of every Yoga. You have first to hear about it and understand what it is; and many things which you do not understand will be made clear you by constant hearing and thinking. It is hard to understand everything at once. The explanation of everything is after all in yourself. No one was ever really taught by another; each of us has to teach himself. The external teacher offers only the suggestion which rouses the internal teacher to work to understand things. Then things will be made clearer to us by our own perception and thought, and we shall realise them in our own souls; and that realisation will grow into the intense power of will. First it is feeling, then it becomes willing, and out of that willing comes the tremendous force for work that will go through every vein and nerve and muscle, until the whole mass of your body is charged into an instrument of the unselfish Yoga of work, and the desired result of perfect self-abnegation and utter unselfishness is duly attained. This attainment does not depend on any dogma, or doctrine, or belief. Whether one is Christian, or Jew, or Gentile, it does not matter. Are you unselfish? That is the question. If you are, you will be perfect without reading a single religious book, without going into a single church or temple. Each one of our Yogas is fitted to make man perfect even without the help of the others, because they have all the same goal in view. The Yogas of work, of wisdom, and of devotion are all capable of serving as direct and independent means for the attainment of Moksha.[4]

The vision of God as Vivekananda upholds and puts in practice is very remarkable. It makes a real and living relationship between god and man. It glorifies man because it makes God visible and prepares the latter for living worship. In a poem titled "The Living God" and written from New York on 6th January 1896 to a Western lady-disciple, Vivekananda serenely presents:

He who is in you and outside you,
Who works through all hands,
Who walks on all feet,
Whose body are all ye,
Him worship, and break all other idols!
He who is at once the high and the low,
The sinner and the saint,
Both God and worm,
Him worship— visible, knowable, real, pmnipresent,
Break all other idols!
In whom is neither past life
Nor future birth nor death,
In whom we always have been
And always shall be one,
Him worship. Break all other idols!
Ye fools! who neglect the living God,
And His infinite reflections with which the world is full.
While ye run after imaginary shadows,
That lead one to fights and quarrels,
Him worship, the only visible!
Break all other idols![5]

A radical thinker of man par excellence, Vivekananda asserts God in everything and boldly inspires to be devoted to the vision of unison between man and man. As there is no real separation between atom and atom, moon and earth, sun and moon, nation and nation, so Oneness of life is the universal truth. Referring to the Vedanta, Vivekananda poignantly observes on the real identity of man:

In the heart of things there is Unity still. If you go below the surface, you find that Unity between man and man, between races and races, high and low, rich and poor, gods and men, and men and animals. If you go deep enough, all will be seen as only variations of the One, and he who has attained to this conception of Oneness has no moredelusion. What can delude him? He knows the reality of everything, the secret of everything. Where is there any more misery for him? What does he desire? He has traced the reality of everything to the Lord, the Centre, the Unity of everything and that is Eternal Existence, Eternal Knowledge, Eternal Bliss. Neither dath, nor disease, nor sorrow, nor misery, nor discontent is there. All is Perfect Union and Perfect Bliss. For whom should he mourn then? In the Reality, there is no death, there is no misery; in the Reality, there is no one to mourn for, no one to be sorry for. He has penetrated everything, the Pure One, the Formless, the Bodiless, the Stainless. He the Knower, He the great Poet, the Self-Existent, He who is giving to everyone what he deserves. They grope in darkness who worship this ignorant world, the world that is produced out of ignorance, thinking of it as Existence, and those who live their whole lives in this world, and never find anything better or higher, are groping in still greater darkness. But he who knows the secret of nature, seeing That which is beyond nature through the help of nature, he crosses death, and through the help of That which is beyond nature, he enjoys Eternal Bliss. "Thou sun who hast covered the Truth with the golden disc, do thou remove the veil, so that I may see the Truth that is within thee, I have known what is the real meaning of thy rays and thy glory and have seen That which shines in thee; the Truth in thee I see, and That which is within thee is within me, and I am That.[6]

The excellence and ascent of man is inherent in feeling. It is the treasure of all treasures . It has no parallel in the true identity of man. It calls forth greatest urgency and topmost care in the making of man. Unless the spirit of feeling is ignited, man becomes a machine with no role for him to exercise his own qualities. His interests, likings or dislikings, his attitudes, interests or skills, his motivations, interpretations or aptitudes— all are turned into illusions or myths. He cannot be transparent in his thoughts and actions. He cannot be distinct in ideations and accomplishments. The inevitable result is the ruthless moratorium of man. Being thus bereft of the exercise of feelings, man digs his own graveyard of futility and hopelessness.

A practical and positive humanist, Vivekananda gives a clarion call to man to earnestly exercise feeling:

Feel like Christ and you will be a Christ; feel like Buddha and you will be a Buddha. It is feeling that is the life, the strength, the vitality, without which no amount of intellectual activity can reach God. Intellect is like limbs without the power of locomotion. It is only when feeling enters and gives them motion that they move and work on others. That is so all over the world, and it is a thing which you must always remember. It is one of the most practical things in Vedantic morality, for it is the teaching of the Vedanta that you are all prophets, and all must be prophets. The book is not the proof of your conduct, but you are the proof of the book. How do you know that a book teaches the truth? Because you are truth and feel it. This is what the Vedanta says. What is the proof of the Christs and Buddhas of the world? That you and I feel like them. That is why you and I understand that they were true. Our prophet-soul is the proof of their prophet-soul. Your godhead is the proof of God Himself. If you are not a prophet, there never has been anything true of God. If you are not God, there never was any God, and never will be. This, says the Vedanta, is the ideal to folow. Every one of us will have to become a prophet, and you are that already. Only know *it. Never think there is anything impossible for the soul. It is the greatest heresy to think so. If there is sin, this is the only sin— to say that you are weak, or others are weak.*[7]

That man is the only decider of religion is the new philosophy which Vivekananda has introduced in order to assure fool-proof evaluation from different perspectives and finer platforms for transfer and transcendence and transfer. How far the constitution of man is transparent should be at the backdrop of understanding and appreciating any religion. The ideas and ideals of religion in the light of such evaluation of man provide ample room for exercise of freedom to think and freedom to reflect in a scientific and objective way. As Vivekananda explicitly observes:

The proof of religion depends on the truth of the constitution of man, and not on any books. These books are the outgoings, the effects of man's constitution; man made these books. We are yet to see the books that made man. Reason is equally an effect of that common cause, the constitution of man, where our appeal must be. And yet, as reason alone is directly connected with this constitution, it should be resorted to, as long as it follows faithfully the same. What do I mean by reason? I mean what every educated man or woman is wanting to do at the present time, to apply the discoveries of secular knowledge to religion. The first principle of reasoning is that the particular is explained by the general, the general by the more general, until we come to the universal. For instance, we have the idea of law. If something happens and we believe that it is the effect of such and such a law, we are satisfied; that is an explanation for us. What we mean by that explanation is that it is proved that this one effect, which had dissatisfied us , is only one particular of a general mass of occurrences which we designate by the word "law". When one apple fell, Newton was disturbed; but when he found that all apples fell, it was gravitation, and he was satisfied. This is one principle of human knowledge. I see a particular being, a human being, in the street. I refer him to the bigger conception of man, and I am satisfied; I know he is a man by referring him to the more general. So the particulars are to be referred to the general, the general to the more general, and everything at last to the universal, the last concept that we have, the most universal— that of existence. Existence is the most universal concept.

We are all human beings; that is to say, each one of us, as it were, a particular part of the general concept, humanity. A man, and a cat, and a dog, are all animals. These particular examples, as man, or dog, or cat, are parts of a bigger and more general concept, animal. The man, and the cat, and thr dog, and the plant, and the tree, all come under the still more general concept, life. Again, all rhese, all beings and all materials, come under the one concept of existence, for we all are in it.[8]

The quest for Truth as the ideal is the desirable goal of man in life. It is a real challenge for him as long as he lives in this world. But the struggle for this ideal is really very tough for him because he must undergo diverse constraints like antithetical forces known or unknown, mild or severe, strong or weak, transitory or permanent as these appear. Just as paradise lost welcomes man to regain it with renewed zeal, so he must always be prepared for learning by mistakes. The march of man for advancement and ascent necessitate a warm embrace with darkness through relentless struggle to welcome the efflorescence of light eternal.

How does Vivekananda inspire man to march for advancement? Here is a dynamic vision portrayed, as it were, in the canvas of positive humanism:

It is not truth, but development, that is the great aim. The struggle is the great lesson. Mind you, the great benefit in this life is struggle. It is through that we pass. If there is any road to Heaven, it is through Hell. Through Hell to Heaven is always the way. When the soul has wrestled with circumstance and has met death, a thousand times death on the way, but nothing daunted has struggled forward again and again and yet again—then the soul comes out as a giant and laughs at the ideal he has been struggling for, because he finds how much greater is he than the ideal. I am the end, my own Self, and nothing else, for what is there to compare to my own Self? Can a bag of gold be the ideal of my Soul? Certainly not! My Soul is the highest ideal that I can have. Realising my own real nature is the one goal of my life.

There is nothing that is absolutely evil. The devil has a place here as well as God, else he would not be here. Just as I told you, it is through Hell that we pass to Heaven. Our mistakes have places here. Go on! Do not look back if you think you have done something that is not right. Now, do you believe you could be what you are today, had you not made those mistakes before? Bless your mistakes, then. They have been angels unawares. Blessed be torture! Blessed be happiness! Do not care what be your lot. Hold on to the ideal. March on! Do not look back upon little mistakes and things. In this battlefield of ours, the dust of mistakes must be raised. Those who are not so thin-skinned that they cannot bear the dust, let them get out of the ranks.[9]

The practice of true religion that man should do with all earnestness requires a positive bent of mind for a march towards realisation of life. This realisation calls forth undergoing all kinds of experiences that lead to perfection. How to understand religion in terms of man and vice versa? In reply to a question by one of his admirers and playmates, Vivekananda's viewpoints are significant:

Don't you see that circumstances have changed now? Have the men of our country the power left in them to take up and practise true religion? What they have is only pride in themselves that they are very Sattvika. Time was when they were Sattvika, no doubt, but now they have fallen very low. The fall from Sattva brings one down headlong into Tamas! That is what has happened to them. Do you think that a man who does not exert himself at all, who only takes the name of Hari, shutting himself up in a room, who remains quiet and indifferent even when seeing a huge amount of weong and violence done to others before his very eyes, possess the quality of Sattva? Nothing of the kind, he is only enshrouded in dark Tamas. How can the people of a country practise religion who do not get even sufficient food to appease their hunger? How can renunciation come to the people of a country in whose minds the desires for Bhoga (enjoyment) have not been in the least satisfied? For this reason, find out, first of all, the ways and means by which men may get enough to eat and have enough luxuries to enable them to enjoy life a little; and then gradually, true Vairagya (dispassion) will come, and they will be fit and ready to realise religion in life.[10]

To realise true religion in life is to realise the divinity inherent in every human being. Man must strive for that wholeheartedly and unendingly. It is a challenge eternal and abiding, persistent and living for manifestation of purity and perfection already in him. It is also a challenge to bring back the serene identity of Man the Divine blessed with continuous experience synchronised. That is evolution. In the words of Vivekananda:

All human knowledge proceeds out of experience; we cannot know anything except by experience. All our reasoning is based upon generalised experience, all our knowledge is but harmonised experience. Looking around us, what do we find? A continuous change. The plant comes out of the seed, grows into the tree, completes the circle, and comes back to the seed. The animal comes, lives a certain time, dies, and completes the circle. So does man. The mountains slowly but surely crumbleaway, the rivers slowly but surely dry up, rains come out of the sea, and go back to the sea. Everywhere circles are being completed, birth, growth, development, and decay following each other with mathematical precision. This is our everyday experience. Inside of it all, behind all this vast mass of what we call life, of millions of forms and shapes, millions upon millions of varieties, beginning from the lowest atom to the highest spiritualised man, we find existing a certain unity. Every day we find that the wall was thought to be dividing one thing and another is being broken down, and all matter is coming to be recognised by modern science as one substance, manifesting in different ways and in various forms; the one life that runs through all like a continuous chain, of which all these various forms represent the links, link after link, extending almost infinitely, but of the same one chain. That is what is called evolution.[11]

Meanwhile, let man muse for That in him:

Existence was not then, nor non-existence,
The world was not, the sky beyond was neither.
What covered the mist? Of whom was that?
What was in the depths of darkness thick?
Death was not then, nor immortality,
The night was neither separate from day,
But motionless did That *vibrate*
Alone, with Its own glory one—
Beyond That *nothing did exist.*[12]

1. Swami Vivekananda: *The Complete Works of Swami Vivekananda*, Advaita Ashrama, Kolkata, Mayavati Memorial Edition, 1989, Vol. III, pp. 130-131.
2. *Ibid*., pp. 387-388.
3. *Ibid*., p. 42.
4. *Ibid*., Vol. I, pp. 92-93.
5. *Ibid*., Vol. VIII, p. 169.
6. *Ibid*., Vol. II, pp. 153-154.
7. *Ibid*., pp. 307-308.
8. *Ibid*., Vol. I, pp. 369-370.
9. *Ibid*., Vol. V, pp. 252-253.
10. *Ibid*., pp. 352-353.
11. *Ibid*., Vol. II, pp. 226-227.
12. *Ibid*., Vol. VI, p. 178.

POSTSCRIPT

Man wants to have his real identity. To have his real identity is to live a life of perfection well crystallised through sincerity and devotion, serenity and submission. That he is an eternal warrior against all constraints in the forms of sorrow, pain, bereavement, loneliness, desolation, devastation, loss and so on is the symbol of his inherent divine power. He must see God within him. He must try his best to reach God anywhere and everywhere. He must prepare himself to be always in the prized quest for perfection and the beyond. Only then he connotes himself as Man the Divine Being.

Swami Vivekananda, an incomparable reminder and introducer of the real identity of man, emphasises on the ascent and excellence of man in terms of purity and perfection by means of being able to enjoy the blessings of God all the time. In the paper read at the Parliament of Religions on 19th September, 1893, referring to the Hindu religion, he strongly reminds us:

> *The Vedas teach that the soul is divine, only held in the bondage of matter; perfection will be reached only when this bond will burst, and the word they use for it is therefore, Mukti—freedom, freedom from the bonds of imperfection, freedom from death and misery.*
>
> *And this bondage can only fall off through the mercy of God, and this mercy comes on the pure. So purity is the condition of His mercy. How does that mercy act? He reveals Himself to the pure heart; the pure and the stainless see God, ye, even in this life; then and then only all the crookedness of the heart is made straight. Then all doubt ceases. He is no more the freak of a terrible law of causation. This is the very centre, the very vital conception of Hinduism. The Hindu does not want to live upon words and theories. If there are existences beyond the ordinary sensuous existence, he wants to come face to face with them. If there is a soul in him which is not matter, if there is an all-merciful universal Soul, he will go to Him direct. He must see Him, and that alone can destroy all doubts. So the best proof of a Hindu sage gives about the soul, about God is: "I have seen the*

soul; I have seen God." And that is the only condition of perfection. The Hindu religion does not consist in struggles and attempts to believe a certain doctrine or dogma, but in realising—not in believing, but in being and becoming.

Thus the whole object of their system is by constant struggle to become perfect, to become divine, to reach God and see God, and this reaching God, seeing God, becoming perfect even as the Father of Heaven is perfect, constitutes the religion of the Hindus.

And what becomes of a man when he attains perfection? He lives a life of bliss infinite. He enjoys infinite and perfect bliss, having obtained the only thing in which man ought to have pleasure, namely God, and enjoys the bliss with God.[1]

To live a life of being blessed with the blessings as above, is to baptise oneself with the spirit of love and selfless service to man and society. Vivekananda time and again reminds us of that religion which wipes out the tears of the distressed, the woes and sufferings of the hapless and the deserted, the ignored and the despised. In fact, he boldly asserts to love every one irrespective of caste, colour, race, community, etc. and wants to serve mankind unselfishly.

In an inspiring letter written from Washington on 27th October, 1894 to Alasinga Perumal, Vivekananda advises:

I am only the figurehead. I am a Tyagi (detached) monk. I only want one thing. I do not believe in a God or religion which cannot wipe the widow's tears or bring a piece of bread to the orphan's mouth. However, sublime be the theories, however well-spun may be the philosophy— I do not call it religion so long as it is confined to books and dogmas. The eye is in the forehead and not in the back. Move onward and carry into practice that which you are very proud to call your religion, and God bless you!

Look not at me, look to yourselves. I am happy to have been the occasion of rousing an enthusiasm. Take advantage of it, float along with it, and everything will come right. Love never fails, my son; today or tomorrow or ages after, truth will conquer. Love shall win the victory. Do you love your fellow men? Where should you go to seek for God— are not all the poor, the miserable, the weak, Gods? Why not worship them first? Why go to dig a well on the shores of the Ganga? Believe in the omnipotent power of love. Who cares for these tinsel puffs of name? I never keep watch of what the newspapers are saying. Have you love?— You are omnipotent. Are you perfectly unselfish? If so, you are irresistible. It is character that pays everywhere. It is the Lord who protects His children in the depths of the sea. Your country requires heroes; be heroes! God bless you![2]

To be real heroes, men must be prepared for undergoing any sacrifice to control themselves through discipline. What kind of discipline does man require fundamentally? It is the discipline that prompts him continually to realise fully the presence of the All Good within him. The incomparable glory of man bears testimony to the realisation of "absolute oneness with the Divine". While referring to the aim of Raja-Yoga, Vivekananda characteristically observes:

Certain positions, certain modes of breathing help to harmonise and concentrate the mind, but with these must go purity and strong desire for God, or realisation. The attempt to sit down and fix the mind on one idea and hold it there will prove to most people that there is some need for help to enable them to do this successfully. The mind has to be gradually and systematically brought under control. The will has to be strengthened by slow, continuous, and persevering drill. This is no child's play, no fad to be tried one day and discarded the next. It is a life's work; and the end to be attained is well worth all that it can cost us to reach it; being nothing less than the realisation of our absolute oneness with the Divine. Surely, with this end in view, and with the knowledge that we can certainly succeed, no price can be too great to pay.[3]

The greatest challenge of man today is to realise his true identity. It is the identity with which his real worth is associated. It is also the identity that is in perfect fusion with true religion. That is yet again the identity that brings forth a new religion of man. That region shows the way for every man the path to attain Rishihood as Vivekananda christens and become a Mantra-drastra. In his soul-stirring words:

Our scriptures declare again and again that even the knowledge of the external senses is not religion. That is religion which makes us realise the Unchangeable One, and that is the religion for every one. He who realises transcendental truth, he who realises the Atman in his own nature, he who comes face to face to God, sees God alone in everything, has become a Rishi. And there is no religious life for you until you have become a Rishi. Then alone religion begins for you, now is only the preparation. Then religion dawns upon you, now you are only undergoing intellectual gymnastics and physical tortures.

We must, therefore, remember that our religion lays down distinctly and clearly that every one who wants salvation must pass through the stage of Rishihood— must become a Mantra-drastra, must see God. That is salvation; that is the law laid down by our scriptures. Then it becomes easy to look into the scriptures with our own eyes, understand the meaning for ourselves, to analyse just what we want, and to understand the truth for ourselves. This is what has to be done. At the same time we must pay all reverence to the ancient sages for their work. They were great, these sages, but we want to be greater. They did great work in the past, but we must do greater work than they.[4]

Today's man is the path-finder of tomorrow in many avenues of perfection and poignancy of vision. His vision requires the warmth of costant pursuit of knowledge and wisdom, erudition and edification. His urge for forging ahead under numerous constraints must be more than what he thinks or does. His progress must be evaluated in terms of experiences achieved or likely to be achieved in future. He must be a Jnana-Yogi in order to be able to live in freedom. He must be non-attached in living in this world. He must prove the fact that he is "the highest of all beings".

In a lecture delivered in New York, 1896, Vivekananda clarifies the real role of man in this world:

Philosophy is no joke or talk. It has to be realised; this body will vanish, this earth and everything will vanish, this idea that I am the body or the mind will for some time vanish, or if the Karma is ended it will disappear, never to come back; but if one part of the Karma remains, then as a potter's wheel, after the potter has finished the pot, will sometimes go on from the past momentum, so this body, when the delusion has vanished altogether, will go on for some time. Again this world will come, men and women and animals will come, just as the mirage came next day, but not with the same force; along with it will come the idea that I know its nature now, and it will cause no bondage, no more pain, nor grief, nor misery. Whenever anything miserable will come, the mind will be able to say, "I know you as hallucination." when a man has reached that state, he is called Jivanmukta, "living-free". He is Jivanmukta who can live in this world without being attached. He is like the lotus leaves in water, which are never wetted by the water. He is the highest of human beings, nay, the highest of all beings, for he has realised his identity with the Absolute, he has realised that he is one with God. So long as you think that you have the least difference from God, fear will cease you, but when you have known that you are He, that there is no difference, entirely no difference, that you are He, all of Him, and the whole of Him, all fear ceases. "There, who sees whom? Who worships whom? Who talks to whom? Who hears whom? Where one sees another, where one talks to another, where one hears another, that is little. Where one sees none, where none speaks to none, that is the highest, that is the great, that is the Brahman." Being That, you are always That. What will become of the world then? What good shall we do to the world? Such questions do not arise. "What becomes of my gingerbread if I become old?" says the baby! "What becomes of my marbles if I grow? So I will not grow," says the boy! "What will become of my dolls if I grow old?" says the little child! It is the same question in connection with this world; it has no existence in the past, present, or future. If we have known the Atman as It is, if we have known that there is nothing else but this Atman, that everything else is but a dream, with no existence in reality, then this world with its poverties, its miseries, its wickedness, and its goodness will cease to disturb us. If they do not exist, for whom and for what shall we take trouble? This is what the Jnana-Yogis teach. Therefore, dare to be free, dare to go as far as your thought leads, and dare to carry that out in your life. It is very hard to come to Jnana. It is for the bravest and most daring, who dare to smash all idols, not only intellectual, but in the senses. This body is not I; it must go. All sorts of curious things may come out of this. A man stands up and says, "I am not the body, therefore my headache must be cured"; but where is the headache if not in his body? Let a thousand headaches and a thousand bodies come and go. What

> *is that to me? I have neither birth nor death; father or mother I never had; friends and foes I have none, because they are all I. I am my own friend, and I am my own enemy. I am Existence-Knowledge-Bliss Absolute. I am He, I am He.*[5]

When would man stand up and pronounce with all serenity: "I am Existence-Knowledge-Bliss Absolute. I am He, I am He?"

1. Swami Vivekananda: *The Complete Works of Swami Vivekananda,* Advaita Ashrama, Kolkata, Mayavati Memorial Edition, 1989, Vol. I, pp. 12-13.
2. *Ibid.,* Vol. V, pp. 50-51.
3. *Ibid.,* p. 294.
4. *Ibid.,* Vol. III, pp. 283-284.
5. *Ibid.,* pp. 10-12.

INDEX